DIPLOMATIC IMMUNITY

D1032781

THE INSTITUTE FOR THE STUDY OF DIPLOMACY concentrates on the *processes* of conducting foreign relations abroad, in the belief that studies of diplomatic operations are a useful means of teaching or improving diplomatic skills and of broadening public understanding of diplomacy. Working closely with the academic program of the Georgetown University School of Foreign Service, the Institute conducts a program of publication, teaching, research, conferences, lectures and special awards. Its associates program enables experienced practitioners of international relations to conduct individual research while sharing their firsthand experience with the university community.

GRANT V. McCLANAHAN

Diplomatic Immunity

Principles, Practices, Problems

WITH A FOREWORD BY SIR NICHOLAS HENDERSON

*Published for the Institute for the Study of Diplomacy
Georgetown University, Washington D.C.*

ST. MARTIN'S PRESS, NEW YORK

Copyright © 1989 by the Institute for the
Study of Diplomacy, Georgetown University
All rights reserved.

For information write:
St. Martin's Press, Inc.,
175 Fifth Avenue, New York, NY 10010

ISBNs
Cased: 0-312-12832-6
Paperback: 0-312-02833-4

Printed in England on long-life paper

Excerpts from *Diplomatic Law: Commentary on the Vienna
Convention on Diplomatic Relations* by Eileen Denza, copyright
© 1976 by Oceana Publications, Inc., are reprinted by permission
of Oceana Publications.

Library of Congress Cataloging-in-Publication Data

McClanahan, Grant V.
    Diplomatic immunity / Grant V. McClanahan ; foreword by Sir
Nicholas Henderson.
      p.   cm.
    Bibliography: p.
    ISBN 0-312-02833-4 : $39.95 (est.). -- ISBN 0-312-02832-6 (pbk.) :
$15.95 (est.)
    1. Diplomatic privileges and immunities. 2. United States-
-Diplomatic and consular service--Privileges and immunities.
3. Great Britain--Diplomatic and consular service--Privileges and
immunities.   I. Title.
JX1672.M34   1989
341.3'3--dc19   89-4161
                                                                   CIP

To Cleo Noel and George ("Curt") Moore of the United States and Marcel Dupret of Belgium, three among the many gifted and dedicated officers who in recent years have given their lives heroically at their posts far from home in pursuit of diplomatic duties. They were treasured friends.

Sideribus recepti — "May they dwell among the stars."

CONTENTS

FIGURES

TABLES

FOREWORD

Sir Nicholas Henderson

Having served as a diplomat at home and abroad for forty years, and having known many others of the same profession from different countries, I realise to what extent one is seen as a *rara avis*, a strange bird set apart from one's fellows. Nor does our distinct plumage neccssarily make us popular or respected. On the contrary, it seems to excite envy and often resentment.

In a recent book of memoirs, a former British foreign secretary opened his remarks on his staff by writing: "Foreign Office officials are the butt of many jokes, but whatever their short-comings . . . they will accept any challenge . . . and work tirelessly and with skill." We mere officials have to get used to this sort of thing, however unfair or patronising, much as the caged inmates of a zoo have to become accustomed to receiving the irrelevant exclamations and titbits cast by passersby, notwithstanding the placarded injunctions against the teasing and wrong-feeding of wild creatures.

The trouble is that the public resents seeing us accorded the privilege that our status requires. It is the privilege of diplomatic immunity that is the badge of all our tribe and that brings such public disfavour upon our heads. We have to face the fact that privilege is unpopular nowadays, just as status is. Even Winston Churchill, who was no demagogue, said on one occasion that while he had no objection to inequality, he disliked privilege.

In recent times this subject of diplomatic immunity has been very much alive for the following main reasons:

1. The tendency of revolutionary regimes to condone, or participate in, the flouting of the rules of diplomatic immunity laid down in the Vienna Convention of 1961 on Diplomatic Relations, an international agreement accepted by 145 states. One example noted herein was the attack on the British embassy and chargé d'affaires in Beijing in 1967 carried out by supporters of the Cultural Revolution; another was the violation of the U.S. embassy and the taking of hostages in Tehran after Khomeini came to power in 1979.

2. The exploitation of diplomatic immunity to escape prosecution for various nondiplomatic activities: petty offences such as wrongful parking; the misuse of the diplomatic bag, premises or status; the appointment as members of diplomatic missions of persons not carrying out legitimate diplomatic functions; and serious criminal offences including terrorism. Examples of recent activities cited in this book that fall within these categories are: the attempt by the

Nigerians in 1984 to abduct a former minister, Dr. Umaru Dikko, from London in diplomatic luggage; the shooting of a guard outside a night club by the son of the Brazilian ambassador in Washington in 1982; and the shooting of the young British policewoman, Yvonne Fletcher, from the window of the Libyan People's Bureau (as they called their embassy) in London.

3. The widespread criticism of these incidents by the public; and the difficulty many people have in understanding why a diplomat and his family have immunities, and what, to be sure, they are.

Grant McClanahan's book explains why anyone who is engaged in the art of resolving international problems peacefully, which is what diplomacy is about, or who is responsible for those involved in it, will insist that without immunity the task is impossible. This is certainly my experience. It is a difficult and risky business. Finding out what is going on in a strange country and what may be likely to go on is hard enough, particularly in a totalitarian state. Many have been the attacks on diplomats in the Middle East. Terrorism is the disorder of the day. Since 1965, as McClanahan points out, over seventy American diplomats have been killed abroad and others wounded; in the past decade seven British diplomats have been attacked by terrorists, four of them fatally.

The essence of immunity is reciprocity, by which I mean that one state accords to the diplomat of another assurances as to inviolability of person, premises and correspondence and immunity from local jurisdiction, provided its own diplomats are treated simi-larly. Another essential feature of diplomacy is that everyone is equal. To paraphrase George Orwell, the diplomat of a great power is no more equal than that of a small country. Immunity from jurisdiction does not signify that a diplomat has the right to break laws of the country in which he resides. On the contrary, the Vienna Convention stipulates precisely that "it is the duty of all persons enjoying such privileges and immunities to respect the laws and regulations of the receiving state."

Given the widespread abuse of privilege and the understandable public reaction to the flouting of the accepted rules governing international life, much discussion has taken place recently on what should be done about it. Why, it is often asked, should those of us who are law-abiding have to put up with the behaviour of those who break the law and then retreat behind the sanctuary of an embassy? Imagination has focussed particularly on the idea of revising the Vienna Convention. While I understand the fury and frustration generated by the sort of incidents to which I have referred, I am sure it would be fatal to start tinkering with the wording of the conven-tion. If, for instance, language were to be added to give automatic legal enforcement to the passage I have quoted above about the need to respect the laws and regulations of a receiving state, the danger would be that diplomats from a Western European country or from the United States might find themselves open to arbitrary arrest in a country where there is no respect for freedom under the rule of law.

The way to deal with the abuse of privilege is to enforce more strictly the provisions of the Vienna Convention, rather than shrink from doing so for fear of political repercussions. Administrative means, including pressure on the heads of missions, can be part of the answer to the problem. Thus there is an article in the Vienna Convention which enables the receiving state to limit the size of foreign missions. There seems no reason why governments should be afraid of exercising this option. As regards diplomatic bags, it is worth noting that the British government have invoked "the over-riding right of self defence" to justify opening a bag if they think that its contents might endanger national security. On the vexed question of parking offences, governments should tell diplomats who persistently disregard the regulations and refuse to pay penalties that they cannot be accepted as members of a diplomatic mission.

More generally, there seems no reason why governments should not do more to pressure the governments of offending diplomats to waive their immunity so that they can be tried in court for some offence for which they are accused. For a charge of a grave criminal offence, governments should either request the waiver of immunity or declare the offender *persona non grata*. Finally, to meet the terrorist threat, governments should co-operate closely with each other both in exchanging information and in action.

There remains the question of the public's indignation over what it regards as the unjustifiable privilege of diplomatic immunity. I happen to have my own resentment on this score, the fruit, no doubt, of my own professional formation. For various reasons, the political leaders of democratic countries seem as little inclined to explain, let alone vaunt, the tasks of diplomats as they are eager to praise, and seek reflected glory from, the activities of members of the armed services, notwithstanding the fact that in the modern world diplomats are exposed to as great, if not greater, physical dangers than the military. Diplomacy is no longer the art of a small coterie that affects the few. It is a business that touches on the political, economic, and security interests of all. More people should be more aware of what it is all about, and I am confident Mr. McClanahan's work will make an important contribution towards this objective.

AUTHOR'S PREFACE

This book was commissioned early in 1986 by the Institute for the Study of Diplomacy of Georgetown University as part of its program of studies and publications on the process of diplomacy. The Institute saw the need for an updated guide to "the principles and practices of diplomatic immunity as they affect the conduct of diplomacy." I have felt honored to be entrusted with this task.

My gratitude and that of the Institute go also to the J. Howard Pew Freedom Trust for its generous support of this project.

A study of recent and contemporary practice in any field of diplomacy becomes more interesting and extensive as one considers actual events, incidents, and government reactions. In the present study, a large reservoir of such incidents was culled for useful examples; selected cases illustrate concepts, issues, and new developments. Many equally useful examples could have been chosen instead.

Diplomatic immunity, one international lawyer has remarked, is one of the most active and vital fields in which international law comes into play. I became acutely aware of the truth of that observation as new incidents and issues constantly obtruded to prolong the preparation of this book. I did not, however, attempt to incorporate every pertinent case from the steady flow of new incidents, but only to note significant new developments. The resulting volume is neither an up-to-the-minute compendium of historical incidents and statistics nor a legal casebook.

This study frequently uses the phrase "diplomatic privileges and immunities," the term most often heard in popular discussions or in the media. Among experts, who think and speak more precisely, the terms are not quite interchangeable. As the 5th edition of Sir Ernest Satow's indispensable *Guide to Diplomatic Practice* explains (p. 120): "In general, a privilege denotes some substantive exemption from laws and regulations such as those relating to taxation or social security, whereas an immunity does not imply any exemption from substantive law but confers a procedural protection from the enforcement process in the receiving state." To put "immunity" more concretely, the diplomat, continues Satow,

is not exempt from the obligation to obey the local criminal law, or the duty to pay his debts, or to seek local planning permission before rebuilding his residence, or from local regulations regarding the maintenance and insurance of his vehicle when he drives. But if he breaks any of these laws he cannot be arrested or detained by the executive authorities of the receiving

xv

state and he cannot be tried, sued or made to testify before the judicial authorities of that state.

This authoritative clarification of "diplomatic immunity" places responsibility to be law-abiding squarely on the individual diplomat, as on any other citizen. In fact, the diplomat has a specific moral duty to be responsible and above reproach.

But let the layman Daniel beware as he steps among the expert lions. My own preference, to abstain from subtle distinctions of this kind as much as possible, was reinforced by encountering in Michael Hardy's 1968 *Modern Diplomatic Law* a footnote (p.9) relating to the clause "that body of international and national law known as diplomatic privileges and immunities." In it Hardy says:

The word "privilege" is sometimes used to denote a benefit over and above that ordinarily granted by national law (e.g., in respect of communications) and "immunity" to describe an exemption from a specific provision of local law (e.g., immunity from taxation), but there is no uniformity of usage and much difficulty in applying the terms consistently with these meanings. Throughout the present lectures the words "privilege" and "immunity" are therefore used as synonyms.

Mr. Hardy, a graduate in law from Oxford and Cambridge, practiced law, taught at two universities, and in 1968 was on the staff of the UN Office of Legal Affairs, and *he* chose to use the terms interchangeably.

The latest edition of *Satow's Guide to Diplomatic Practice*, edited by Lord Gore-Booth and Desmond Pakenham, has been an invaluable aid to my study, as the many quotations from and references to its contents indicate. Another work on which I have frequently relied is Eileen Denza's excellent *Diplomatic Law*, of which copies are now unfortunately frustratingly scarce. C.E. Wilson's *Diplomatic Privileges and Immunities*, one of few monographs on the subject, was a scholarly treatment which assisted me greatly as technical background.

At several stages in my work, knowledgeable persons helped me with advice, suggestions, and documents. In the State Department, I would like to mention Richard Gookin of the Office of Protocol, Ronald Sol Mlotek of the Office of Foreign Missions, and William Michael McQuade of the Office of the Legal Adviser.

Early in my researches, a conversation with John Lawrence Hargrove, executive vice president of the American Society of International Law, was helpful in illuminating the path before me.

In London, the library of the Royal Institute of International Affairs provided me with a reader's ticket in the summers of 1986 and 1987. I appreciated the courteous assistance of their staff during many hours spent in their reading room on St. James's Square. The staff of the Foreign and Commonwealth Relations Library also assisted my researches in their rooms. At the library of the American Society of International Law in Washington, D.C., I was given good advice, suggestions, and the opportunity to read in the society's extensive collection. The present librarian, Jill Watson, and her predecessor, Helen Philos, both aided me in locating materials, checking sources, and many other ways.

Ambassador David D. Newsom, director of the Institute for the Study of Diplomacy, kindly read the first draft shortly after its completion and made many constructive suggestions both on the ideas and on some of the information, based on his exceptionally wide experience of practical diplomacy. He later took a helpful interest in the successively expanded and refined drafts.

To the Institute's editor, Margery R. Boichel, I am profoundly indebted. It was always a pleasure to meet with her on problems, and her encouragement and specific ideas for greater clarity and order have improved the substance and presentation of hundreds of points.

My wife Pauli devoted many hours and sometimes days to the typing of early drafts and helped give me extra freedom from distractions at key times.

Of course, I accept responsibility for the book's limitations and for any errors which may, in spite of my best efforts, still appear in the finished text.

I should like to close with a mention of the motivation that was most powerful in impelling me to move ahead when discouragements arose. This was my wish to do something to repay some of the debt I owe both to diplomacy as a career and, in particular, to the many American Foreign Service officers and diplomats of other nations whom I have known and admired and who have been my friends. It is my deep conviction that diplomats can and do make a great contribution to the effective conduct of good relations among governments and peoples. My studies for this work have confirmed my belief that a status of immunity, in its modern form, continues to be essential to their effectiveness.

1
INTRODUCTION

One of the few things most members of the public know about diplomats is that they enjoy, as diplomats, certain privileges and immunities. There is much less clarity in the typical citizen's understanding of the extent and limits of such immunity, and still less of the practical reasons for it. The subject's general obscurity is indicated by the frequent feelings of envy or resentment often aroused by the visible exercise of diplomatic immunity, as when a diplomat's car is seen to be unticketed in a "no parking" zone or a tourist in customs sees a diplomat's luggage go through unsearched. At times public opposition intensifies to the level of outrage in the wake of flagrant abuses of immunity.

What then are diplomatic privileges and immunities? And why are they needed? Why do governments accept them? Why should citizens tolerate their governments' doing so? Are they really useful under late twentieth century circumstances, or are they merely a quaint tradition from the times when ambassadors rode about in carriages and danced at balls at the Congress of Vienna? What has been happening and changing with respect to diplomatic immunity in the past twenty or thirty years? Should it be reformed? Is it on its way out like many venerable institutions?

In the discussion that follows we shall take the term to mean the immunities from local jurisdiction enjoyed by diplomatic agents (ambassadors and their staffs of officers) in doing their work and maintaining their dignity as persons representing one national state (a "sending" government) within the territory of another state (the "receiving" government, also referred to as a "host" government). The U.S. Department of State Office of Protocol provides another useful formulation in a 1981 paper: "Diplomatic immunity, a principle of international law, is broadly defined as the freedom from local jurisdiction accorded duly accredited diplomatic agents and members of their immediate household." The analogous but somewhat more limited immunities of consuls will also be distinguished and explained.

More specifically, we shall describe the areas of activity where immunity is now *in practice* generally recognized to be necessary for an ambassador, one of his or her officers, or a consul to function effectively. The actual categories in which their freedom is not to be constrained include (1) movement - no arrests or summonses; (2) property use - no entry into or taxation of their offices and, by a

1

modern extension, their automobiles, nor (3) into their homes, for there their dignity and their work are also inviolate. Similarly, (4) their communications with their fellow citizens within the receiving state are sacrosanct, because their work requires such access to fellow citizens.

These immunities rest on a long tradition of usage, many court judgments, a number of specific bilateral agreements, and, most importantly, on a few multilateral, almost universal, conventions of recent decades.

It is true that diplomatic immunities have their legal complexities and their uncertain outer boundaries. Furthermore, because they are in effect a limitation that one sovereign state places on its own actions toward another such state, they are not actually enforceable; for there is no way a sovereign state can be put in prison or forced to pay a fine for violating a diplomat's immunity.

Nevertheless, as diplomats know from experience, most governments behave themselves most of the time and, outwardly at least, take great pains to keep their written agreements, as well as to polish their images of honor and respectability. Respect for diplomatic immunity is generally taken, today as in the past, as a measure of a modern civilized state's good behavior. As C.E. Wilson has written, "The international rules of diplomatic privileges and immunities, which are among the oldest examples of international law, are firmly entrenched in practice, treaties, and municipal legislation."[1]

Considerations of reciprocity give powerful support to maintaining the customary and treaty status of diplomats. In the words of Eileen Denza, a seasoned British expert in this field, "Every government is both a sending and a receiving State and its own diplomats abroad are sureties for its behavior."[2]

This study will emphasize mainly the present era. During the years since 1945, diplomatic immunity has been extended to apply to the embassies of new states, of which many have appeared on the world scene, especially in the 1960s. At the same time, many of the older states have established embassies in the new nations' capitals.

Within embassies, staffs have grown in numbers, with more diplomats in the traditional roles of minister, secretary, and attaché, and many new categories of specialized attachés, such as treasury

---

[1] C.E. Wilson, *Diplomatic Privileges and Immunities* (Tucson: University of Arizona Press, 1967), p. vii.

[2] E. Denza, "Diplomatic agents and missions, privileges and immunities," in *Encyclopedia of Public International Law*, Installment 9, edited by R. Bernhardt (Amsterdam: North-Holland, 1986), p. 95.

representatives, civil air attachés, science attachés and cultural attachés. All these have been accorded diplomatic immunity.

There have also been many more nonresident special missions and representatives, officials who go abroad to attend conferences or bilateral meetings. While travelling and working abroad, they often have immunity. Sometimes famous or powerful individuals travel officially on ad hoc missions with ad hoc diplomatic titles, as in the case of special presidential envoys. They and their spouses, for reasons of honor and courtesy, are often given immunity.

All these nonresident categories are parts of the factual picture of the conduct of international relations. In a more comprehensive discussion of diplomatic immunity than this one, they might well have to be included. We shall leave them aside but indicate where they may be found in the works in the "suggested reading" bibliography.

Our focus, then, within the period since World War II, is primarily on resident diplomats in embassies and on consuls. The diplomatic immunities of military and commercial attachés and information officers at embassies are treated more generally.

Immunities of officers of development assistance missions will also be discussed (chapter 3). The expansion since World War II of bilateral and multilateral economic and other assistance programs has resulted in a large body of "cooperation" agreements between and among the governments concerned. These agreements include provisions for certain immunities and privileges for the foreign resident directors and technical experts of such assistance programs as the U.S. Agency for International Development (A.I.D.). This was a new development in the field of immunities, and its practices have been influenced by the long tradition of diplomatic immunity.

In examining the administration of immunity, the emphasis is further narrowed to the period since 1961. That was the year the Vienna Convention on Diplomatic Relations was signed – a great landmark event in the development of the subject. The discussion will necessarily take account also of the 1963 Vienna Convention on Consular Relations, the most influential guide to the practices of immunity in its field. These conventions were almost universal agreements and have been almost universally accepted and applied.

While the study concentrates, among national practices, on the United States and Great Britain, attention is given to other nations' practices and experience, including the Soviet Union's. These are taken into account for comparative purposes in describing such problems as immunity from taxation and the immunity of diplomatic pouches. The study also touches upon the degree to which the diplomatic immunity practices of other nations reflect the trend of the 1970s and 1980s in the United States and Britain toward more restrictive interpretation of applicable international law and the Vienna Conventions of 1961 and 1963.

A phenomenon of international relations since the war has been the emergence and prominence of the United Nations and regional international organizations such as the North Atlantic Treaty Organization, the Arab League, the Association of Southeast Asian Nations, and a host of others. Officials of such organizations, too, enjoy privileges and immunities, often very extensive ones.

The nature and scope of their immunities and the way they function in practice, however, seem to be a separate subject from diplomatic immunities, interesting for comparative purposes but fundamentally and increasingly distinct. Articles 104 and 105 of the UN Charter provide that the United Nations shall have the necessary legal capacity in the territory of its members to carry out its functions and shall have "such privileges and immunities as are necessary for the fulfillment of its purposes." To spell this out, the UN General Assembly adopted the General Convention on the Privileges and Immunities of the United Nations and the Convention on the Privileges and Immunities of the Specialized Agencies in 1946 and 1947 respectively. In 1975, a specially convened UN conference, once again in Vienna, adopted the Convention on the Representation of States in Their Relations with International Organizations.

Most members have acceded to these conventions. The United States, however, has never done so and instead regulates such matters under an agreement between the United States and the United Nations concerning UN Headquarters. Switzerland, which is not a UN member, also has a headquarters agreement with the United Nations to cover the extensive UN premises and activities in Switzerland.[3] In a standard work on the subject, C.W. Jenks states: "The law governing international immunities no longer consists primarily of a general principle resting on the questionable analogy of diplomatic immunities; it has become a complex body of rules set forth in detail in conventions, agreements, statutes and regulations."[4]

The light that international immunities in practice can throw on the kindred subject of diplomatic immunities stems from certain similarities between the two institutions: (1) Both are on the defensive against a world political climate adverse to immunity from local

---

[3] *Satow's Guide to Diplomatic Practice*, 5th ed., edited by Lord Gore-Booth assisted by D. Pakenham (London and New York: Longman, 1979), pp. 368–69 and 377 (hereafter cited as Satow, 5th ed.).

[4] C. Wilfred Jenks, *International Immunities* (London: Stevens and Sons, 1961), p. xxxv.

jurisdictions and to privileges and immunities. Jenks quotes Eli Lauterpacht, a great modern authority on international law, on this point: "Exemption from legal process is not congenial to the climate of the modern state."[5] (2) Both, and especially international immunities, survive on the grounds of real, contemporary usefulness (an example of the theory of functional necessity in action). (3) Both are increasingly regulated by written agreements. (4) Both cover an increasing number of persons in a wider and wider range of activities. This study therefore includes some works on international immunities in the annotated bibliography of suggested readings, and a few further comments on international immunities at the end of chapter 3.

Diplomatic Immunity in Action: Some Recent Illustrations

"Conventions, agreements, statutes, and regulations" on immunity are the stuff of international law and may appear deceptively dry and arcane. Not so their applications. These invariably involve the interactions of individual diplomats and their families with the laws, customs, and people of host countries and range from minor irritants to major crises. One too readily recalls recent examples of the latter.

In a tragic incident on 17 April 1984, a young British policewoman, Yvonne Fletcher, was killed in London by shots of automatic gunfire from a window of the Libyan People's Bureau (as the Libyans called their embassy). The affair precipitated a severance of diplomatic relations between Britain and Libya and endangered the safety of British diplomats and nationals in Libya. It was dramatically publicized in the media worldwide. In ensuing months it led to a review of the whole question of the inviolability of embassy premises and the immunity of diplomats by a House of Commons committee, the British Foreign Office, and a U.S. Senate subcommittee. There was a general public reaction of resentment and impatience because in the end no one was punished or even indicted. The lasting result of the whole incident seems to be that while certain procedures will be tightened, the fundamental legal situation, as laid out in the Vienna Convention of 1961, has not been changed.

The affair had begun about the middle of February 1984, when the chancery building of the Libyan People's Bureau was taken over by a group of Libyan students.[6] The official Libyan news agency, JANA, called them a provisional committee who would operate the

---

[5] Ibid.
[6] The narrative of these events is based on *Keesing's Contemporary Archives* (London: Keesing's Publications, 1931 et seq.) XXX, July 1984, pp. 33004–6.

bureau (i.e., embassy) in a revolutionary manner. On March 10, a bomb explosion in London's Mayfair seems to have aroused suspicions of a Libyan connection. On March 11, the foreign secretary notified the Libyans that the use of British territory for terrorist attacks was totally unacceptable. Eleven Libyans were arrested in connection with bombings in March. Four were charged and five deported on the grounds that their presence was "not conducive to the public good."

During this period of strained UK-Libyan relations, the Foreign Office could get no answer as to who exactly was in charge at the Libyan embassy. Finally, on April 9, the British ambassador in Tripoli was notified orally that Mr. Muftah Fitouri was in charge, but he was not one of the students; and on April 17 when the shooting occurred he was not in the embassy!

On the morning of April 17, a planned demonstration was held in front of the embassy by a coalition of at least three Libyan opposition groups. The demonstrators numbered about seventy. A pro-Qadhafi counter demonstration of about twenty persons, some from the embassy staff, was staged simultaneously. The police, who had been notified, were present and had erected crash barriers outside the embassy. Suddenly, after about half an hour of demonstrations, a burst of automatic gunfire came from the embassy's windows. (Later, the inquest report suggested two Sterling submachine guns as the source.) The bullets mortally wounded Constable Fletcher and injured eleven demonstrators. The police immediately evacuated everyone from the area, closed the square, and cordoned off the building. That evening the home secretary announced that the UK government's first objective was to evacuate the embassy to enable the police to search it.

The Libyan government in Tripoli on April 17 officially stated to the world press that no shots had been fired from the embassy and there had been no weapons in the building. That evening, Libyan militia prevented anyone from leaving the British embassy in Tripoli. Soon after, two British businessmen were detained, and in May four more. No British consul was permitted to visit the six until June 25.

The Foreign Office negotiated in London with Mr. Fitouri. He, and later the embassy staff, expressed regrets about WPC Fletcher's death, but denied any shots had come from the embassy. In London, the police allowed food to be taken into the embassy; and in Tripoli, on April 18, the Libyans again allowed people to enter and leave the embassy.

On April 22 the British announced they were severing relations with Libya, to take effect April 29. The reason was Libya's "unacceptable and unprecedented breaches of British law, of international law and of the Vienna Convention."

The Libyan government sent a three-man group headed by a Colonel Shaibi to London to supervise withdrawal from the embassy. Two of the student "provisional committee" were deported, one had left before the incident, and the fourth seems to have remained in Britain.

The staff of the embassy left under police escort on April 27. They were searched and invited to give information on the April 17 shooting, then taken to the airport, where they departed for Libya. The grounds given by the Foreign Office for the physical search of the persons leaving the embassy was the right of self-defense under both domestic and international law, whether or not the persons searched were diplomats. The Libyans made no objection to the search.[7] The British diplomats from Libya arrived in London by air on the same day.

British interests in Libya were to be protected by Italy, and Libya's in Britain by Saudi Arabia. From April 29 to May 1, British police, in the presence of a representative of the Saudi embassy, searched the vacated building. They reported finding six handguns and some ammunition.

The Libyans said these had been planted. They searched the British embassy in Tripoli and stated they found small arms and gas canisters. The British Foreign Office denied there had been weapons in the Tripoli embassy and suggested planting by the Libyans.

The Foreign Affairs Committee of the House of Commons in May 1984 commenced a study of the abuse of diplomatic immunities and privileges. The foreign secretary also "instituted a full review of the Vienna Convention." Some of their conclusions will be discussed in a later chapter. The Commons committee and the Foreign Office eventually concluded that, in general, the British government's handling of the crisis had been satisfactory under the circumstances.

The political restraints on British action had been strong. They included the long-term need to abide by the 1961 Vienna Convention's provisions for the inviolability of embassy premises and for full immunity for diplomatic agents from the jurisdiction of local

---

[7] House of Commons, First Report from the Foreign Affairs Committee, Session 1984-85, *The Abuse of Diplomatic Immunities and Privileges*, Report with an Annex; together with the Proceedings of the Committee; Minutes of Evidence taken on 20 June and 2 and 18 July in the last session of Parliament; and Appendices, 12 December 1984, Ref. no. 127 (London: HMSO), p. xxxii (hereafter cited as House of Commons Report, December 1984).

courts. Furthermore, the welfare of British diplomats in Libya and some eight thousand British nationals living and working in Libya, as well as British commercial interests, all weighed in the decisions.

The U.S. Senate Subcommittee on Security and Terrorism of the Committee on the Judiciary held hearings on "firearm felonies by foreign diplomats" in July and September 1984. Their work was greatly assisted by cooperation from the British government in sharing information and ideas on the Libyan embassy incident of the previous April. The views expressed in this Washington study were sometimes bolder than London's had been. The American experts and senators seemed especially concerned that no one had been put on trial for killing in such circumstances.

For Americans, the most politically important and highly publicized incident involving diplomatic immunity in the postwar period was the seizure on 4 November 1979 of the American embassy in Tehran and the holding of its entire staff as hostages. The whole affair was extensively discussed in the press and dramatically covered by the television networks. We will here discuss briefly some of the aspects directly involving the established rules on diplomatic privileges and immunities.

On 16 January 1979, the Shah left Iran in the aftermath of a successful revolution led from abroad by the elderly, charismatic Islamic leader, the Ayatollah Khomeini. Khomeini returned to Iran on February 1, and his regime took over on February 11. Though the United States recognized the Khomeini government on February 12, U.S.-Iranian relations were strained and precarious. On the morning of February 14, the U.S. embassy was attacked by gunmen, two Marine guards were injured, and the whole staff, including the ambassador, were taken prisoner while the embassy building was ransacked. The ambassador was able to telephone for help, and in a few hours some of the forces loyal to Khomeini released the Americans and handed back control of the embassy.

On 4 November 1979, the embassy was again occupied and its staff detained. This time it was a group of several hundred armed "students." They said they were holding the staff as hostages, whom they would not release until the U.S. government extradited the Shah and in effect apologized for its involvement in internal Iranian political affairs for the previous decades. The U.S. government immediately protested, and the State Department on November 6 announced that the government would not accede to the students' demands.

The Iranian government did nothing on the spot to help the embassy. On November 6, in fact, the Iranian minister responsible for supervising the Foreign Ministry said, "This occupation is certainly positive."[8]

There had been sixty-three Americans in the embassy when it was occupied. Three American diplomats, including the chargé, were held at the Foreign Ministry, where they happened to be at the time. Almost all the detained Americans were diplomatic or consular personnel as defined in the Vienna Conventions of 1961 and 1963, although a few were businessmen or others with no diplomatic status. Thirteen of the sixty-three, all black or female, were released on 18 and 20 November 1979, and one American was later released on health grounds. The remaining fifty-two were held in Iran in various conditions of humiliation and discomfort until 20 January 1981, a total of 444 days.

The United States instituted proceedings before the International Court of Justice (the World Court) on 29 November 1979. Its application cited the relevant articles of the Vienna Conventions of 1961 and 1963, the Convention on Prevention and Punishment of Crimes against Internationally Protected Persons, and the bilateral Treaty of Amity, Economic Relations and Consular Rights. The court was asked to find that Iran was violating international obligations and was obliged to release the hostages, to pay reparations, and to put the persons responsible on trial.[9]

The United States also submitted a request to the court to indicate provisional measures to be taken promptly to preserve the rights of the U.S. government. This meant that Iran should take prompt, effective measures to protect "the lives and physical and emotional well-being of the hostages." It should also "restore the premises to United States control."

The United States maintained that the detention of the hostages created "dangers to the fabric of diplomatic relations and international law," and that if Iran proceeded to carry out a threat to put diplomats on trial for alleged criminal acts, "the principles of international law and the fundamentals of diplomatic relations will have been irreparably damaged."[10]

The court on 15 December 1979 did render an order which called on the Government of Iran to restore the embassy premises to the possession and control of the United States, to release the U.S. nationals who had been held hostage, and to afford all U.S. diplomatic and consular personnel the full "protection, privileges, and

---

[8] *Keesing's Contemporary Archives*, 21 March 1980, p. 30150.

[9] Marian Lloyd Nash [Leich], *Digest of United States Practice in International Law 1979*, Department of State, Office of the Legal Adviser (Washington: U.S. Government Printing Office, 1983), pp. 581–82.

[10] Ibid., p. 583.

immunities" to which they were entitled under treaties and general international law.

The Iranian government on December 9 had told the court in a telegraphed letter that the court should not take cognizance of the matter, for it "only represents a marginal and secondary aspect of an overall problem," namely, the actions of the United States in Iran for "more than twenty-five years."[11] Iran maintained that any examination of the numerous repercussions of its revolution was "essentially and directly a matter within the national sovereignty of Iran."

The court on December 15 ruled that it did have jurisdiction and endorsed "the provisional measures" the United States had requested. Later, on 24 May 1980, the court pronounced judgment. It unanimously called on Iran to redress the situation and to carry out the steps ordered on December 15 as provisional measures.[12]

Unfortunately Iran refused to follow the court's decision and orders. The case increasingly shifted to nonlegal spheres. The United States on 24 and 25 April 1980 had taken unsuccessful military action to rescue the hostages. The Canadian government gave secret asylum to some six American diplomats and managed to remove them safely from Iran.

Complex negotiations commencing in October 1980 through third parties[13] finally reached agreement some three months later, on 19 and 20 January 1981, on the release of the American diplomatic hostages and, simultaneously, of some Iranian assets in the United States. The broad agreement under which the hostages gained freedom was detailed and fairly complex. Perhaps because the Iranians sensed the indefensibility of their actions under international law concerning diplomats, the wording of the agreement played down any relation between what had happened and what would have been required had customary procedures been followed.

The agreement took the form of a declaration by the government of Algeria that several "interdependent commitments" had been made by the United States and Iran in order to resolve "the crisis in their relations arising out of the detention of the 52 United States nationals in Iran." More than nine-tenths of the agreement dealt with the procedures for settling several billion dollars of U.S. claims

[11] Ibid., p. 587.

[12] Alfred P. Rubin, "The Hostages Incident," in *The Yearbook of World Affairs* XXXVI, issued by the London Institute of World Affairs (London: Stevens and Sons, 1982), p. 228. Excerpts from the World Court's judgment of 24 May 1980 appear as Appendix C of this book.

[13] Ibid., p. 237.

against Iran and Iranian claims to recover Iranian assets frozen in the United States. The embassy hostages were never referred to as diplomats or even officials but repeatedly as "United States nationals." The only mention of the Tehran embassy was in an article in which the United States undertook that when Algeria had certified "that the 52 United States nationals have safely departed from Iran," the United States would then "promptly withdraw all claims" pending before the World Court and bar "prosecution against Iran of any pending or future claims of the United States *or United States nationals*" [emphasis added], including "injury to the United States property or property of the United States nationals within the United States embassy compound in Tehran after November 3, 1979."[14]

The United States thus secured the release of its hostages but only after 444 days and at a moment (the last day of the Carter administration) chosen by the Iranians. The new administration of President Reagan, after study and apparent hesitation, announced on 18 February 1981 that the agreement would be honored.

This was the first case since the Vienna Convention of an embassy's being seized and its personnel taken hostage in which the host government for a period of months refused to set matters right. It was also the first time the World Court had given so fundamental a ruling on the immunities of diplomats and embassy premises.[15] The U.S. recourse to the court's judgment, when it came, did much for the firm establishment of diplomatic immunity in this century and for the Vienna Conventions as the preeminent guiding rules for diplomatic immunity.

Probably the lesson to be drawn for the outlook for diplomatic immunity is that the Tehran hostage crisis fully vindicated the wisdom of adopting general conventions on diplomatic and consular immunity. Because of the Vienna Conventions, the United States' legal initiative and the court's decision in favor of the release of the hostages and the embassy property both moved with unusual certainty and speed (only sixteen days between the U.S. complaint and the court's first order).

It is surely an overstatement to put the story, as international law professor Alfred P. Rubin has done, as one of "how the United

---

[14] *Keesing's Contemporary Archives*, 18 Sept. 1981, pp. 31082–86.

[15] A convenient summary of the ICJ's actions, the highlights of its reasoning in making its statements on interim measures, and its judgment of 24 May 1980 confirming them is to be found in Karin Oellers-Frahm, "United States Diplomatic and Consular Staff in Tehran Case," *Encyclopedia of Public International Law*, Instalment 2 (1981), pp. 282–86. The author includes a brief selected reading list of specialized articles in legal journals.

States decided to use the tools of the international legal order to help resolve the situation, how it abandoned those tools without any apparent consideration of the consequences or with any better prospect of success using any other tools, how the extraneous claims issues came to dominate the situation, and how the resulting arrangement led to the release of the hostages only, and unnecessarily, at the expense of the stability and security that might have been preserved by more adroit leadership."[16]

International issues so politically and even electorally important as the Iranian hostages will never be left to be settled entirely by even the most eminent courts and the most widely accepted treaties. They will continue to be resolved by all available means, including military, financial, and propaganda. Certainly this seems likely so long as there are sovereign states and revolutionary regimes. We may take some comfort from this tragic episode in that the United States, a superpower, used a legal approach; that the World Court spoke clearly; and that although the Iranian government may have survived an adverse court order, it was at a heavy moral and political price, which it is still paying and which should be pondered by any government tempted to follow the Khomeini regime's example.

There have been regrettable indications that, in spite of World Court judgments and world public opinion, the Iranian government does not regard itself as having done anything detrimental to international law in the hostage affair. It has repeatedly issued postage stamps, for example, that treat its condemned actions as heroic, with religious and patriotic connotations.[17] These officially promoted images surely mark one of the low points in international practice in the matter of respect for the principle of diplomatic immunity.

The actions of the World Court and the general attitude of

---

[16] Rubin, "The Hostages Incident," p. 213.

[17] A 1983 28-riyal stamp showing demonstrators climbing over the American embassy gates, a blindfolded American hostage, and the stars and stripes being burned was inscribed in English, "The takeover of the U.S. spy den." On United Nations Day that year, a 32-riyal stamp showed a sword with the name of Allah on its hilt severing at the wrist a long-nailed hand labeled "veto" emerging from the UN Secretariat building. In 1985, a 40-riyal stamp commemorated "Takeover of U.S. den of espionage." The background showed documents stamped "Top Secret," the middle ground was the embassy gates with the broken red letters "C.I.A." and the foreground was a shattered "Embassy of the United States" shield. The next year's 40-riyal stamp commemorated the failed American military rescue attempt with a dead American soldier lying face down in the desert beside a wrecked helicopter. An Arabic inscription quoted the Quran on the defeat of a Christian Ethiopian army in pre-Islamic Arabia, and one in English said "Failure of U.S. Military Aggression against Iran, Tabas – 1980." Color photos, *New York Times Magazine*, 15 Feb. 1987.

governments and public opinion in most nations, including those in the Soviet bloc, supported the principle of diplomatic immunity in the Tehran affair. The ten nations of the European Community imposed trade and economic sanctions on Iran in May 1980, and the Foreign Ministers of the Community on 20 January 1981 officially welcomed the release of the hostages. Typical of many governments' feelings was the Australian Foreign Ministry's 21 January statement that the "sense of relief and joy on the hostages' release should not obscure the fact that their seizure had gravely violated international law and morality."[18]

The death of a policewoman in London and the seizure of the American embassy in Tehran were major events. In one, diplomatic immunity was abused by its beneficiary. In the other, immunity was flagrantly violated over a long period by governmental action and inaction.

At the other end of the scale of importance, diplomatic immunity creates daily public irritation in cities when diplomats park their cars illegally and obstructively. Almost any resident of a capital city has personally witnessed such offenses. On a typical working day in Washington, D.C., for example, two or more diplomatic cars are parked on the sidewalk of a certain block of Que Street Northwest. Often such cars are there for hours at a time, and pedestrians are forced to step into the street in order to get around them.

Martin Mayer tells how in 1980 he invited the cultural counselor of the Soviet embassy to luncheon at the Cosmos Club. This official "picked up an embassy car from the (legal) parking rank across Sixteenth Street, drove the few blocks to the club, and without troubling to look for a parking space pulled into the bus stop on Florida Avenue." After a ninety-minute luncheon there was a ticket on the car. The "counselor did not trouble to look at it: he tore it up" and "stuffed the pieces in his overcoat."[19]

Parking offenses by diplomats are a long-standing problem. For a number of years, it had been getting worse in London, as probably elsewhere. In fact, the figures for parking tickets cancelled on grounds of diplomatic immunity in 1983 and 1984 were "double those for 1979 and 1980" and had "reached unacceptable levels," according to a White Paper of April 1985. The proportion of diplomatic offenses had also increased from 2.9 percent in 1982 to 4.3 percent in 1984.[20]

18 *Keesing's Contemporary Archives*, 18 Sept. 1981, p. 31087.

19 Martin Mayer, *The Diplomats* (New York: Doubleday, 1983), p. 40.

20 Her Majesty's Government, *Diplomatic Immunities and Privileges*, Government Report . . ., Miscellaneous No. 5 (1985), Cmnd. 9497 (London: HMSO, April 1985), p. 26 (hereafter cited as Command Paper 9497, April 1985).

Fortunately, this problem can be reduced by various administrative measures permitted under the Vienna Conventions. In London, for example, the tightening of administrative measures reduced the annual rate of parking tickets from 108,000 in 1984 to under 30,000 in 1986.[21] Later, in April 1987, when the totals for the latter year were available, the government gave the House of Commons an even more favorable account. To a question on parking offenses by diplomats at the Nigerian High Commission, Mr. Timothy Eggar, under secretary of state for foreign and Commonwealth affairs, responded that "the number of foreign diplomats sheltering behind diplomatic immunity for offences committed in this country had fallen and was still falling, since the introduction of stricter standards in April 1985." Unpaid fines had gone down "to 23,000 in 1986 and were falling fast,"[22] dropping to 14,437 in 1987, according to the Foreign Office.[23] The practice of Foreign Office warnings of possible expulsion of chronic offenders, begun in 1985, had resulted in twelve such warnings in 1987, but no expulsions as of April 1988.[24] U.S. attempts to deal with similar problems are treated in chapter 4.

The public is particularly aroused to anger by cases in which a diplomat or a diplomat's dependent commits a criminal offense but cannot be arrested and tried because the diplomat enjoys immunity. Such a case occurred in Washington in 1982.[25]

On November 29 that year, Antonio da Silveira, Jr., the 23-year-old son of the Brazilian ambassador to Washington, took time off from his studies at American University to visit a night club. His father was away in Brazil to assist with a visit there by President Reagan. At the night club, the young man got into an argument with the club's manager. His voice was raised and the manager suggested he leave. Instead, he went into the men's room, then emerged carrying a pistol and threatened to kill the manager. The club's part-time bouncer, Kenny Skeen, a muscular young carpenter, moved to eject da Silveira, who pointed the pistol at him and pulled the trigger repeatedly, but the weapon did not fire. The Brazilian youth backed to the rear entrance followed by the manager and Skeen, who had

---

[21] *Times* (London), 28 June 1986.

[22] *Times* (London), 23 April 1987.

[23] *New York Times*, 1 May 1988. Egyptian diplomats accounted for the highest total, 799, in 1987, followed by the Soviets with 622, Chinese 551, French 513, and Spanish 435. U.S. diplomats accounted for 77.

[24] Ibid.

[25] The account that follows is based on C. Ashman and P. Trescott, *Outrage: An Investigation into the Abuse of Diplomatic Immunity* (London: W. & H. Allen, 1986), pp. 127–34.

seized a piece of piping. Hiding in the shadows just outside the building, da Silveira pulled a second pistol, a .32 caliber, from his coat and fired at the two men. Skeen tackled the youth, who then shot Skeen in the stomach. Skeen grabbed at the armed hand of da Silveira, but the latter managed to empty the gun. Two more of his shots wounded the bouncer, one in the hand, the other in the leg. Skeen managed to hit him with the pipe, causing a small cut in his mouth.

The police came, and Skeen was taken to Georgetown University Hospital for surgery and intensive care. The bullets were removed from his stomach, thigh, and hand. The ambassador's son was taken to D.C. General Hospital and treated for his light wounds. Because he would not initially give his name to the police, he was detained under a $2,000 bond. He then gave what turned out to be the false name of "Frank Sanchez," could not post the bond, and was taken to police headquarters to await trial. Late the next day, the Brazilian embassy asked the police and the F.B.I. to search for the ambassador's son. That evening, the detained young man revealed his name to the police, thus ending the search. An embassy representative and a State Department official came to the police station and identified him. He was immediately released, and charges against him were dropped.

The hospital bill for Skeen's major injuries was about $10,000.

The young Brazilian and his mother departed from the United States on December 3. His mother had denied that her son was even at the night club, and his father, the ambassador, told a news agency his son was a victim of cruel treatment.

The State Department received many calls, and Senator Robert Byrd expressed amazement "that the relative of a diplomat can . . . shoot an American citizen [and] cannot be brought to trial: can just be turned loose on the street."

The State Department explained: "Mediation procedures to settle disputes between diplomats and American citizens begin with the aggravated citizen's filing of a written claim with supporting details to the Office of Protocol. We use our good offices, when appropriate, to bring the matter to the attention of the diplomat's embassy with a request that it use its best efforts to promote a just settlement of the dispute."

During his convalescence, Skeen hired a lawyer, filed a suit for damages in U.S. District Court, and wrote a letter to President Reagan, which was forwarded to the State Department. State Department officials met in confidence with the Brazilian embassy. Months passed, the Brazilian ambassador departed permanently on 3 March 1983, and his deputy took no action. Skeen's lawsuit was dismissed on July 6, and Skeen moved on to the Court of Appeals. Eventually in September 1983 a replacement for the Brazilian ambassador arrived in Washington. Shortly thereafter the State Department was able to come to Skeen's lawyer with an *ex gratia* offer from the new ambassador of cash for Skeen. This voluntary payment was accepted, as was the condition that Skeen not discuss it publicly and that he drop his suit.

In August 1987, Chief of Protocol Selwa Roosevelt testified before the Senate Foreign Relations Committee that the incident would have been forestalled had the Justice Department notified her office of an earlier incident in which da Silveira had been accused of assault, instead of waiting until after the attack on Skeen. Said Mrs. Roosevelt: "Had I known about the first offense . . . that guy would have been out so fast it would have made your head go round."[26]

The occurrence of incidents involving diplomats or their dependents who flagrantly abuse their immunity in stable Western countries while simultaneously in other parts of the world radical and extremist regimes are threatening or mistreating Western and other diplomats has been a disturbing feature of recent years. It has had a profound effect on practice affecting diplomatic immunity. Such incidents, together with the sharp increase in numbers of diplomats and posts, have led to a definite and significant shift throughout the world, especially in the Western world, to a more restrictive attitude on immunities.

One such change takes the form of underlining the principle of Article 41 in the 1961 Vienna Convention that diplomats *are not* immune from the laws of the country where they are accredited, but only from the usual methods of enforcement. Therefore, there is room for much new attention to assembling evidence whenever diplomats infringe the laws of the host state. Wherever possible, as with driving offenses, governments may proceed to institute preventive measures, issue systematic warnings, and announce possible penalties to diplomats. At the same time, full weight is also being given to the older procedure of expelling seriously erring diplomats on the grounds that they have become *persona non grata* to the host government.

Diplomatic immunity has always been a noteworthy facet of international relations because of its practical importance to all governments, large or small, Western, Eastern, or Third World; for they all have their diplomats. Particular cases that test diplomatic immunity are frequently dramatic, involving individual diplomats

---

[26] *Washington Post*, 6 Aug. 1987.

and novel situations. To these interesting aspects, changes are now to be added in the philosophic basis of this ancient institution, which is undergoing a rethinking in many countries. These new ideas are being translated into innovations in practice, with the outcome still uncertain.

2

FROM CUSTOM TO INSTITUTION: THE EMERGENCE OF DIPLOMATIC IMMUNITY

This chapter offers a brief, simplified account of the idea of immunity through several millennia of the history of diplomacy and of the broader history of intergovernmental relations. The interested reader may wish to explore the subject further in the sources cited and in the list of suggested readings at the end of the book. The books of Garrett Mattingly, R. Numelin, and C.E. Wilson are especially helpful.

Immunity before the Age of Resident Embassies

The Vienna Convention of 1961 begins: "*Recalling* that peoples of all nations from ancient times have recognized the status of diplomatic agents. . . ."

How far back do these "ancient times" extend? Into prehistory and the postglacial age in Europe, say 12,000 to 10,000 B.C.? Perhaps so. Modern scientific studies of prehistoric man, such as Grahame Clark's *Archaeology and Society*,[1] by ingenious reasoning from the settlements, graves, and pictographs of that age, have established that prehistoric men were organized into communities that practised agriculture and the division of labor. They had oral literature and laws, religion and priests, and they traded and made war. Thus they may well have had some sort of relations between different communities, which were probably tribes and larger linguistic groups.

A learned diplomat, Dr Ragnar Numelin, the Minister of Finland in Brussels in 1949, studied the anthropological evidence of existing primitive peoples at this elemental level of social development. He deduced from a host of published evidence that primitive societies develop customary procedures for starting wars, making peace, discussing trade, and sending intercommunity messengers who conduct business and are recognized as entitled to free movement and personal immunity.[2]

[1] Grahame Clark, *Archaeology and Society: Reconstructing the Prehistoric Past*, 3rd ed. (London: Metheun University Paperbacks, 1960), pp. 219–51.
[2] Ragnar Numelin, *The Beginnings of Diplomacy: A Sociological Study of Intertribal and International Relations* (London: Oxford University Press, and New York: Philosophical Library, 1950).

18

Life in an early society may have been psychologically cramped, routinized, and boring. The arrival of a well-selected messenger with an important agenda to discuss with local leaders may have been an interesting and welcome event. If he proved his peaceful intentions, he could benefit from the generous treatment we know most early societies accorded to a guest. The host tribe would provide food and shelter for the duration of his stay. Numelin noted that "sexual privileges are also included in primitive hospitality." He quotes the anthropologist B. Malinowski, who, in studying the people of the Northwest Melanesian Islands, was told that it had been "considered the duty of a girl from the village to act as the stranger's partner for the night. Hospitality, curiosity and the charm of novelty would make this duty perhaps not very arduous."[3]

With this sort of anthropological data, Sir Harold Nicolson created his charming and partly convincing picture of the first envoys being sent out from a Cromagnon cave by a wise old chief to meet with a hostile neighboring tribe to try to work out a truce or cessation of fighting between them.[4] However, such explorations of the probable origins of fundamental institutions, like Rousseau's "social contract," have a misty, unprovable quality.

When the age of written records begins, we can see the picture of primitive diplomatic institutions in a much clearer light. The records of the early kingdoms of the Middle East and India and China offer glimpses of rudimentary diplomatic activity.

When Egypt was admitted to the League of Nations in 1937, the leader of the Turkish Delegation in his welcoming speech discussed the treaty of peace and alliance and extradition between the Hittite King Hattushilish III and Pharaoh Rameses II about 1271 B.C., of which the text has been found in the Hittite language in Turkey and in hieroglyphics on the walls of an Egyptian temple at Luxor. This treaty is so detailed and important that it must have been negotiated in secret by officials of the two kingdoms.

Even earlier, a recorded event in the history of Egyptian-Hittite relations about 1350 B.C. illustrates the diplomatic activities of the area. Hittite clay tablet archives from their capital at Boghaz-Keui in modern Turkey contained a sort of aide-mémoire on earlier troubles between the Hittites and Egypt in Syria. They record that an Egyptian queen became widowed. From the context it seems to have been Merit Amun, the royal wife of Tutankhamen. She sent a letter to the Hittite king saying she now had no husband and no sons,

---

3 Ibid., p. 113.
4 Harold Nicolson, *Diplomacy*, 3rd ed. (New York: Oxford University Press, Galaxy Book, 1964; Washington: Institute for the Study of Diplomacy, Georgetown University, 1988), p. 6.

and if he would send one of his sons to marry her, that son could become Pharaoh of Egypt. The Hittite king was suspicious and sent an envoy to Egypt, who returned and confirmed to the king that the young queen was making a sincere offer. The king allowed the Egyptian queen to select one of his sons, but when this prince was proceeding to Egypt with an escort, he was attacked and killed in Syria by Egyptians. The cuneiform tablet describes the Hittite government's reaction in terms easily recognized by any diplomat who has read the policy options of a confidential national security crisis study in the 1980s: "The Hittite army marched into Syria, captured the murderers, and led them to the Hittite capital to be tried and condemned in accordance with international law."[5]

For our purposes here, the significance lies in the picture of the confidential message from the widowed queen to a neighboring head of state, the travel back and forth of the Hittite envoy, with what must have been a written memo of a conversation quoting the queen's words in such a way as to reveal her mood of desperation and sincerity. The envoy's account was believed by his government and action taken on his report. One may guess plausibly that he had immunity while on his mission and that he carried some form of sealed, inviolate pouch containing his papers, or rather clay tablets. After the incident, some sort of second millennium B.C. desk officer wrote a background memo and filed it for possible use in case the subject was raised again. That cuneiform record is what was excavated in the ancient capital of the Hittites.[6]

Abba Eban, in *The New Diplomacy,* finds "there is a great deal of political and military diplomacy in the biblical narrative" and that "kings, queens, generals and other dignitaries are portrayed as sending messengers to adversaries in the region, usually with such unwelcome tidings that they would need every ounce of immunity that they could get."[7] He cites the Assyrian envoy of Sennacherib who met King Hezekiah's negotiators just outside the walls of Jerusalem about the year 700 B.C.[8] The envoy presented Sennacherib's warnings and threats against Hezekiah's alliance with Assyria's enemy, the "bruised reed" Egypt, so

---

[5] John A. Wilson, *The Burden of Egypt: An Interpretation of Ancient Egyptian Culture* (Chicago: University of Chicago Press, and London: Cambridge University Press, 1951), p. 235

[6] A translation of the Hittite document is given in Christiane Desroches-Noblecourt, *Tutankhamen: Life and Death of a Pharaoh* (London: George Rainbird, 1963), pp. 275–76.

[7] Abba Eban, *The New Diplomacy: International Affairs in the Modern Age* (London: Weidenfeld and Nicolson, and New York: Random House, 1983), p. 335.

[8] 2 Kings 18:26–35.

emphatically and loudly in Hebrew that the soldiers on the wall overheard. When Hezekiah's negotiators begged him to speak in Aramaic, the language of diplomacy, which the soldiers would not understand, the envoy undiplomatically refused and said his master's message was for those very men, not the negotiators.[9]

A more peaceable style of diplomacy is surely implied in the narrative of the Queen of Sheba's possibly legendary state visit to Solomon about 940 B.C.[10] So grand a political, cultural, and economic head-of-state visit would undoubtedly have involved envoys to sound out the intentions of the parties in advance and to negotiate the agreed positions with regard to gifts at the end of that summit meeting.

Ancient Greece was a land of small city-states each fiercely attached to its independence and claiming equality with the others. Since these states spoke a common language and respected the same religious and moral values, there was both a need and a means for active diplomacy among them.

In the Homeric age, circa 1000 to 800 B.C., the Greek kings had heralds who served as their accredited messengers.[11] They carried a herald's staff as symbol of their office, and their persons were inviolate while on such missions. They were personages of high standing who between heraldic duties managed the royal household, kept order at public gatherings, and conducted religious rites. They are mentioned in both the *Iliad* and the *Odyssey*. The office was often hereditary, but the technical qualifications included a good memory and a loud voice (presumably there was some sort of oral entry examination).

The Greek states, mainly democracies in the classic age (750–350 B.C.), were unfortunately all too fond of making war on each other and of forming loose leagues and temporary alliances to help themselves against their enemies. Ambassadors sent by the states to promote these alliances or to make peace were accorded immunity and were even regarded as under the protection of Zeus. Any molesting of them would be a grave offence against the gods and the city that sent them. As privileged guests of the receiving state, they might be introduced to prominent men or the public assembly by the permanently resident *proxenos*, a sort of honorary consul of the sending

[9] A.T. Olmstead, *History of Palestine and Syria to the Macedonian Conquest* (New York and London: Charles Scribner's Sons, 1939), p. 478.

[10] 1 Kings 10.

[11] Numelin, *Beginnings of Diplomacy*, pp. 296–97; *Oxford Classical Dictionary*, 2nd ed., 1970, pp. 501, 1137.

state.[12] They would address the receiving state's assembly and answer questions on policy. They were assured of the right to return to their home city in safety and dignity.

Immunity for envoys was only one of many customary rules that together almost constituted a system of international law among the Greek states. Other parts of the system were that wars should be formally declared, that an enemy should be granted a truce to bury his dead, and that no fighting should occur during the seasons set apart for sacred athletic games like those at Olympia.

The Macedonian kings, Philip II and his son Alexander, conquered the Greek states in the fourth century B.C. and set up a brief Greek-Oriental Empire. This soon broke up into large Greco-Macedonian kingdoms, which endured for two or three centuries. They continued to observe much of Greek customary international law, including the inviolability of envoys.[13]

The governments of these Hellenistic states in Anatolia, the Levant, Egypt, and Macedonia were hereditary monarchies. Their dynastic politics involved sending envoys to arrange marriages, discuss boundaries, combine in alliances against other dynasties, or lend ships and crews to each others' naval campaigns. There were questions of hostages held, ransoms paid, and political asylum granted.

Ancient Rome's practice with respect to diplomatic immunity followed the custom of respect for the sacred character of envoys during the early republican era when Rome was a city-state, with neighboring states in the Italian peninsula and Sicily. But the history of even republican Rome was one of increasingly successful military expansion, carried eventually to the limits of the Mediterranean region. As Nicolson noted, "Their methods were those of the legionary and the road-maker rather than those of the diplomatist."[14] The concepts of immunity and inviolability were known, but they were reserved for the consuls and tribunes during their terms of office, or for the vestal virgins, or the premises of the great state temples, such as Jupiter's on the Capitol.

Institutional diplomacy was barely tolerated under the Roman Empire. As Abba Eban noted:

Courtesy to foreigners was not the distinguishing feature of Imperial Rome. The soul of the diplomatic idea is reciprocity, and this was an unfashionable notion in the domineering environment of Roman politics after victories in war.[15]

[12] Numelin, p. 299.
[13] Ibid, p. 300.
[14] Nicolson, *Diplomacy*, p. 9
[15] Eban, *The New Diplomacy*, p. 336.

The messengers who came through the frontiers of the empire with requests from other states or peripheral client-kings were required to pass "suspicious scrutiny" and to wait patiently on the convenience of the Senate before entering the city. Foreign ambassadors also endured long waits before addressing the Senate, "even longer to receive the imperial reply," after which they were hastened out of the capital "with all possible dispatch." Roman ambassadors, in keeping with this attitude, kept their visits to other lands short, returning swiftly to their usual occupations after reporting to the Roman Senate.[16]

Emperor Trajan's heroic political image as a second century Roman of ideal qualities was so well accepted that crowds would hail later emperors, often usurpers, with shouts of *Melior Traiano! Felicior Augusto!* ("May you be more virtuous than Trajan, more fortunate than Augustus!") Yet Trajan once publicly received a young Parthian prince, Parthamasiris, in camp at Erzurum in Armenia and then arranged to have the prince assassinated on the highway as he was proceeding back to his homeland.[17] Theoretically speaking, one could say that to the Romans privileges and immunities for non-Romans served no functional purpose.

In ancient India, kings and princes sent envoys to one another and had at least tenuous diplomatic relations with the Hellenistic kingdoms formed out of Alexander's brief empire, especially those in Syria and Egypt.[18] Envoys were accorded immunities and personal inviolability. For example, according to the fourth century B.C. Indian classic work on foreign relations, Kautilya's *Artha-Sastra*: "Messengers are the mouth-pieces of Kings . . . hence messengers who, in the face of weapons raised against them, have to express their mission as exactly as they are entrusted . . . do not . . . deserve death."[19]

There was, however, an early Indian tradition that an envoy should use his position to make trouble in the receiving state. Some of the secret actions prescribed for him to undertake would inevitably put him in the *persona non grata* category if discovered. Thus, he should publicly uphold the claims of his own king at the receiving court, but secretly ascertain the strengths and weaknesses

16 Ibid.

17 F. Stark, *Rome on the Euphrates: The Story of a Frontier* (New York: Harcourt Brace, 1966), p. 208.

18 G.V.G. Krishnamurty, *Modern Diplomacy: Dialectics and Dimensions* (New Delhi: Sagar Publications, 1980), p. 48, and B. Sen, *A Diplomat's Handbook of International Law and Practice* (The Hague, London, and Boston: Martinus Nijhoff, 1979), p. 4.

19 Krishnamurty, p. 49.

of the host government. He should use bribes to get information and to encourage opposition. His tactics might include giving gifts to the favorite maid of the queen and planting astrologers in positions where they could arouse disloyal ambitions among the host king's high officers.[20]

During the years of antiquity, the Middle Ages, and the Renaissance in Europe, China was a civilized nation which did not recognize the existence of other civilized nations. It saw no need or even possibility of any equivalent of the idea of diplomatic relations that was emerging elsewhere. Indeed, Professor Immanuel Hsü notes[21] that, under its "Mandate of Heaven," traditional China's "highest political idea . . . extended to the ordering of the whole known world, East Asia."

The Chinese, as we know, are not alone in history in believing their own culture to be the only true culture and all other peoples barbarians. The great size and populousness of their country, their isolated geographic situation, and, one must concede, the high quality of their civilization, however, permitted them to avoid considering other states as equals many centuries longer than had pharaonic Egypt or the Roman Empire.

Nevertheless, although the Chinese could not conceive of "foreign relations" or feel any need for intercourse with other peoples, they did, in practice, have relations of sorts outside their own administered territory. They conducted "tributary relations" with such peripheral states as Korea, Annam, Siam, and Burma, and intermittently accommodated invading barbarian tribes. From the sixteenth century onward, there were also trade relations by sea with European countries and overland with Russia.

The Chinese attitude toward envoys of other peoples and something of the sophisticated, haughty picturesqueness of Chinese institutions are suggested by the names they used in conducting external relations. Under the Ming Emperors, there was the "Common Residence for Envoys" and the "Residence for Barbarian Envoys," both supervised by the "Court of Sacrificial Worship." The subsequent Ch'ing Dynasty in 1748 reorganized the two, combining them into the "Common Residence for Tributary Envoys," which was under "a senior secretary of the Board of Rites."

Hsü notes further that relations with Russia were separate and were grouped "with Mongolian, Tibetan and Muslim affairs"

[20] G.K. Mookerjee, *Diplomacy: Theory and History* (New Delhi: Trimurti Publications, 1973), Vol. 1, p. 8.
[21] Immanuel C.Y. Hsü, "The Development of the Chinese Foreign Office in the Ch'ing Period," in *The Times Survey of Foreign Ministries of the World*, Zara Steiner, ed. (London: Times Books, and Westport, CT: Meckler, 1982), pp. 119–34.

under the "Court of Colonial Affairs." After 1727, the Russians were even allowed to have a semi-diplomatic mission in Peking, and Russian priests and language students were admitted every ten years by treaty.[22]

It is not possible to find the Chinese accepting the idea of diplomatic privileges and immunities before the late nineteenth century. In 1860, when they reluctantly conceded the right of foreign legations to be resident in Peking, it was "a totally unprecedented situation . . . [in] Chinese external relations, necessitating a complete reexamination of the existing system."[23]

It is an example of constructive institutional change that 115 years later, in 1975, the People's Republic of China acceded to the Vienna Convention of 1961, with its modern norms for diplomatic privileges and immunities. This deliberate, fundamental decision is particularly significant in light of the history of China's external relations in the past century, when "alternate patterns of exaggerated xenophilia and xenophobia" and "ambivalence and tensions" have underlain China's dealings with the outside world.[24]

Resident Ambassadors: Renaissance Beginnings of Modern Diplomatic Immunity

The modern form of diplomatic immunity could not take shape until the establishment of resident ambassadors. This innovation occurred first in Italy and spread to other European states around the mid-fifteenth century. Resident ambassadors "have been the most characteristic officers of Western diplomacy ever since. They differentiate our system strikingly from any other we know about elsewhere."[25] Mattingly offers a working definition of a resident ambassador as "a regularly accredited envoy with full diplomatic status sent . . . to remain at his post until recalled, in general charge of the interests of his principal."[26] This concept has been further refined by Paolo Selmi, who stipulates another modern requirement: The office "begins to exist when one has the institution of a permanent *officium* of which the ambassador, provided with a general mandate, is the titulary during his assignment; and when the existence of such an *officium* is not diminished if it should be

[22] Ibid.
[23] Ibid.
[24] Michael B. Yahuda, "The Ministry of Foreign Affairs of the People's Republic of China," in Steiner, *Times Survey of Foreign Ministries*, p. 158.
[25] Garrett Mattingly, *Renaissance Diplomacy* (Boston: Houghton Mifflin, and London: Cape, 1955), p. 64.
[26] Ibid.

temporarily deprived of a titulary, when such a vacancy creates the necessity of nominating a successor''[27] – the chargé d'affaires ad interim.

For the sake of historical precision, it would be interesting to be able to identify the first ambassador who fitted the job descriptions provided by Mattingly and Selmi, presumably someone in the fifteenth century.[28] This question will have to be left for the time being to the historians and the Venetians. Some day the almost infinite archival records of Italy may provide an answer. In the meantime, one can discern the main dates in the historical trend leading to the institution of resident ambassadors with diplomatic privileges and immunities.

By 1500 or so, the major European powers were exchanging resident ambassadors between their courts. As Mrs. J.G. Russell notes, ''This development, from the use of 'special' ambassadors with specific short-term missions, began in Italy and became normal after the peace of Lodi in 1454. It was a way of obtaining and retailing [*sic*] regular information.''[29]

After inventing the institution, the Italian states later sent resident ambassadors to other parts of Europe. Milan had one in France, as did Venice from 1478. In the 1490s, Milan had a resident ambassador in Spain, in England, and at the imperial court of the Holy Roman Empire. Spain sent a resident ambassador to Rome in the 1480s and to England by 1495. The Pope sent resident nuncios to Spain, France, England, Venice, and the Holy Roman Emperor by 1505.[30]

The privileges and immunities of resident ambassadors in the sixteenth and seventeenth centuries were something of a new situation, different from the special ambassadors and heralds of the Middle Ages. One is reminded of some of the problems that have arisen in the post–World War II period due to the proliferation of often inexperienced diplomatic missions. As in our time, the national governments were disposed to be more liberal in their treatment of the foreign diplomats' inevitable minor offenses than were local citizens and municipal authorities. According to Mattingly,

Sovereigns were usually anxious to preserve diplomatic contacts, and consequently tolerant of the incidental frictions which such contacts entailed. At the same time the growing embassy staffs, groups of specially privileged foreigners resident among populations quick to suspect them of misbehavior and evil intentions, multiplied the opportunities for friction. Embassy staffs

---

[27] In D.E. Queller, *The Office of Ambassador in the Middle Ages* (Princeton: Princeton University Press, 1967), p. 76.

[28] An historical note on this question appears at the end of chap. 2.

[29] J.G. Russell, *Peacemaking in the Renaissance* (London: Duckworth, 1986), pp. 67–68.

[30] Ibid., p. 68.

ranged from grave secretaries and young aristocrats through tough couriers and lackeys. . . . They were not always carefully selected. . . . As such groups began to realize that their immunity from local prosecution could be extended by the insistence of the ambassador . . . it is not surprising that municipal authorities and city mobs responded to their provocations with violence. Embassy servants were attacked in the streets. Embassy precincts were forcibly invaded by local officers. Now and then some ambassador's residence stood for days what almost amounted to a siege.[31]

So in the sixteenth and seventeenth centuries, the limits of diplomatic immunity were something to argue and brawl about. The prince of the receiving state had the last word, and he generally paid less attention to "the principles of international law than [to] the truculence of the ambassador involved and the importance of the power he represented." The situation varied from capital to capital.[32] One of Mattingly's observations about this period – "On the whole, no government willingly conceded privileges as extensive as its envoys claimed abroad"[33] – has a long and continuing validity, although in our time this has been clearer in the case of Communist governments than in the West.

Out of the confusions and uncertainties emerged an idea, articulated by Grotius in 1620, the notion of exterritoriality. Though now on the whole rejected, this theory was useful in its day, especially, for example, in justifying the famous *droit de chapelle* by which Protestant or Catholic envoys could hold religious services in their embassies in countries of the contrary faith. "When all Europe had been Catholic, everyone had been able to take communion everywhere. But after Martin Luther, John Calvin, and Henry VIII, the *droit de chapelle* was needed." First to grant this privilege were France and England, reluctantly followed a great deal later by Catholic Spain and Italy and Protestant Scandinavia and The Netherlands. In the end, tolerance for "heretical" chapels was gradually conceded. Because of the delicacy of the subject, the toleration was tacit rather than written.[34]

Theories of Diplomatic Immunity

Since the mid-sixteenth century, there have been three major theories of diplomatic immunity, commonly identified as personal

---

[31] Mattingly, *Renaissance Diplomacy*, pp. 278–79.
[32] Ibid., p. 279.
[33] Ibid.
[34] Ibid., pp. 280–81.

representation, exterritoriality, and functional necessity.[35] Functional necessity fits the conditions of the period since 1945 most effectively and seems to have the most promising future. However, some ideas and terms from the other two theories still have validity and appear in court rulings, international law treatises, and popular discussions of diplomatic immunity. All three theories in varying degree are therefore helpful, as a good theory should be, in providing an intellectual framework for the mass of rules, judgments, incidents, and opinions that are the substance of diplomatic immunity.

We will therefore briefly describe the first two, mentioning the surviving influence of each and its weaknesses for contemporary purposes. We will then discuss the third, functional necessity, in greater detail, and suggest, finally, that even it has a few inadequacies, which await the refinements of future thinkers.

Personal representation. The theory of personal representation has the deepest roots. Long before the term diplomat or diplomatist or even anything resembling a Renaissance ambassador, there were rulers who sent representatives. These representatives were given specially respectful treatment because, in honoring them, one pleased the ruler and avoided offending him. One gave the representative freedom of movement and access to one's own ruler and respected his person, so that the ruler who sent him would hear about it and be satisfied, whether he was Peter the Great or the tribal chieftain of a neighboring valley. In a world where state power was lodged in individuals and dynasties, this theory was a clear guide to practice. The representative was treated as though the sovereign himself were there, conducting negotiations, giving gifts and promises, making alliances or refusing requests, conducting most of the business of diplomacy at an elemental level.

In our own times, there are lingering traces of the theory in the idea that an ambassador is a personification of the head of the sending state or of that state itself. In Baghdad, this writer was always impressed by the special aura of prestige which Marcel Dupret, the respected Belgian ambassador, could generate by referring to his position as *"l'ambassadeur du roi des Belges."* To the sensitive ear, there is a particular fullness and resonance when a French diplomat, in a discussion of the position taken by the Quai d'Orsay on even a technical or commercial issue, uses a phrase such as *"du point de vue de la France."*

As a desk officer assisting a new American ambassador preparing

---

[35] C.E. Wilson, *Diplomatic Privileges and Immunities*, p. 1.

for his departure to Libya, this writer felt the force of the idea that nothing could be more worth his time than the arrangements for his predeparture call at the White House. To discuss relations with Libya, even perfunctorily and briefly, face-to-face with President Kennedy in the Oval Office would symbolize with maximum clarity to anyone the ambassador met in Libya that he was entitled to the fullest privileges and immunities of the office of an ambassador.

"Divinity doth hedge a king" and, psychologically, immunity doth hedge an ambassador, and even his (or her) staff of officers, when the ambassador is personally and directly acquainted with the person who directs his government and symbolizes his nation. British ambassadors to major posts are frequently knights, sometimes peers, and it is more than a matter of picturesque history. One knows that Sir James or Sir Ronald is not only accredited like all other ambassadors in the capital, but invested personally with an honor by his sovereign.

The inadequacies of the theory in modern times are said to be that it is less and less appropriate as constitutions of national states increasingly vest sovereignty in the nation instead of a monarch[36] One of the reasons the U.S. government did not appoint ambassadors until late in the nineteenth century was that it was thought by our public that ambassadors were personal representatives of monarchs.[37]

Another weakness is that the theory would not suffice to cover the privileges and exemptions accorded to the private acts of diplomats, especially those below the rank of chief of mission. Even ambassadors in our time cannot realistically expect to be treated as personifications of kings, presidents, and sovereign states, and how much less are the chances of a vice-consul or assistant administrative officer?

The theory of personal representation, nevertheless, will long survive in fusion with the dominant theory of functional necessity. In 1958, in preparing drafts for the 1961 Convention on Diplomatic Relations, the UN's International Law Commission reported that, while it was guided by the theory of functional necessity when current practice was unclear, it "was also bearing in mind the representative character of the head of mission and of the mission itself."[38]

---

[36] Ibid., pp. 4–5.

[37] M. Ogdon, *Juridical Bases of Diplomatic Immunity* (Washington: John Byrne, 1936), p. 144, quoted in Wilson, *Diplomatic Privileges and Immunities*, p. 4, footnote 18.

[38] Wilson, p. 5, with citation of UN document in footnote 23.

Exterritoriality.[39] The second theory, that of exterritoriality, has had a relatively short run, a mere four centuries, in the long history of political ideas. It held that the offices and homes of diplomats and even their persons were to be treated at all times as though they were on the territory of the sending state and not the receiving one. What could be simpler as an idea to explain diplomatic immunity? On the other hand, what could be more difficult or even silly in practice in modern situations?[40]

The theory of exterritoriality was considered to be a useful principle in the early centuries after the coming of permanent resident missions in the fifteenth century. It was enunciated by early authorities, notably Emmerich de Vattel, who wrote in 1758 that "an ambassador's house is, at least in all common cases of life, like his person, considered as out of the country."[41] As late as 1883, in his treatise on international law, James Lorimer stated that "an English ambassador, with his family and his suite, whilst abroad in the public service, is domiciled in England."[42]

Yet in this century it has been steadily devalued as a guide to courts or even commentators on cases of diplomatic immunity. The term was always a legal fiction and now seems to be used only in a historical sense, going the way of "capitulations," "mixed tribunals," and "international enclaves," such as Tangier or Shanghai. Contemporary treatises on international law generally use such qualifiers as "dangerous fiction," "palpable fiction," "little more than a fiction," "worn-out fiction," or "picturesque metaphor" when alluding to the theory.[43]

The idea that an embassy is part of the country of the sending state occasionally crops up rhetorically, for emphasis. An instance occurred when U.S. Secretary of State George P. Shultz, at a State Department press conference on 8 April 1987 concerning the security situation at the U.S. embassy in Moscow, said: "[The Soviets] invaded our sovereign territory, and we're damned upset about it."[44]

The United States historically has often taken a pragmatic line on such practical forms of exterritoriality as consular courts and international zones. In the nineteenth century, American consuls in

---

[39] Traditionally "extraterritoriality," but now most commonly in the shorter form used here.

[40] D.P. O'Connell, *International Law*, 2nd ed. (London: Stevens and Sons, 1970), p. 888; and Wilson, pp. 5–16.

[41] In Wilson, p. 6, footnote 34.

[42] Cited in ibid.

[43] Wilson, pp. 8-9 and 13–14.

[44] *State: The Newsletter*, May 1987, p. 8.

the Orient often exercised jurisdiction over Americans where the receiving state was willing to permit the system. French-speaking American judges served on the Mixed Courts in Egypt until, by agreement, those courts ceased to function in 1949. Yet American policy was not to make stubborn objections when national governments abolished such practices, for example, in the territory of the Ottoman Empire and elsewhere. Sometimes the situation was ambiguous or even confused, but when exterritoriality was clearly resisted, the United States accepted its absence.

This happened in U.S. relations with the Sultanate of Oman. The consular agreement of 1833 between the two governments suggested, in the English version, that the American consul would have jurisdiction over cases involving Americans in Oman. The Omani translator, however, apparently altered the Arabic text to give local courts jurisdiction. The difference was not known to the American negotiator, Edmund Roberts, nor was it noted by the Department of State until early in the next century, when the Dutch orientalist, Christiaan Snouck Hurgronje, commissioned by the Department of State to compare the texts of Arabic and Turkish treaties with their English versions, brought this fact to light.

The 1833 agreement was replaced by a modern treaty, negotiated in 1957 and 1958, signed in the latter year, and put into force with an exchange of ratifications in 1959. Only then was the point cleared up. During the negotiations, the U.S. side did not mention exterritoriality, but sought to assure adequate special protection for American businessmen and putative investors in Oman. The Sultan of Oman diligently and successfully resisted the idea.

U.S. diplomat Hermann Eilts, who kindly provided this information concerning Oman, was the officer sent by Secretary of State Christian Herter to exchange ratifications with the Sultan in 1959. He recalls that the Sultan examined with great care "the document that he had signed the previous year in order to check that we had not reinstituted some kind of extraterritoriality provision."[45]

Perhaps the clearest evidence of the vestigial survival of exterritoriality is in occasional incidents of political asylum in embassies.[46] Cardinal Mindzenty was given asylum in the American legation in Budapest, but this was at the time an exceptional case.[47] The practice of asylum has been especially common in Latin America and continues to be so.[48]

---

[45] Letter to author, 22 Dec. 1987.
[46] O'Connell, *International Law*, p. 734.
[47] Wilson, *Diplomatic Privileges and Immunities*, p. 15.
[48] Ibid., p. 15 and footnote 87.

Asylum in an embassy was deduced from the theory of exterritoriality. Now, on the basis of custom and treaties, it endures despite the discarding of its original theoretical basis. The United States, especially since the 1950s, in practice accepts the idea of asylum in its own embassies and consulates when the person seeking asylum is in imminent danger of mob violence or, as in the Mindzenty case, claims to be in danger of persecution on political grounds in a Communist country.[49] In earlier decades, the United States attached reservations to two Latin American multilateral conventions on political asylum – in Havana in 1928 and Montevideo in 1933 – stating that the United States did not recognize a right of asylum.[50]

The decline of exterritoriality as a viable theory of diplomatic immunity is further seen, indirectly, in its abandonment by major academic groups seeking to draft codifications of international law. It was also rejected by the UN International Law Commission, which worked out the language eventually adopted in the Vienna Convention of 1961, by far the most important agreement on diplomatic immunity.[51]

Functional necessity. The theory of functional necessity is also rooted in ideas that have been present for many centuries. Yet its broad acceptance in modern times stems from the fact that it is more dynamic and adaptable than the other two.

According to this theory, the rationale for a diplomat's privileges and immunities is that they are necessary to enable him to perform his diplomatic functions. Modern diplomats need to be able to move freely and to be unhampered as they represent their governments, report in confidence, observe actual conditions in the receiving country, negotiate agreements, and so on. Their private actions need to be immune from local jurisdictions and taxation, for they need to be free at all times to perform official duties. In this century, as governments have required their diplomats to take on additional and, in some cases, new tasks, immunity can logically be provided for those functions, too. Thus the theory is adaptable to change and expansion. However, it can also apply to reforms covering needed limitations. It has a built-in safeguard against excessive demands for new privileges and immunities, because its principle is pragmatic. Are expanded or new immunities really necessary? Will they work well in practice? The theory demands that both these questions

---

[49] O'Connell, *International Law*, pp. 737 (on embassies) and 922 (on consulates).
[50] Ibid., p. 735.
[51] Wilson, *Diplomatic Privileges and Immunities*, p. 10.

be answered in the affirmative before an immunity is conceded.

The rudiments of the theory go back at least to the eighteenth century, when the English Lord Chancellor, in Barbuitt's case in 1737, observed that diplomatic privileges stem from "the necessity of the thing, that nations may have intercourse with one another."[52] His words contain also the idea of mutual interest and hence reciprocity, a further aspect of the theory.

Functional necessity as a theory seems thoroughly to deserve the respect it has gained, but it also has at least a few inadequacies. For example, it does not quite cover the real need for diplomatic immunities to be limited by the interest or even convenience of the society of the receiving country. Even when doing their diplomatic duties, diplomats should not exercise immunity to the point of becoming a nuisance in their neighborhood or an obstacle in urban traffic. They have been accredited to help their work, not licensed to override accepted behavior. They have privileges, but they are foreigners and should act in the spirit of the Arabic proverb "*Ya ghareeb, khalleek adeeb*" ("O stranger, be thou courteous").

Even more seriously, a diplomat should function in good faith in the matter of the host nation's security. The theory of immunity as based on functional necessity should at least be qualified to mean that a diplomat's immunity assumes the sending government will not include in the diplomat's duties any threat to the security of the host nation.[53]

Wilson finds the theory also inadequate to explain why diplomatic immunity should be equally accorded to all missions in a given capital. Some are more important, have more urgent business and keep busier schedules than others. These are functional differences.[54] One must presume, however, that the theory is applied equally, regardless of the level of need for immunity on grounds of urgency or importance of functions, because it would not be possible to draw a line between those diplomats whose work requires immunity and those whose work does not.

As an embassy political officer in London in the 1960s, I had the pleasure of calling from time to time on the ambassador of a certain Middle Eastern kingdom. He was not only courteous and charming; he was also obviously not busy. His phone did not ring, the papers on his desk often did not move between my calls, even weeks apart. His outer office was usually quiet and unoccupied There was obviously no clear functional reason why he would not have had

[52] Ibid., p. 19.
[53] Ibid., p. 25.
[54] Ibid., p. 23.

adequate time to find a legal parking place for his car or even to answer a court summons as a witness, though he, like all of his counterparts, was exempt from such requirements.

Clearly, any failure to grant immunity equally, without regard to the status of a diplomat's country or the size of his work load, would set a dangerous precedent certain to be challenged. It is the older theory of representation that applies here, not the theory of functionalism.

A Growing Body of Court Judgments, Laws, and Practices

The practice of giving immunity to diplomats and to their historical predecessors, the messengers, envoys, and heralds, clearly has a long history, but not so its embodiment in laws. In Britain, there was no legislation on the subject until 1708, when a law was passed in the aftermath of a famous incident. The Russian ambassador of Peter the Great was pulled out of his coach and arrested in the streets of London by bailiffs acting for his creditors. He was released on bail paid by his friends, and Queen Anne ordered the secretary of state to express regret to him. The ambassador was told that all persons who had committed the offense against him would be tried. However, "his excellency Andrew Artemenovitz Matueof [*sic*] ambassador extraordinary of his Czarish Majesty Emperor of Great Russia and her [Majesty's] good friend and ally" (so-styled in the language of the preamble to the subsequent Act of Anne)[55] was not in the least mollified and left the country in a huff without presenting his letters of recall. When Peter the Great learned of the incident, he interrupted the British ambassador, Lord Whitworth, in St. Petersburg one day to ask that all the persons be not tried but summarily executed.[56] Ambassador Whitworth was commissioned to convey to the Czar at a public audience Queen Anne's regret for the insult to his ambassador.

As a further effort to appease the Czar's anger, a law was enacted, known in history as the Act of Anne, or the Statute of Anne, of 1708. It said that all writs and processes to arrest or imprison ambassadors or their servants were null and void, and anyone who attempted to sue them with such a writ could be tried before a special court of three high judicial officers. This law was later interpreted as declaratory of the common law. It stayed on the books until repealed to make way in 1964 for Britain's Diplomatic Privileges

---

[55] Satow, 5th ed., p. 125.

[56] *Dictionary of National Biography*, Vol. 21 (London: Oxford University Press, 1921–22), p. 161.

Act, which put into force in Britain the provisions of the Vienna Convention of 1961. According to D.P. O'Connell, the Act of Anne is still in force in some countries of the Commonwealth.[57]

Perhaps because of the particular crisis that occasioned it and the haste in which it was enacted, the Act of Anne made no reference to such important subjects as the inviolability of diplomatic premises or pouches. Later judgments have held that it could be taken to bring international law into British law, and it has had that effect. In any case, as O'Connell says, "Whether the Act was declaratory of the common law as it was in 1708, or whether it was subsequently absorbed by a rule of international law which operates as part of the common law, is a matter of no moment save for academic discourse."[58] Certainly, international law in Queen Anne's reign had accorded immunities to ambassadors and their residences.

The American colonies were presumably guided by the Act of Anne. When in the early years of American independence a case arose involving an assault on a French diplomat, a judge in Philadelphia ruled that it was a crime under international law which "is part of the law of this state."[59] Congress agreed with him when it passed a law in 1790 closely analogous to the Act of Anne, but more comprehensive.[60] This law made it an offense to arrest an ambassador or his servants or to seize their goods, and penalized any person who issued or executed an order to do so This was the basic legislation until 13 December 1972, when the Vienna Convention of 1961, by presidential proclamation, entered into force in the United States.[61]

The act of 1790, however, was not explicitly repealed until 1978. The legal situation in the United States with respect to diplomatic immunities was somewhat anomalous during that six-year interval. Following the 1972 presidential proclamation, the Vienna Convention of 1961 became the law of the land without any further implementing legislation (article IV, clause 2 of the U.S. Constitution). As to differences in the scope of immunities between the old statute and the new treaty, the Justice Department's official view, set forth on 3 May 1973, was that both were "the supreme law of the land"; that "when the two relate to the same subject, an endeavor should be made to give effect to both," if reasonably pos-

---

57 O' Connell, *International Law*, p. 890, footnote 14.

58 Ibid., p. 891.

59 Ibid., p. 893.

60 I Stat. 117; now 22 U.S. Code 252 and 253.

61 Presidential Proclamation of 24 November 1972, in Dept. of State, *United States Treaties and Other International Agreements* (T.I.A.S.), vol. 23, pp. 3227–28. The Senate resolution advising ratification had been passed on 14 September 1965.

sible; and that "in general, it would be lawful to accord the broader privileges and immunities provided for in the statute," although separate analysis may be required in specific cases.[62]

The Diplomatic Relations Act of 1978 happily cleared up this state of affairs.[63] In section 3, it first repealed the Act of 1790 and then stated that missions of nonconvention countries "shall enjoy the privileges and immunities specified" in the Vienna Convention.

Both the Act of Anne in Britain and the U.S. Act of 1790 had come to be regarded in the mid-twentieth century in those two countries as being far too sweeping in their grants of immunity. The British and American participants in the drafting of the Vienna Conventions fully supported the limitations contained in the conventions, especially on the categories of persons entitled to full immunity. As a lawyer in the State Department Legal Adviser's Office characterized the situation prior to the Vienna Conventions, when the Act of 1790 was the operative U.S. law: "When a diplomat assigned to this country saw his name on the diplomatic list, he could figure he was home free."[64]

An entertaining and legally accurate fictional narrative which illustrates that remark is Rex Stout's short story "Immune to Murder."[65] In it, foreign ambassador Theodore Kelefy is discovered by private detective Nero Wolfe to have been the perpetrator of the mysterious murder of David M. Leeson, assistant secretary of state for Kelefy's own oil-rich region. Ambassador Kelefy's motive is resentment of an earlier affair of Assistant Secretary Leeson with Kelefy's glamorous wife Adria. Wolfe, after assembling complex clues and comparing alibis, has all the suspect house guests assemble in one room, with the attorney general of New York and the district attorney of the county as witnesses. Wolfe first insists on having the secretary of state on the phone. He gives the secretary his chain of reasoning pointing to Ambassador Kelefy's guilt, then quotes from a pocket notebook the appropriate section on diplomatic immunity from the U.S. Code (the Act of 1790) and the derivatory passage in the penal code of New York State. He concludes, "That last, Mr. Secretary, explains why I insisted on speaking to you. If I had reported to the officers of the law who are here, and if in their zeal for justice they had maltreated the ambassador, not only would they have been subject to prosecution under federal

---

[62] A.W. Rovine, *Digest of United States Practice in International Law*, 1973, Department of State Publication 8756, July 1974, pp. 143–45.

[63] PL 95–393, 95th Cong., 30 Sept. 1978.

[64] Interview with W.M. McQuade, Department of State, on 16 April 1986.

[65] *American Magazine*, November 1955; and in *Three for the Chair* (New York: Bantam, 1958).

law, but so would I . . . , and I chose the expedient of reporting directly to you." The ambassador then rises to his feet and says to his wife, "Come, my dear." The two, followed by the ambassador's aide, move toward the door.

The narrator, Wolfe's assistant Archie, describes the workings of diplomatic immunity. "That was a sight I had never expected to see and don't expect to see again. Standing there were an attorney general, a district attorney, a sheriff, and three state troopers in uniform, not to mention a pair of private detectives; and none of them moved a muscle while a murderer calmly walked out of the room, taking with him his wife, who had driven him to murder, and a member of his staff, who had certainly known he was guilty."

Down-to-earth Archie ends the story: The ambassador "left for home the next day, taking his wife, and a month later they shot him, but whether it was for murder or for ruining negotiations I can't say. Diplomatically speaking, I doubt if he cared much."

To return to the Act of Anne, by a curious coincidence it seems that a later eighteenth century czar displayed a degree of touchiness and bad temper with another British Ambassador Whitworth. (This incident, however, had no particular impact on diplomatic history and no damaging effect on the ambassador's career, which subsequently included the embassy in Paris and the Lord Lieutenancy of Ireland.) The czar was Paul I, who reigned from 1796 to 1801, a ruler characterized as "tyrannical and mentally unbalanced."[66] This Lord Whitworth apparently finished his tour in St. Petersburg in a crisis of diplomatic protocol.

The circumstances of Lord Whitworth's recall had been in the last degree mysterious. Various rumours were current; amongst others, that he had offended the Czar in the following somewhat ludicrous manner: the Czar having forbidden that any empty carriage should pass before a certain part of his palace, Lord Whitworth, uninformed of the regulation, ordered his coach to meet him at a certain point which would entail passing over the forbidden area. The sentry held up the coach; the servants persisted in driving on; they came to blows; and the Czar, when the affair came to his ears, ordered Lord Whitworth's servants to be beaten, the horses to be beaten, and the coach to be beaten too. Lord Whitworth, in a fit of rage and petulance, dismissed his servants, ordered the horses to be shot and the coach broken into pieces and thrown into the Neva.[67]

It would take a legal historian to trace even in outline the way different states have evolved their domestic legislation on

---

[66] W.L. Langer, comp. and ed., *Encyclopedia of World History*, 5th ed. (Boston: Houghton Mifflin Co., 1972), p. 518.

[67] V. Sackville-West, *Knole and the Sackvilles*, 4th ed. (London: E. Benn, 1958), p. 194.

diplomatic immunity. A general impression may be formed from the published results of the UN International Law Commission's systematic work in this area. The UN secretary-general in October 1955 sent a circular to governments requesting reports on their laws and regulations on diplomats and consuls. Long, significant passages from their official replies, up to November 1957, were published by the United Nations in 1958 as *Laws and Regulations Regarding Diplomatic and Consular Privileges* (ST/LEG/SER.B/7).

Approximately sixty national replies came in from states ranging from the two superpowers to Luxembourg and the Vatican. Ironically, Iran did not reply in time for the deadline. Its statement would have made interesting reading about twenty years later.

The following sampling from that UN publication treats mainly the reports of the nations' earliest or most basic legislation, i.e., their nearest equivalent, if any, to the Act of Anne.

For Britain, Australia, and New Zealand, the Act of Anne had indeed been the starting point, and for the United States, the Act of 1790.

For France, a decree of "12 ventôse, an II" (i.e., 1793) protected the persons of foreign envoys and directed that *"réclamations"* against them should be addressed to the Committee of Public Safety. A subsequent decree of 22 messidor, an XIII, eleven years later, changed the authority from the Committee to the Ministry of Foreign Affairs.

Austria quoted a law from 1762, when the ruler in Vienna was still the Holy Roman Emperor, the symbolic successor of Augustus, Trajan, and Constantine. The Austrians cited a court decree of 23 September 1817, which in turn had stated: "By virtue of the provisions of the Instruction of 31 August 1762 all consuls of foreign Powers, whether they are Austrian or foreign nationals, shall be subject to the jurisdiction and laws of the place in which they are authorized to reside." (The ghosts of the ancient Caesars would probably have approved.) However, the Austrians also quoted their Imperial Civil Code of 1811, Article 38, that "representatives, public ministers and persons employed by them enjoy the exemptions laid down by international law and in public treaties."

The Republic of China (Taipei) cited only the Chinese text of a law of 1929 giving customs exemptions to diplomats and consuls.

Israel, still a relatively new state on the modern scene in 1956, submitted an interesting, well-drafted, 14-page essay, in the donnish manner of Abba Eban in an American television interview. It could have been taken as a chapter of a scholarly introduction to the legal system of the country. There was "no comprehensive Israeli legislation on the topic of diplomatic and consular immunity as a whole," so questions were "resolved either administratively or by what the courts might decide in a given case to be the applicable rule of international law. . . . Judicial precedents of England . . . [had] high persuasive authority." There had been a Transition Law 5709/1949 enabling the president of Israel to receive diplomatic representatives and confirm consuls. One sensed, however, that at this stage there was in practice a certain deliberate tentativeness, an advantageous untidiness about the status of diplomats and consuls in the new state. There had been, of course, no diplomats in mandatory Palestine. The consuls who had exequaturs from the British-controlled mandatory government were now "recognized in their status on a de facto basis." There were a few consuls in Israel whose governments did not recognize the new state. They were being allowed to "carry on their activities without any exequatur" and were normally accorded privileges and immunities, but "it cannot be stated with any certainty that their jurisdictional immunity would be upheld in a case involving a private litigant."

In Brazil, diplomatic and consular immunities of representatives of the American republics were governed by the provisions of the Havana Conventions of 1928. With other states' representatives, immunities were on condition of reciprocity.

In the Soviet Union's reply, the basic law was an order of 14 January 1927 of the Central Executive Committee and the Council of People's Commissions, which contained a general statement that diplomats "shall enjoy, subject to reciprocity, all the rights and privileges attaching to their status under the rules of international law." The same principle was said to apply to consuls. Earlier, in 1924, there had been an Order of the Central Executive Committee of the USSR which provided that in criminal cases "the question of the criminal liability of foreign citizens enjoying exterritoriality shall be resolved through the diplomatic channel."

Luxembourg's response to the UN inquiry stated that the only text with regard to the general subject of diplomatic immunity from the local jurisdiction was a French law of March 1804 "which has remained in force in Luxembourg since the annexation of the country by France during the French Revolution." The forty-word law, almost word-for-word the same as the 12 ventôse law in Paris, was quoted by Luxembourg in full with the comment: "This very vague text permits a rather free jurisprudential interpretation."

From Nepal came the reply that Nepal "very much regrets to inform" the United Nations that "there is not as yet any publication . . . on the laws on diplomatic and consular immunities," but such immunities are "accorded to the Diplomatic Corps" on the basis of "conventions and general international practice."

Norway cited an ordinance of 8 October 1708, which protected diplomats ("foreign ministers"), their servants, and their goods from seizure for debts.

Pakistan had "not yet formulated any rules" but accorded immunities admissible "under international law on a basis of reciprocity."

Cuba, in addition to the usual reference to "the universally accepted principles of international law," cited its "Code of Social Defence (Offences against international peace and international law)." This code provided that an offence against a diplomat was liable "to the penalty applicable to the offence plus one-third to one-half of the penalty." This seems, at least superficially, a milder form of Peter the Great's personal reaction to the assault on his ambassador in 1708.

Finland had no laws concerning diplomatic immunity and in practice observed the general principles of law, international courtesy, and generally accepted usages.

West Germany went back to a law of 1877 organizing the judicial system, in which certain persons "in virtue of generally recognized rules of international law or under a treaty, are exempt from German jurisdiction."

India reported no legislation on diplomatic immunity except Article 86 in the Code of Civil Procedure, which said there could be no suits against or arrests of a head of mission nor of such members of his staff or retinue as the Central Government may by order specify.

Ireland's constitution in Article 29(3) accepts the generally recognized principles of international law as part of the law of Ireland.

From Italy came a response which was *minimissimo* in extent. Italy had no laws or regulations on diplomatic or consular immunities but accorded them on the basis of "the usual principles which are applied by the different states."

The Vatican replied that the Holy See does not have a consular service itself, that diplomats accredited to it reside normally in Italian territory, and their status is governed by the treaty of 1929 between the Holy See and Italy. The relevant article, 12, gives these diplomats in Italy "the prerogatives and immunities which pertain to diplomatic agents in accordance with international law."

Even these brief selections from the UN's survey indicate that national governments already in 1957 were in general harmony on the principle arising out of their separate national legislative histories and their practical experience with diplomacy. Based on these facts and proceeding by discussion and compromise, there was clearly room for a major step forward toward reaching a worldwide, universal agreement on a text covering diplomatic and consular immunities.

International agreement might not be quite so comprehensive as on the technical topics of postal systems or international electronic and telephone communications. However, all governments (except the Vatican) wanted to have both diplomats and consuls, and they all had a stake in keeping diplomats and consuls secure and effective in their work on behalf of national interests. In 1961–63 the time was ripe.

Regional and Universal Conventions

As we have seen, well into the twentieth century the rules for diplomatic immunity could still only be ascertained by consulting national legislation and cases and the treatises of private authorities on the subject. In the case of consular immunities, one had to consult these same sources and, frequently, the terms of bilateral treaties.

There had long been a dream and increasingly a hope that international law on immunities could be codified, and several draft codes had been sketched by learned writers. Starting in the 1920s, more serious efforts were undertaken. Two of these significantly pointed the way toward what was later achieved in Vienna in 1961 and 1963.

The first was regional in scope: the Havana Convention on Diplomatic Officers, signed in 1928.[68] However, this treaty was put into force only by fourteen Latin American states, and its text acknowledged that it was intended as a provisional instrument until something more complete could be achieved.

A second effort was the Harvard Research Draft Convention on Diplomatic Privileges and Immunities, published in 1932.[69] If Harvard had been a Great Power, or better yet an international organization, instead of only a prestigious university, this might have been an immense step forward. However, though the "document had great persuasive authority . . . it did not lead states to modify the provisions of their domestic law where these diverged."[70]

In 1957, the International Law Commission of the United Nations undertook the herculean task of preparing a draft

---

68 Satow, 5th ed., p. 108.
69 *A.J.I.L. Supplement*, Vol. 26, 1932; and ibid.
70 Satow, 5th ed., p. 108.

Convention on Diplomatic Relations that could make the dream of a universal comprehensive law on the subject almost a reality. The commission worked carefully and, inevitably, slowly. Information and then comments were requested from all governments on an evolving succession of drafts. All members of the United Nations and its Specialized Agencies and the parties to the Statute of the World Court were invited to the final conference in 1961 in Vienna[71] (now symbolically a neutral capital but still the historic site of the great Congress of 1815 and forever haunted by the ghosts of Metternich, Talleyrand, Castlereagh, and Czar Alexander I). The conference bore such good fruit that by 1975, when the People's Republic of China acceded, the adherents included all the important actors on the world stage, and in 1985, numbered 145.[72] Without doubt, "the Vienna Convention constitutes the modern law in regard to the privileges and immunities of diplomats."[73]

The Vienna Convention on Consular Relations of 1963 was achieved by following a similar path, although the substantive situation was different in several important respects. The institution of consuls and consulates is considerably older than that of resident ambassadors and permanent diplomatic missions, and there is a large body of customary international law concerning consuls. In modern times it has often been convenient for states to conduct consular relations under bilaterally negotiated consular conventions.

The whole subject of consuls and their role is somehow more precise, down-to-earth, and less conspicuously political than that of diplomats. Much of a consul's work directly and visibly benefits and protects both individuals and commercial interests – those of the consul's own nation and of local businessmen and citizens. As one who has worked contentedly as a consul and later as an embassy political officer, the author recalls that this direct, tangible benefiting of individuals is seldom a characteristic of other diplomatic work. The consul gets midnight phone calls because some individual has been hurt or arrested. The political officer is wakened at 2:00 a.m. because someone in the State Department has to brief the assistant secretary in an hour and wants to be able to say "I had the embassy on the phone a few minutes ago and they think . . ."

The 1963 Consular Convention is longer than the 1961 Diplomatic Convention; it is more precise and closely descriptive and gives its subjects (the consuls and their posts) immunities that are

---

[71] Ibid.
[72] Command paper 9497 of April 1985, p. 6
[73] Satow, 5th ed., p. 108

much more limited and much more closely related to their official functions. Nevertheless, it was drafted, negotiated, signed, and generally accepted just as efficiently as the 1961 Convention.

*   *   *

Historical note on the first ambassador. Nicodemo Tranchedini da Pontremoli, the agent of Francesco Sforza of Milan in Florence for over 17 years (circa 1446–67), began to be considered the first resident ambassador by historians as early as 1894. However, his claim to the honor has been considerably qualified by more recent historians of diplomacy. They note that during his first years in Florence, his future sovereign, Sforza, was only a promising, ambitious *condottiere*, not yet duke of Milan. "Sweet Nicodemus," as he was known in his day,[74] was sent by Sforza to be "his personal liaison to his old friend Cosimo de' Medici," at the time neither the ruler of Florence nor its foreign minister, but rather its "most influential private citizen." When Sforza became Duke of Milan, in 1450, Nicodemo became "the regularly accredited orator resident of Milan at Florence," a position he held for seventeen years. In Mattingly's view, "It is for length and distinction of his diplomatic career, not its priority, that he deserves to be remembered."[75]

Mattingly did not nominate a particular candidate to replace Nicodemo. Likewise, D.E. Queller's more recent study on early European diplomacy did not accept Nicodemo's claim. Queller explains why he was also unconvinced by a "rather tentatively" nominated "new candidate," Othon de Grandson. Mrs. E.R. Clifford in 1961 had presented the claims of Grandson, "who spent the greater part of ten years in the early fourteenth century at Avignon on the business of the English king."[76] Queller is also not able to accept two other possibilities who have their champions, namely, the Venetian consul in Naples of 1257, whose claims have been pressed by two or three leading modern Venetian historians, including their dean R. Cessi, writing in the *Enciclopedia italiana*. Nor did Queller buy the theory that a holder of the very early office of the *baiulo* of Venice in Constantinople was the first resident ambassador.

---

[74] Wilson, *Diplomatic Privileges and Immunities*, p. 5, footnote 26.
[75] Mattingly, *Renaissance Diplomacy*, pp. 69, 85.
[76] Queller, *Office of Ambassador*, p. 79.

3

THE COVERAGE AND SCOPE OF DIPLOMATIC IMMUNITY

Much of this chapter will be devoted to a review of the contents of the Vienna Conventions of 1961 and 1963. Of special value in this task have been the commentaries and analyses of Eileen Denza, whose work on the Diplomatic Convention, published in 1976, is widely regarded as authoritative. Readers will find it a most useful source.[1] Mrs. Denza also shared responsibility for rewriting the relevant chapters in the 5th edition of *Satow's Guide to Diplomatic Practice*, heavily cited here. The texts of the 1961 and 1963 Vienna Conventions are reproduced as appendix A and appendix B.

Governments may issue administrative guidelines, which clarify the actual practices through which the language of the conventions is applied. One such useful example is a booklet currently in use by the Office of Protocol of the Department of State, entitled *Guidance for Law Enforcement Officers*. It distills the practice of the U.S. government as it relates to the immunity of persons and illustrates the subject of this chapter in practical terms. A portion of the text is reproduced as Appendix D.

The Significance and Value of the Vienna Conventions

The Vienna Convention on Diplomatic Relations, signed on 18 April 1961, came into force on 24 April 1964. The Vienna Convention on Consular Relations was signed on 24 April 1963 and came into force on 19 March 1967. Together they constitute the starting point for any discussion of contemporary practice on diplomatic and consular privileges and immunities. Now almost universally accepted, they continue to grow in authority.

Professional diplomats and international lawyers and any person interested in an orderly world might well observe a moment of silent reflection on April 24, the coincidental anniversary of the signing of the Consular Convention and the entry into force of the Diplomatic Convention a year later. There may be regrets and mental reservations about some details on the part of some governments and some expert individuals. Even the most cynical and skeptical observers of postwar international relations should concede, however, that the

---

[1] Eileen Denza, *Diplomatic Law: Commentary on the Vienna Convention on Diplomatic Relations* (Dobbs Ferry, NY: Oceana, 1976).

two conventions have proved themselves to be solid achievements, demonstrating that sovereign governments can behave responsibly, that international organizations (the United Nations and its Law Commission, in this case) can be effective, and that lawyers and legal departments can be well worth their cost.

The fifty-three articles on diplomacy and the seventy-nine on consular relations are so well organized and drafted and so relatively free of technical legal terminology that they can be read conveniently by a layman and almost entirely understood. In this chapter, we will attempt to summarize the contents of both conventions as they relate to diplomatic and consular privileges and immunities.

Two important principles are stated in the preambles of both conventions. One is that an agreement on privileges and immunities contributes to the development of friendly relations "irrespective of differing constitutional and social systems." The other is that privileges and immunities are not intended "to benefit individuals but to ensure the efficient performance of functions." The conventions' purposes are thus consonant with those of the UN Charter – to maintain international peace and security and promote friendly relations among sovereign states.

Definitions. The first article of each convention tidily covers definitions. The expressions chosen are ones which turn out to be important to diplomatic and consular immunity, as covered by later articles, and are a guide to the usage in the conventions.

For example, in the diplomatic convention, the "premises of the mission" are the buildings and ancillary land "irrespective of ownership, used for the purposes of the mission including the residence of the head of the Mission." In the consular convention, the "consular premises" are the buildings and ancillary land "used exclusively" for the purposes of the post. "Consular archives" include not only papers but "films, tapes and registers . . . together with the ciphers and codes, the card-indexes and . . . furniture intended for their protection or safekeeping."

Persons covered by at least a degree of immunity are also "defined" in what is essentially a list of terms; for in practice it is up to the sending state to give titles to its personnel at a mission, subject only to acceptance of those titles by the receiving state. As Denza points out, a sending state could decide to style all its "private servants" as "service staff."[2] The 1961 convention distinguishes between the head of mission, members of the mission, members of the staff, members of the diplomatic staff, a diplomatic agent,

---

[2] Denza, *Diplomatic Law*, p. 13.

administrative and technical staff, service staff, and a private servant. Other persons entitled to full or limited immunity include, for example, the family members of diplomatic agents and of administrative and technical staff if they form "part of the household" and if they are not nationals of the receiving state (article 37).

Consular convention articles 40 through 52 cover the immunities and exemptions of consular officers and staffs, which are much more restricted than those of diplomatic staffs. In addition, as noted earlier, consular immunities are described in more precise detail and, usually, closely and specifically tied to their official duties.

Bilateral conventions. Consular relations are often the subject of bilateral agreements, and the degree of specific immunity can be defined only in the light of these. Both the United States and the United Kingdom have bilateral consular agreements with the Soviet Union and several East European governments. These agreements extend much fuller immunity than the 1963 Vienna Convention would afford. Because of the contrast in legal and political systems and the occasional periods of tensions in diplomatic relations, both sides wish a particularly full freedom from local criminal, civil, and administrative jurisdictions for their consulates in the receiving states.

Following World War II, as Satow notes, states such as Britain having large consular services found it in their best interest to increase the use of career, as opposed to honorary, consuls. It was also more efficient to merge their consular and diplomatic services so that many individual officers could be assigned either to embassies or to consulates. To improve upon customary taxation and customs privileges, major states negotiated a network of bilateral consular conventions. Beginning in 1948, the United Kingdom, for example, concluded consular conventions with the United States and fourteen other states, mostly Western European. Subsequent consular conventions negotiated with Eastern European governments for the purpose of providing greater protection conferred "full diplomatic immunities and personal inviolability" on consuls, junior staff, private servants, and their families.[3]

In the case of the United States, agreements with Hungary, the People's Republic of China, Poland, the Philippines, and the Soviet Union provide, on a reciprocal basis, that consular personnel and members of their families shall have full criminal immunity. Special U.S. agreements with the People's Republic of China and the Soviet

---

[3] Satow, 5th ed., pp. 221–22.

Union, also on a reciprocal basis, give full criminal immunity to all embassy personnel and members of their families.[4]

A clear illustration of the growing acceptance of the Vienna Convention of 1961 as an accepted and convenient guide to diplomatic practice occurred when the United States and the Mongolian People's Republic established diplomatic relations at the ambassadorial level for the first time on 27 January 1987. The two governments had worked out the agreement over several months through their delegations at the United Nations in New York.[5] They signed a memorandum giving the framework of their relations under six points, the second of which was that relations would be governed by the 1961 Vienna Convention. Any questions not covered therein would be governed by customary international law. In the fifth point, both governments agreed to the use of wireless transmitters by their embassies, citing article 27 of the convention.[6]

Such bilateral arrangements are reflected in article 73 of the 1963 convention, which expressly recognizes the right of states to conclude "international agreements confirming or supplementing or extending or amplifying" the convention's provisions. One must therefore be aware of the terms of any existing bilateral conventions, even between states that are parties to the Vienna Convention. Satow points out that the United Kingdom and its treaty partners have agreed that "where a bilateral convention accorded [consuls] a lower standard of privilege or immunity, the Vienna scale of privilege or immunity should be accorded." Those affected thus "enjoy the higher immunities set out in the Vienna Convention and the higher tax privileges specified in the bilateral consular conventions."[7]

The System of Immunities under the Conventions

The two Vienna Conventions set forth the system of immunities and privileges for diplomats and consuls principally in terms of: (1) the functions it is intended to cover; (2) the "premises," i.e., buildings and spaces; (3) the persons; (4) customs duties and inspection; (5) the records and communications; and (6) certain other provisions. In matters not regulated by the Vienna Conventions, the rules of customary international law continue to apply.

[4] "Diplomatic Immunity and U.S. Interests," *Current Policy*, No. 993, U.S. Department of State, Bureau of Public Affairs, August 1987, p. 3.

[5] *Washington Post*, 28 Jan. 1987.

[6] Marian Nash Leich, *American Journal of International Law*, Vol. 81, No. 3 (July 1987), pp. 641–42.

[7] Satow, 5th ed., p. 222.

The functions. As the stated purpose of privileges and immunities is to "ensure the efficient performance" of diplomatic and consular functions, it is important to note what the conventions state these functions to be. As set forth in the 1961 convention (article 3),

The functions of a diplomatic mission consist, *inter alia*, in:
(*a*) representing the sending State in the receiving State;
(*b*) protecting in the receiving State the interests of the sending State and of its nationals, within the limits permitted by international law;
(*c*) negotiating with the Government of the receiving State;
(*d*) ascertaining by all lawful means conditions and developments in the receiving State, and reporting thereon to the Government of the sending State;
(*e*) promoting friendly relations between the sending State and the receiving State, and developing their economic, cultural and scientific relations.

The list of functions of a consular post, enumerated in article 5 of the 1963 convention, is longer (thirteen items instead of five) and more specific and detailed than that of a diplomatic mission. There is no reference to "*inter alia*," only a final miscellaneous item, paragraph (*m*), indicating that consular functions consist also in

performing any other functions entrusted to a consular post by the sending State which are not prohibited by the laws and regulations of the receiving State or to which no objection is taken by the receiving State or which are referred to in the international agreements in force between the sending State and the receiving State.

The specific consular functions, which are officially recognized and therefore covered by immunity are, in summary:

(*a*) protecting the interests of the sending state and its nationals, including corporate bodies;
(*b*) furthering commercial, economic, cultural, and scientific relations and "otherwise promoting friendly relations";
(*c*) "ascertaining by all lawful means conditions and developments in the commercial, economic, cultural and scientific life of the receiving State, reporting thereon to the Government of the sending State and giving information to persons interested";
(*d*) issuing passports to sending state nationals and visas or appropriate travel documents to receiving state nationals;
(*e*) assisting individuals and corporate bodies of the sending state;
(*f*) acting as notary and civil registrar;
(*g*) safeguarding the interests of sending state individuals and corporate entities in cases of death in the receiving state;
(*h*) safeguarding the interests of "minors or persons lacking full capacity who are nationals of the sending State";
(*i*) representing or arranging representation for nationals of the

sending state before tribunals and other authorities of the receiving state where, because of absence or other reasons, the nationals are unable to appear at the proper time;

(*j*) transmitting judicial documents or executing commissions to take evidence for the courts of the sending state;

(*k*) exercising supervision and inspection in respect of sending state vessels and aircraft and their crews;

(*l*) assisting such vessels, aircraft, and crews, examining their papers, and conducting investigations into incidents during their voyages and settling disputes between the master, officers, and seamen.

Functions (*f*) through (*j*), (*l*), and (*m*) are expressly limited by the need to conform to the laws and regulations of the receiving state.

The question naturally arises as to whether the receiving state has any obligation under the convention to facilitate a consul's actions under this long list of recognized consular functions. Most important, what about consular access to sending State nationals when they are detained?

On facilitating *"communication and contact with nationals of the sending State"* (article 36), there are three provisions: (1) that consuls shall be free to communicate with and have access to their nationals and vice versa; (2) that the authorities of the receiving state shall inform the consul without delay if a foreign national who is arrested, imprisoned or "detained in any other manner" so requests, that any other communication from him shall be forwarded to the consul without delay, and that the authorities shall inform the detainee of these rights; and (3) that consuls shall have the right to visit such a person "to converse and correspond with him and to arrange for his legal representation." In addition, the "laws and regulations of the receiving State" on this subject "must enable full effect to be given to the purposes for which the rights accorded under this article are intended."

These general requirements are sharpened in some bilateral consular conventions. In the aftermath of a troubling case of delayed access, the British government insisted that its consular convention with the Soviet Union oblige the receiving state to notify the consul of the arrest of one of his nationals and grant him access on a recurrent basis. The British government has included similar provisions in bilateral consular conventions with nearly all Eastern European countries, as has the United States.[8]

Formal consular assistance and right of access to all those persons the sending state wishes to treat as its nationals have in some cases

---

[8] Satow, 5th ed., p. 219.

met resistance by the receiving state for policy reasons. Satow cites the U.S. refusal in 1962 to allow the consul general of West Germany to act on behalf of Germans living in East Germany, or to allow the Soviet consul to act on behalf of Estonian and Lithuanian nationals."[9]

Premises. The places, or premises, that for functional reasons are to be inviolate under the two conventions are, in general, where the work is done and the records kept and where the diplomatic agents and consular officers live.

DIPLOMATIC PREMISES DEFINED. The 1961 convention defines the premises of the mission as "the buildings or parts of buildings and the land ancillary thereto, irrespective of ownership, used for the purposes of the mission including the residence of the mission" (article 1).

INVIOLABILITY. These premises "shall be inviolable. The agents of the receiving State may not enter them, except with the consent of the head of the mission" (article 22). Further, the premises, "their furnishings and other property thereon and the means of transport of the mission shall be immune from search, requisition, attachment or execution." A short phrase sometimes used for this particular immunity is freedom from "jurisaction."[10] The same inviolability and protection applies to the private residence of a diplomatic agent (article 30). In situations where diplomatic relations are broken off or a mission is recalled, the receiving state must "respect and protect the premises of the mission, together with its property and archives," even in cases of armed conflict (article 45).

TAXATION. The premises of the mission are "exempt from all national, regional or municipal dues and taxes . . . other than such as represent payment for specific services rendered" (article 23), e.g., utilities and trash collection.

EXPROPRIATION FOR PUBLIC PURPOSES. In the latter half of this century, large cities, including national capitals, are constantly being replanned and rebuilt. Venerable structures and prominent landmarks are often displaced or completely eliminated from new "paths of progress." How would an "inviolable" embassy building fare in such circumstances?

The question of expropriating embassy premises in the public interest was extensively discussed when the Vienna Convention of 1961 was being prepared. Most governments advocated cooperation

---

9 Ibid., p. 213.
10Denza, *Diplomatic Law*, p. 78.

by the sending state, subject to bilateral negotiation, but did not accord the receiving state "any right to override a refusal by the sending State to give up mission premises or diplomatic residences." The U.S. position, however, was "that international law did not absolutely preclude the requisitioning of diplomatic property or its taking 'by exercise of the right of eminent domain,' " at least in "exceptional circumstances and subject to a duty to make prompt compensation and assist the mission to find alternative accommodation."[11] In the end, the 1961 convention made no reference to this question of expropriation.

What, then, is the pattern of practice on this necessarily delicate subject? Denza, writing in 1976, offers an indirectly relevant case involving the construction of the Fleet Line underground railway in 1966. Since the line was to run under the premises of many diplomatic residences in London, the Foreign Office sought their consent to proceed. "General compulsory procedures were not used . . . out of concern to protect [the embassies'] peace and dignity." None objected, "although several asked for confirmation that compensation would be paid in the event of resulting damages to their premises."[12]

The British embassy in Moscow, long established in a fine, formerly private mansion across the Moscow River from the Kremlin, was subjected to decades of attempts to move it by Soviet leaders reportedly upset by the "unavoidable sight of the Union Jack from the Kremlin windows." Finally, in May 1986, despite British reluctance to give up such a historic, beautiful, and commanding site, the Foreign Office accepted another riverside site after Soviet authorities had informed them that "the choice of sites for the new embassy would be withdrawn and a new site 'imposed' if a decision was not made quickly." In reciprocation, the Soviet embassy in London was to be modernized and expanded.[13]

ABANDONED PREMISES. Although diplomatic premises are inviolate and the receiving state is under an obligation to protect them, the Vienna Convention leaves open the question of what to do about such buildings when they are temporarily or indefinitely abandoned by the sending state. An article by Leana Pooley in the London *Evening Standard* of 7 October 1987 surveyed the situation in London. A new Diplomatic and Consular Premises Act had been

---

[11] Ibid., p. 85.
[12] Ibid.
[13] *The Times* (London), 17 Sept. 1986.

passed in May and was to come into force by the end of 1987. Under the act, the foreign secretary would be able to take title to diplomatic or consular buildings which were "lying empty (or without diplomatic occupants)" if the buildings "could cause damage to pedestrians or neighboring buildings because of their neglect." The foreign secretary would sell the buildings, use the proceeds to pay debts, and return the balance to the sending state.

Pooley observed that the Iranian embassy residence in Princes Gate, part of a row of fine terrace houses, had become dilapidated since its abandonment in 1980. The neighbors on each side complained it was causing damp and weakening their buildings. The embassy building was being guarded by the police of the Diplomatic Protection Group. The former Cambodian embassy building in Avenue Road, London N.W.8, abandoned eleven years earlier, had been informally occupied in the interim by a group of squatters calling themselves the Guild of Trans-Cultural Studies and "occasionally organizing talks about mysticism and ley lines." The two Libyan embassy buildings, one on St. James's Square and the other on Princes Gate, were in better condition. The latter had been occupied for a time by squatters, who had been evicted by the police.

Shortly before Ms. Pooley's survey, the unused Libyan embassy building on St. James's Square, where WPC Fletcher had been killed in April 1984, acquired a new tenant. In mid-September 1987, Elders, an Australian brewing company, signed a twenty-year lease and began preparing to restore the premises. A Libyan embassy document shredder, correspondence, a film about Col. Qadhafi, and other paraphernalia had to be cleared. This transaction removed the abandoned property, estimated to be worth around £15 million, from the protective custody of the Saudi Arabian embassy.[14]

Disposition of the abandoned Iranian embassy building in Princes Gate was on the agenda of British-Iranian talks held in London in early June 1988. The three-day talks covered reparations for damages done to the two countries' diplomatic property. Iran had claimed damages of £1.8 million suffered in 1980 during the dramatic seizure of its embassy by British commandos rescuing hostages held there by anti-Khomeini Iranians. For its part, Britain claimed £900,000 for damages to its Tehran embassy by Iranians from 1978 to 1980. The two governments reached "broad agreement" on June 10, with only minor details remaining to be settled, based on Britain's offer to pay Iranian claims, with Iran to pay

---

[14] *The Observer* (London), 20 Sept. 1987.

Britain's.[15] In addition, the British government reportedly expected to pay about $370,000 (over £200,000) compensation to the borough of Westminster for eight years' upkeep on the Princes Gate embassy building.[16]

In Washington, embassies temporarily abandoned due to broken relations may be sequestered and turned to other uses pending resumption of relations. This has been the case with the Iranian embassy facilities since the break in diplomatic relations that occurred in April 1980.

CONSULAR PREMISES. The Vienna Convention of 1963 defines premises in the same language as that used in the 1961 convention, except that consular premises are those "used exclusively for the purposes of the consular post." However, the inviolability of consular premises is clearly less comprehensive (article 31). For example, authorities may not enter the premises of the consulate without the consent of the head of the consular post, his representative, or the head of the diplomatic mission of the sending state. However, this rule applies only to that part of the consular premises "used exclusively for the work of the consular post." Consent is assumed in case of fire or other emergency. Further, expropriation of consular property is clearly contemplated as a possibility if deemed necessary "for purposes of national defence or public utility."[17] The caveat to this point is that "all possible steps shall be taken" to avoid disrupting consular functions and to provide "adequate and effective compensation."

Exemption from taxation is provided for consular premises and the consular head's residence on the same terms as for mission premises (article 32). However, in the 1963 convention this exemption "shall not apply to such dues and taxes if under the law of the receiving State, they are payable by the person [e.g., a landlord] who contracted with the sending State or with the person acting on its behalf." These distinctions limiting the inviolability and tax exemption of consulates seem to reflect the fact that consulate premises are often suites in office buildings or apartment buildings or even hotels, with shared hallways, entrances, and elevators and often are rented from the building owner.

ASYLUM. The question of whether embassy or consulate premises can provide asylum is not directly covered in the Vienna Conventions of 1961 and 1963. The premises are simply declared to be

15 *Times* (London), 11 June 1988.
16 *Washington Post*, 6 June 1988.
17 In Satow's view, "such expropriation could not take place in regard to diplomatic premises except with the express consent of the sending state." 5th ed., p. 223.

inviolable, and officials of the receiving state may not enter them except with the consent of the head of mission or of the consular post respectively. Thus inviolability is set forth in such a way as to leave open the possibility of asylum.

In the preparatory work of the International Law Commission, according to Denza, "the majority of members of the Commission were of the opinion that it was possible to separate the question of diplomatic asylum from that of inviolability of embassy premises, since in modern law and practice it was not seriously contended that a failure on the part of the mission to comply with the rules relating to asylum entitled the receiving State to enter the premises." This tactic was a prudent side step that averted possible political acrimony at the Vienna Conference over the question of asylum.[18]

In practice, asylum in diplomatic and consular premises is often permitted in Latin America.[19] There was even a Convention on Diplomatic Asylum drafted at the Tenth Inter-American Conference held in 1954 in Caracas, Venezuela.[20] The procedure under this convention provides that the person seeking asylum stay only long enough to be allowed to leave the territory of the receiving state under that state's guarantee of safe passage. If the receiving state requires the post to be closed, the departing diplomat can take the asylee with him, or if that is not feasible, transfer him to asylum in another post's premises. If the asylees are too numerous for the existing premises, the post can provide additional premises, which shall also be inviolable. Such pro-asylum arrangements are not countenanced in Europe or most other regions.[21]

The U.S. government's policy in recent years has been to try to avoid giving asylum except in cases of mob violence. However, recent administrations have made exceptions due to congressional and public sympathy toward persons who seek asylum in U.S. diplomatic and consular premises in Communist countries. There is a feeling that any such asylum seeker claiming to be in danger because of political or religious views should be given the benefit of the doubt. While nothing should be done to entice or even encourage asylum, once persons take the initiative to seek asylum, they will not be expelled from the premises.

The attitude the United States would take toward cases where an American or other national sought asylum in an embassy in Washington has not been tested. Such an instance almost occurred on

[18] Denza, *Diplomatic Law*, p. 82.
[19] Satow, 5th ed., p. 113.
[20] For the terms of this convention, see R.G. Feltham, *Diplomatic Handbook*, 4th ed. (London and New York: Longmans, 1982), pp. 108–9.
[21] Satow, 5th ed., p. 114.

21 November 1985 when Jonathan Pollard and his wife, who were under FBI surveillance, attempted to seek asylum in the Israeli embassy. The embassy declined to let them stay, but did immediately send home Pollard's official Israeli contacts, both of whom had diplomatic immunity. Pollard later pleaded guilty to a charge of espionage.[22]

Persons enjoying immunity. The Vienna Conventions have greatly clarified the categories of persons who enjoy full or limited diplomatic or consular privileges and immunities and have reduced the categories of those entitled to full immunity.[23]

DIPLOMATIC CATEGORIES. Those accorded immunities are the head of the mission and its members. These include: "members of the diplomatic staff," defined as those who have diplomatic rank; "members of the administrative and technical staff," defined as those "employed in the administrative and technical service of the mission"; "members of the service staff," defined as those "in the domestic service of the mission"; and any "private servant," defined as "a person who is in the domestic service of a member of the mission and who is not an employee of the sending State" (article 1). The immunity of the technical and administrative staff, the service staff, and the private servants is greatly affected by whether they are nationals of the sending or receiving state. If the latter, their immunity is severely limited.

PROTECTION OF DIPLOMATIC AGENTS. The highest degree of privilege and immunity is enjoyed by diplomatic agents, defined (article 1) as the head of the mission or members of its diplomatic staff. Their persons "shall be inviolable" (article 29), and they are "not . . . liable to any form of arrest or detention." The receiving state must treat them "with due respect" and "take all appropriate steps to prevent any attack on [their] person[s], freedom or dignity." The private residence of the diplomatic agent, as previously noted, is inviolable and protected to the same degree as the premises of the mission. This means that it cannot be entered by the receiving state's officials except with the consent of the head of mission (article 30).

CRIMINAL AND CIVIL IMMUNITIES. Diplomatic agents enjoy full immunity from the criminal jurisdiction of the receiving state (article 31). With some exceptions, immunity from the civil and administrative jurisdiction of the receiving state is also granted, but not immunity from the jurisdiction of the sending state. If a person

---

22 *Washington Post*, 15 Feb. 1987.
23 Denza, *Diplomatic Law*, pp. 4–5 and pp. 225–31 on art. 37.

accorded immunity initiates proceedings against another party, this "shall preclude him from invoking immunity from jurisdiction in respect of any counter-claim directly connected with the principal claim" (article 32, ¶3).

WAIVER OF IMMUNITY. A significant feature of the system is that diplomatic immunity from receiving state jurisdiction may be waived by the sending state (article 32). This is a very real deterrent to abuse of immunity by covered individuals in the case of the U.S., British, and some other governments, as we later note. Waivers of immunity "must always be express" (i.e., not merely implied), and waiver of immunity from jurisdiction in civil or administrative proceedings does not imply waiver of immunity regarding execution of the judgment, "for which a separate waiver shall be necessary" (article 32). A sending state may thus choose to concede that its diplomatic agent deserves indictment and trial by the receiving state, but still reserve the right to reject the resulting judgment, for example, if it is not satisfied the judgment is fair.

PERSONAL EXEMPTIONS. Diplomatic agents are exempt, with respect to services rendered for the sending state, from social security provisions of the receiving state. Such exemption extends also to private servants in the sole employ of the agent unless they are "nationals of or permanently resident in the receiving State" and are not covered by social security provisions in the sending state or a third state (article 33). The diplomatic agent is exempt "from all dues and taxes, personal or real, national, regional or municipal," with certain exceptions. These exceptions include: indirect taxes, such as a value added tax (VAT), "normally incorporated in the price of goods or services"; property taxes, except on property held "on behalf of the sending State for the purposes of the mission"; estate, succession, or inheritance duties, except on movable property not related to the deceased's presence as a member of a diplomatic mission or of such person's family; and several other enumerated categories of local dues, taxes, fees, and charges (article 34).

In commenting on the "great practical importance in every country" of article 34 on taxation, Denza cites as evidence of the functional approach of the article's drafters the types of exceptions to tax exemption found in the article. These cover "matters unrelated to a diplomat's official activities, . . . taxes which are really payment for services rendered, and taxes where refund or exemption would be administratively impractical."[24] She notes "broad agreement that diplomats should not be required to contribute to such

[24] Denza, *Diplomatic Law*, p. 4.

matters as national defence, public education, social security benefits or the general expenses of central government."[25]

Diplomatic agents are also exempted from all personal and public
services, including military obligations, of the receiving state (article
35). Customs exemptions for diplomats, diplomatic missions, consulates, and consular officers are discussed later in this chapter.

FAMILY MEMBERS AND OTHER STAFF. To what extent are these
immunities of diplomatic agents enjoyed by the other members of
the mission, such as the families of diplomatic agents, the administrative and technical staff and their families, the service staff, and
the private servants of members of the mission? Or that separate
category, the diplomatic agents and members and servants of the
mission who are nationals of or permanently resident in the
receiving state?

For *sending state nationals not permanently resident in the
receiving state*, the rules are laid down in article 37:

1. "The members of the family of a diplomatic agent forming part
   of his household" enjoy the full immunities of the agent himself
   (articles 29 to 36), unless they are nationals of the receiving
   state.
2. "Members of the administrative and technical staff . . . together
   with members of their families forming part of their respective
   households, shall . . . enjoy the privileges and immunities" of
   diplomatic agents "except that the immunity from civil and
   administrative jurisdiction . . . *shall not extend to acts performed outside the course of their duties*" (emphasis added). The
   phrase "course of their duties" in the diplomatic convention was
   deliberately selected, in Denza's view, to be wider than that later
   adopted in the corresponding articles (43 and 44) in the consular
   convention – "in the exercise of consular functions." In practice, she believes, if the head of the mission were to state that the
   acts of one of his officers were performed in the course of his
   duties, proving otherwise would be very difficult. A formula of
   "performed in the exercise of diplomatic functions" would have
   been much narrower.[26]
3. The members of the service staff "enjoy immunity in respect of
   acts performed in the course of their duties" and "exemption
   from dues and taxes on the emoluments they receive by reason of
   their employment. . . ."
4. "Private servants of members of the mission" are also "exempt
   from dues and taxes on the emoluments they receive by reason of

25 Ibid., p. 195.
26 Ibid., pp. 230–31.

their employment." Any other privileges and immunities they may enjoy are "only to the extent admitted by the receiving State," which, however, must not "interfere unduly with the performance of the functions of the mission."

For those diplomatic agents and other members of the mission who are *nationals of or permanently resident in the receiving state,* the rules of immunity are explicitly circumscribed. Such a diplomatic agent "except insofar as additional privileges and immunities may be granted by the receiving State . . . shall enjoy only immunity from jurisdiction, and inviolability, in respect of official acts performed in the exercise of his functions" (article 38, ¶1). This severe limitation of privileges is consistent with the general opinion that a diplomat should be a national of his sending state and in particular *not* a national of the state where he serves in a mission. Many foreign services do not take kindly even to the idea of their diplomats having foreign wives. The Vienna Convention on Diplomatic Relations, Article 8, states that diplomats "should in principle be of the nationality of the sending State," that if they are nationals of the receiving state they may be appointed only "with the consent of that State which may be withdrawn at any time," and that "the receiving State may reserve the same right with regard to nationals of a third State who are not also nationals of the sending State."

The other categories of mission staff members and private servants who are receiving state nationals or permanent residents "shall enjoy privileges and immunities only to the extent admitted by the receiving State," which, as in article 37 respecting private servants not nationals or permanent residents of the receiving state, must exercise its jurisdiction without undue interference with the functions of the mission (article 38, ¶2).

CONSULAR CATEGORIES. Under the 1963 Convention on Consular Relations, the privileges and immunities of persons at a consular post are more limited in many respects than those of persons at a diplomatic mission under the 1961 Convention on Diplomatic Relations. The 1963 convention, articles 40–52, covers immunities of career (as distinct from honorary) consular officers and other members of consular posts headed by a career consular officer.

Applicable *categories of persons at a consular post,* as defined in article 1, are the "head of consular post," defined as the person charged with "acting in that capacity"; the "consular officer," anyone, including the head, "entrusted in that capacity" to exercise consular functions; the "consular employee," anyone "employed in the administrative or technical service of a consular post"; and "member of the service staff," one "employed in the domestic service of a consular post." "Members of the consular post" are all of the above, i.e., officers, employees, and service staff members; "members of the consular staff" are all but the head of the post; and "members of the private staff" are those "employed exclusively in the private service of a member of the consular post."

There are different degrees of privileges and immunities for officers, employees, and service staff members. After reviewing them, we shall see that the immunities are also accorded differentially for honorary consuls (articles 58 through 67) and for those consular post members who are nationals or permanent residents of the receiving state.

There is yet another categorical distinction (article 70) concerning applicable immunities. When a member of a diplomatic mission is charged with the exercise of consular functions, for example in the consular section of an embassy, that person's "privileges and immunities . . . shall continue to be governed by the rules of international law concerning diplomatic relations," that is, those of diplomatic agents summarized above under the Vienna Convention of 1961.

PERSONAL PROTECTIONS. The consular convention is more restrictive than the corresponding section of the diplomatic convention, which states unequivocally (article 29): "The person of a diplomatic agent shall be inviolable. He shall not be liable to any form of arrest or detention. The receiving State shall treat him with due respect and shall take all appropriate steps to prevent any attack on his person, freedom or dignity." In contrast, article 40 of the consular convention, on *"Protection of consular officers,"* does not use the word "inviolable." Rather, it provides only that "the receiving State shall treat consular officers with due respect and shall take all appropriate steps to prevent any attack on their persons, freedom or dignity."

As compared to that of diplomatic officers, the personal inviolability of consular officers contains several important limitations (article 41). (1) Consular officers can be arrested or detained "pending trial . . . in the case of a grave crime" when duly ordered "by the competent judicial authority." (2) In such cases only, they may be imprisoned or otherwise restricted, provided these steps are "in execution of a judicial decision of final effect." (3) Paragraph 3 of article 41 even describes the procedure for dealing with a consul accused of "a grave crime," which emphasizes the respect that must be accorded the officer. The proceedings should not unduly "hamper the exercise of consular functions," except in the case of a grave crime, and even then they "shall be instituted with the minimum of delay."

If any member of the consular staff is arrested, detained, or prosecuted, the receiving state must "promptly notify the head of the consular post." If it is the head of the post himself who is the accused, the receiving state must notify the sending state through diplomatic channels.

JURISDICTIONAL IMMUNITY. Consular officers are entitled to immunity from civil and administrative jurisdiction in the receiving state "in respect of acts performed in the exercise of consular functions." Two civil actions not covered by immunity are those "arising out of a contract concluded by a consular officer or a consular employee in which he did not contract expressly or impliedly as an agent of the sending State" and those "by a third party for damage arising from an accident in the receiving State caused by a vehicle, vessel or aircraft" (article 43).

"LIABILITY TO GIVE EVIDENCE" (article 44). The members of a consular post are expected to serve as witnesses in court in some cases, in contrast to diplomatic agents, who, under the 1961 convention (article 31), are "not obliged to give evidence as a witness." Members of consular posts are not, however, obliged to give evidence or to produce documents "concerning matters connected with the exercise of their functions" or "as expert witnesses with regard to the law of the sending State."

A consular witness has some significant privileges in that "no coercive measure or penalty may be applied to him" should he decline to give evidence. This provision could have considerable importance to a consul in some developing or highly authoritarian countries. In addition, evidence may be taken at the consular witness's residence or consular post or in writing, in order to avoid disruption of consular functions.

WAIVER OF IMMUNITY (article 45). Provisions for waiving the privileges or immunities of consuls by the sending state are similar to those for diplomatic agents: the waiver must be express, and a waiver of immunity from proceedings does not imply a waiver from measures of execution, for which "a separate waiver shall be necessary." Likewise, self-initiated proceedings "preclude [a consular post member] from invoking immunity from jurisdiction in respect of any counter-claim directly connected with the principal claim."

PERSONAL EXEMPTIONS. Consular officers and employees who are permanent employees of the sending state and family members of their household are exempt from alien registration and residence permit requirements of the receiving state, excepting those "who carry on any private gainful occupation in the receiving State" (article 46).

Members of the consular post are exempt from work permit

requirements "with respect to services rendered for the sending State," and the private staff of consular officers and employees are similarly exempt if they are not otherwise gainfully employed in the receiving state (article 47).

Like diplomatic agents, members of the consular post and their families are also exempt from social security provisions (article 48) and taxation (article 49), with similar exceptions, including those for private and service staff members. Exemptions from inheritance duties (article 51) and from personal services and contributions, including military (article 52), are also covered under the convention.

Customs duties and inspection. The conventions on both diplomatic and consular relations provide exemption from customs duties and inspection. As in several other categories of exemptions, the consular convention is more restrictive.

EXEMPTION FROM CUSTOMS DUTIES. On these questions, the Vienna conferences found themselves codifying practices that were difficult to generalize. As Denza observes: "Prior to the Vienna Convention there was general agreement among writers, strongly supported by State practice and legislation, that the grant of customs privileges to members of diplomatic missions was not a legal requirement of customary international law but a matter of courtesy, comity or reciprocity only." While "customs privileges were almost universally accorded," when one surveyed the applicable rules, "very little common practice could be deduced." Usually, for example, there were quantitative limits, but many countries did not "disclose officially either the existence of restrictions or the limits set, except by way of complaint of excessive imports to an individual mission."[27]

The diplomatic convention declares (article 36):

1. The receiving State shall, in accordance with such laws and regulations as it may adopt, permit entry of and grant exemption from all customs duties, taxes, and related charges other than charges for storage, cartage and similar services, on:
(a) Articles for the official use of the mission;
(b) Articles for the personal use of a diplomatic agent or members of his family forming part of his household, including articles intended for his establishment.

This formulation leaves room for considerable discretion by individual countries as to how diplomats' immunity from customs will be regulated. In practice, therefore, it is necessary for each embassy to ascertain the applicable local laws and customs regulations.

[27] Denza, *Diplomatic Law*, pp. 211–12.

Issues include procedures to clear official and personal goods; what goods are forbidden without special permission (e.g., firearms); allowable quantities of items such as tobacco; and what customs permission is required before a diplomat sells goods he has imported duty-free.

The foreign ministry is usually the best source for this information. The British Foreign Office, for example, set forth some general rules in a memorandum circulated to diplomatic missions in London in 1966, when the United Kingdom became a party to the Vienna Convention.[28] Briefly, these rules included: (1) relief from customs duties only to goods originating in foreign or Commonwealth countries, except British manufactured cars previously owned and used abroad; (2) the requirement that such goods must be for the personal use of an entitled person or the official use of the mission and must not be sold, hired, lent, or given away; (3) the right of the commissioner of customs to limit quantities to those not "in excess of reasonable genuine requirements"; (4) the right reserved by Customs to examine such duty-free goods "in exceptional circumstances," normally "after consultation with the privileged importer"; and (5) arrangements for the temporary export of a car acquired or imported under diplomatic privilege and the requirement to notify Customs if a vehicle is being permanently exported.

To illustrate the application of the third-mentioned regulation, a senior Foreign Office official told this writer that H.M. Customs discovered a certain ambassador was importing quality cigarettes in quantities that seemed suspiciously large. Before agreeing to clamp down administratively, the officer made an occasion to call on the ambassador so as to tell him personally that he would shortly be receiving a restrictive notice from Customs. The ambassador served coffee, and the call commenced with a general discussion on some matters of mutual interest in the relations between the United Kingdom and the ambassador's country. The senior Foreign Office official soon observed that even in this relaxed social setting the ambassador chain-smoked at a startlingly rapid rate. He decided that the ambassador's personal habits probably accounted for the high level of his duty-free tobacco imports, never raised the intended subject of his call, and forestalled any clampdown by H.M. Customs on the grounds that it was not necessary and might injure good relations.

EXEMPTION FROM INSPECTION. The sometimes touchy subject of baggage inspection is covered in article 36, paragraph 2, as follows:

---

[28] Memorandum on Diplomatic Privileges and Immunities, Annex C, as cited in Satow, 5th ed., pp. 139–40.

The personal baggage of a diplomatic agent shall be exempt from inspection, unless there are serious grounds for presuming that it contains articles not covered by the exemptions mentioned in paragraph 1 . . . or articles the import or export of which is prohibited by the law or controlled by the quarantine regulations of the receiving State. Such inspections shall be conducted only in the presence of the diplomatic agent or of his authorized representative.

In September 1986, the Italian Foreign Ministry announced as an antiterrorist measure that all diplomatic baggage and pouches in Italy would be scanned by metal detectors and possibly by X-ray devices.[29] This seemed to be an innovation in national practice. In April 1985, the British Foreign Secretary had indicated his government's policy was "against the introduction of scanning as a matter of routine," but that Britain would "be ready to scan any bag on specific occasions where the grounds for suspicion are sufficiently strong."[30] The U.S. State Department's Office of Foreign Missions has resisted the practice of scanning when applied to U.S. diplomatic pouches, as described in chapter 4 below.

CONSULAR EXEMPTIONS. The 1963 Convention on Consular Relations (article 50), while granting exemptions along the same lines as the 1961 diplomatic convention (article 36) and in almost exactly the same language, adds several limitations. Articles intended for the consular officer's personal use may not exceed "the quantities necessary for direct utilization by the persons concerned." In addition, consular employees enjoy customs privileges and exemptions only "in respect of articles imported at the time of first installation," but not upon subsequent reentries.

The exemption from customs examination of personal baggage, in the case of consular officers and members of their families forming part of their households, is for "personal baggage *accompanying*" such persons (emphasis added), which may be subject to inspection "if there is serious reason to believe" it contains prohibited or quarantined articles, provided such inspection is conducted in the presence of the consular officer or family member concerned. Since that person must be "accompanying" the piece of baggage that customs may inspect on the grounds of serious suspicions, one can visualize the scenario at the customs officer's counter. This contrasts with the situation of the diplomatic agent's baggage as set forth in article 36 of the 1961 convention, where the relevant language leaves room for him to decline to witness the opening of an unaccompanied suitcase and instead to send an "authorized representative."

29 *Daily Telegraph* (London), 11 Sept. 1986, and *Times* (London), 12 Sept. 1986.
30 Command Paper 9497, April 1985, pp. 20–21

BAGGAGE SEARCHES. This question of what diplomatic or consular personal luggage may be searched and by whom is illuminated by Denza. Prior to the Vienna Convention of 1961, she observes, "there was no uniform rule of international law . . . exempting diplomatic agents from search of their personal baggage," though heads of mission were usually exempted and other diplomats, too, in many countries. Article 30, which makes the property of a diplomatic agent inviolable, would seem to cover his personal luggage. In view of the clear intent of the conference, as expressed in article 36, to provide for possible searches, Denza believes that a proviso to that effect should have been inserted in article 30.[31]

Denza also notes the right of an airline to refuse to carry a diplomat "unless he voluntarily submits to search of his personal baggage in circumstances where there is no reason to suspect him. These searches are carried out by agents of the airlines and not of the receiving State, and the necessity for so doing appears to have been accepted by diplomats in general in view of incidents involving hijacking by persons carrying diplomatic passports." Her observations, published in 1976, seem even more pertinent today.[32]

Records and communications. Protection of the freedom and secrecy of the official communications of diplomatic missions and consular posts with their own government is "probably the most important of all the privileges and immunities accorded under international law."[33] We will survey, first, the situation of pouches and the couriers who move them and, secondly, the increasingly significant channel of electronic communications.

These topics are covered at length in article 27 of the 1961 convention. In furtherance of the general principle expressed in article 25 that "the receiving State shall accord full facilities for the performance of the functions of the mission," article 27 obligates the receiving state to "permit and protect free communication on the part of the mission for all official purposes." Communications expressly covered are those with "the Government and the other missions and consulates of the sending States," for which "the mission may employ all appropriate means, including diplomatic couriers and messages in code or cipher."

DIPLOMATIC BAGS AND COURIERS. All "official correspondence of the mission shall be inviolable," and "the diplomatic bag shall

---

[31] Denza, *Diplomatic Law*, p. 219.
[32] Ibid., p. 220. Also House of Commons Report, 1984, op. cit., p. XIV, and Satow, 5th ed., p. 140.
[33] Denza, *Diplomatic Law*, p. 119.

not be opened or detained." However, the mission is required to conform to rules that "the packages constituting the diplomatic bag must bear visible external marks of their character and may contain only diplomatic documents or articles intended for official use."

The diplomatic courier who carries the mission's bag "shall be provided with an official document indicating his status and the number of packages constituting the diplomatic bag." When so accredited, he "shall be protected by the receiving State in the performance of his functions" and "shall enjoy personal inviolability and shall not be liable to any form of arrest or detention." Not all couriers need be career ones or, apparently, even government employees. "The sending State or the mission may designate diplomatic couriers *ad hoc*." However, in such cases the courier's immunities "shall cease to apply" when he "has delivered to the consignee the diplomatic bag in his charge."

A common arrangement, especially for small posts or developing countries, is to deputize the captain of an aircraft. Though not considered a diplomatic courier, the deputized captain is then entrusted with the diplomatic bag. "The mission may send one of its members to take possession of the diplomatic bag directly and freely from the captain of the aircraft" at the port of entry (article 27).

Hans-Peter Kaul notes that "the principle of inviolability of couriers and despatches of a sending State and its envoys," which had been recognized since the sixteenth century and expressed in many treaties, "was greatly expanded and clarified" by the Vienna Convention of 1961. That convention's rules have been the model for courier status not only in the Convention of 1963 on consuls but also in the 1969 Convention on Special Missions (articles 28 and 42), the 1975 Vienna Convention on the Representation of States in Their Relations with International Organizations of a Universal Character (articles 27, 57, and 81), and many subsequent consular treaties."[34] This is an illustration of the fundamental importance of the work done at Vienna in 1961.

Kaul has observed "a distinct trend in State practice to accord to diplomatic couriers basically the same privileges and immunities" as to diplomatic agents, which is "important with regard to immunity from jurisdiction, but is also relevant in the field of exemptions from personal examination, custom duties and inspections, as well as from dues and taxes." This trend, based on "comity and reciprocity," means that in many states a courier does "not pay customs

---

[34] Hans-Peter Kaul, "Couriers," in R. Bernhardt (ed.), *Encyclopedia of Public International Law*, Instalment 9 (Amsterdam, New York, Oxford, Tokyo: North-Holland, 1986), p. 50.

duties or similar charges for articles imported as personal luggage, which normally is not inspected."[35] Here we seem to see again the influence of the ideas of reciprocity and functional efficiency (i.e., speeding couriers on their way) which underlie so much current practice in the field of diplomatic immunity.

CONSULAR FREEDOM OF COMMUNICATION. The 1963 provisions dealing with consular pouches, couriers, and wireless communications (article 35) are almost the same as for diplomatic missions and in one detail somewhat more liberal, namely, that the consular bag may also be entrusted to the captain of a ship, as well as of a commercial aircraft.

In some respects, the consular bag is slightly less privileged than the diplomatic one. For example, if authorities in the receiving state "have serious reason to believe that the bag contains something other than [official] correspondence, documents or articles . . . they may request that the bag be opened in their presence by an authorized representative of the sending State. If this request is refused . . . the bag shall be returned to its place of origin." No such procedure was mentioned in the case of diplomatic bags.

In addition, the choice of consular couriers, while similar in other respects to diplomatic couriers, is limited, except with the receiving state's consent, to those who are neither nationals of the receiving state nor permanent residents of the receiving state, unless the latter are also nationals of the sending state.

COMMUNICATION WITH SENDING STATE NATIONALS. The 1961 Convention, Article 27, provides that "the receiving State shall permit and protect free communication on the part of the mission for all official purposes." In the opinion of Denza, "It is quite clear that the free communication to be protected includes not only communication between the mission and the sending State and consulates within the territory of the receiving State, but also communication with nationals of the sending State in the receiving State or elsewhere and communication with international organisations." On the other hand, the right to use "specially secure methods such as couriers and codes or ciphers is . . . expressly accorded only in regard to communications with the sending State and any of its other agencies."[36] The idea is that specially secure methods are only appropriate between parts of the same government.

ELECTRONIC COMMUNICATIONS. As for the privilege of operating their own wireless communications, both diplomatic missions and consular posts are on the same basis. They "may install and use a

---

[35] Ibid.
[36] Denza, *Diplomatic Law*, p. 120.

wireless transmitter only with the consent of the receiving State" (article 27, 1961 convention, and article 35, 1963).

At the Vienna conference in 1961, there was a difference of view between industrialized and developing countries. The former wished to have no restriction on the use of wireless transmitters from embassies. Such was the situation, in practice, in London. The developing states wanted to require the consent of the receiving state, not just simple consent but "after making proper arrangements for [their] use in accordance with the laws of the receiving State and international regulations." The point of view of the major industrialized states was adopted. Consent by the receiving state is indeed required, but it need not even be express. Foreign missions in London, for example, have been allowed to set up transmitters "without seeking permission or even notifying the authorities."[37]

However, the State Department Office of Foreign Missions, whose strong regulatory role will be described in chapter 4, in 1985 denied the Soviet embassy's request to install a parabolic dish receiver at its embassy complex.[38] It also ruled that the acquisition of telecommunications goods and services was a benefit that must be obtained through the OFM.[39] To this extent the point of view of the developing countries seemed to be gaining ground in one major industrialized state.

Other provisions. Among other aspects of privileges and immunities covered in the two Vienna conventions are the duration of the status of diplomatic agents and consular officers; obligations of third states; gainful private activity; honorary consuls; and consular agents.

DURATION OF IMMUNITIES. For a member of a diplomatic mission and his family, entitlement to privileges and immunities commences "from the moment he enters the territory of the receiving State on proceeding to take up his post, or, if already in its territory, from the moment when his appointment is notified" to the proper authorities. When his functions in the mission have come to an end, his privileges and immunities "shall normally cease at the moment when he leaves the country, or on expiry of a reasonable period in which to do so, but shall subsist until that time, even in case of armed conflict." However, immunity continues indefinitely in regard to acts performed in the exercise of mission functions. If a

[37] Ibid., p. 122.
[38] "[1985] Annual Report on the Implementation of the Foreign Missions Act of 1982, as amended (P.L. 972–41)," March 1986, Department of State, Office of Foreign Missions, p. 3.
[39] Ibid., p. 6.

member of the mission dies, the deceased's family members continue to enjoy their privileges and immunities "until the expiry of a reasonable period in which to leave the country" (1961:article 39).

For members of a consular post and their families, the duration provisions (1963:article 53) are similar, with the privileges and immunities commencing from the moment of entry to take up the post or, if already in the receiving state, from the moment of entering upon the duties of the consular post. Similarly, consular family and private staff members enjoy the convention's privileges and immunities from the same date as the member of the consular post, or from the date they enter the receiving state or become a member of such family or private staff, whichever comes later. Immunity for members of the consular post at the end of their tour of duty continues until departure or until a reasonable time to depart expires, and immunity from jurisdiction for official acts in the exercise of consular functions "shall continue to subsist without limitation of time."

The privileges and immunities of family members and domestic staff "end when they cease to belong to the household or to be in the service of a member of the consular post." If, however, they plan to leave the receiving state within a reasonable period, their privileges and immunities continue until their departure. Article 53's duration provisions for the family members of a member of the post who dies are similar to those in article 39 of the Convention on Diplomatic Relations.

IMMUNITY IN THIRD STATES. We turn now to the privileges and immunities diplomats and consuls and official communications enjoy when passing through a third state. Article 40 of the 1961 convention and article 54 of the 1963 convention deal with this topic.

When a diplomatic agent is proceeding to take up or return to his post or to return to his own country and has been granted a passport visa by a third country, where required, then "the third State shall accord him inviolability and such other immunities as may be required to ensure his transit or return." The same applies to covered family members accompanying the diplomatic agent, or traveling separately to join him or her, or returning to their country. In the case of administrative and technical or service staff members and their families, the third state "shall not hinder" their passage through its territories.

Official correspondence and communications in transit, including messages in code or cipher, are to be accorded by third states "the same freedom and protection" as are required of the receiving state. Diplomatic couriers having the required passport visa and diplomatic bags in transit are entitled to "the same inviolability and protection as the receiving State is bound to accord."

A final provision of article 40 no doubt sounds particularly welcome to those thousands of diplomats who serve in areas of the world troubled by chronic instability and periodic local conflicts. The obligations of third states mentioned above also apply to the persons mentioned above, and to official communications and diplomatic bags, "whose presence in the territory of the third State is due to *force majeure*."

The consular convention prescribes the same obligations for third states with respect to members of a consular post and their families and the post's communications, except that the immunities are those set forth in the consular convention. The *force majeure* clause is included in the same way.

GAINFUL PRIVATE ACTIVITY. The Vienna Convention of 1963 stipulates that career consular officers "shall not carry on for personal profit any professional or commercial activity in the receiving State" (article 57). Furthermore, the privileges and immunities of consulate members and their families are not accorded to consular employees, service staff, family, or their private staff members who themselves "carry on any private gainful occupation in the receiving State."

HONORARY CONSULS. The contemporary status of members of consular posts with respect to privileges and immunities emerged from the existence of the old and extensive institution of honorary (as contrasted with career) consuls. Honorary consuls may head a consular post and carry out most of the functions of career consuls. They are generally unpaid by the sending government and they can do much useful work, which in part explains their survival. The individuals who are so appointed usually welcome the social prestige thus acquired and may have a genuine feeling of pride in serving the interests of the sending state. From his childhood in a large provincial town in southern Egypt, this writer remembers the handsome consular shields that decorated the gates or doorways of the mansions of several wealthy men in the town. Their names and consulships were known in the local community and they were listed in Baedeker's *Egypt*.

Consular posts headed by an honorary consul enjoy most of the facilities, privileges and immunities of those headed by career consuls (1963 Convention, Chapter III, "Regime Relating to Honorary Consular Officers and Consular Posts Headed by Such Officers"). The receiving state shall accord them full facilities for their functions, permit them to display the flag and coat-of-arms of the sending state, assist them in finding consular premises and accommodations, give members of the post freedom of movement and of communication, treat their official correspondence as inviolable, and permit their use of a consular bag. They are free to maintain contact with nationals of the sending state, address the authorities, and levy consular fees and charges. Third states shall not hinder their official communications or couriers in transit. If they are detained, the head of the post shall be notified or the diplomatic channel used to notify the sending state. Honorary consular officers are not amenable to local jurisdiction in exercising their consular functions, nor may they be required to testify in court concerning matters connected with these functions.

Yet, at almost every turn, the privileges and immunities of honorary consular officers are trimmed down compared to those of career consuls. Although the receiving state is obliged to protect their premises against intrusions, damage, or impairment of dignity (article 59), there is no inviolability. Premises owned or leased by the sending state are exempt from taxation, but not if payable by the local contractor (article 60). Inviolability of consular archives and documents is accorded only if they are kept separate from the consular officer's private and business papers (article 61). Customs exemptions apply only to specified items, such as flags, seals, office material, and the like (article 62). The list does not include such supplies as alcohol or foodstuffs. The family members of an honorary consul have no privileges or immunities (article 58, paragraph 3) nor, apparently, do their personal servants.

Overall, the status of honorary consular officers remains much the same as before the 1963 convention.

One can sense that the State Department's policy in recent years has been hardening against a previously rather liberal attitude toward the acceptance of honorary consuls, and indeed of consular posts headed by career consuls. This shift stems from several considerations. There was an increase in the early 1980s in requests for consular posts and a simultaneous increase in the burden of protecting the security of such consulates. There was also a build-up of congressional concern that there were too many persons entitled to some degree of immunity from U.S. jurisdiction.[40]

On 27 February 1985, the State Department issued a circular setting out new guidelines for the consideration of "requests for the establishment of consular posts, the recognition of consular officers, and the continuation of existing consular posts, particularly

---

[40] *American Journal of International Law*, Oct. 1985, pp. 1051–52.

those headed by honorary consular officers."[41] Foreign missions were thereafter to be required to present detailed, written explanations of the reasons for proposed new posts, and "honorary consular appointments will be reviewed to ensure that there is a need for consular services and that the appointment is not being made due to only political or honorific considerations."[42] Many honorary consuls, and the mayors of American cities who have welcomed the prestige that a consular corps adds to a municipal image, may shiver in the cold wind of this policy pronouncement. Viewed in the broader picture of modern practice in handling diplomatic and consular immunities, the policy is yet another instance of the functional principle at work.

CONSULAR AGENTS. One additional consular category mentioned in the 1963 convention (article 69) is that of the consular agency, conducted by agents "not designated as heads of consular posts by the sending State." The decision to establish or to admit such agencies is entirely optional, and their numbers vary widely. For example, at the start of 1988, there were 77 active consular agents in the United States, of whom 36 were foreign nationals serving as career agents and 41 were U.S. citizens or permanent residents serving as honorary agents.[43] At the same time, there were 41 U.S. consular agencies in other countries, with 38 consular agents and 3 vacancies.[44] Their conditions of work and any privileges and immunities accorded to the agents in charge are determined by bilateral agreements.

Analogous Privileges and Immunities

This study has treated mainly the privileges and immunities accorded to diplomats and consuls, including the specialized attachés, such as military, labor, scientific, or cultural, all of whom are within the scope of the Vienna Conventions. For some governments, particularly the United States, there are many additional categories of officials serving in foreign countries whose status includes at least some privileges and immunities analogous to diplomatic ones.

Development assistance missions. Bilateral agreements determine the privileges and immunities accorded to the overseas missions and personnel of the Agency for International Development (AID). In

[41] Ibid., p. 1052.
[42] Ibid., p. 1053.
[43] Office of Protocol, Department of State, 15 Jan. 1988 (telephone inquiry).
[44] Bureau of Security and Consular Affairs, Department of State, 15 Jan. 1988 (telephone inquiry).

general, an AID mission and its employees are given a status comparable to that of embassy personnel.

As an illustration drawn from practice in a country with a relatively large AID program, one may consider some of the terms of the 1978 U.S.-Egypt agreement, headed "Economic, Technical and Related Assistance Agreement."[45] The two parties "agree that a special mission will be received by the Government of the Arab Republic of Egypt to carry out and discharge the responsibilities of the Government of the United States under this agreement[;] . . . that the special mission will enjoy the same inviolability of premises as is extended to the diplomatic mission" of the United States; and that Egypt "shall accord all United States Government employees who are United States citizens and their families in Egypt to perform work in connection herewith the same immunity as is accorded by the Government of the Arab Republic of Egypt to the personnel of comparable rank of the Embassy of the United States of America in Egypt" (article 4). The agreement provides tax exemption for American contractors financed by the United States for purposes covered under the agreement and to U.S. citizens who are in Egypt to perform work connected with the agreement (article 5). Further particular privileges with regard to importing automobiles and the like are clarified in an accompanying exchange of notes between Ambassador Hermann Eilts and the chief of protocol in the Ministry of Foreign Affairs.

A further indication of the status of AID personnel abroad is the final sentence of article 4: "These employees will be subject to the same obligations and responsibilities as apply to members of the Embassy of the United States of America."[46] Presumably this means such obligations as those in the Vienna conventions, for example, the duty to respect local laws and not to interfere in local affairs.

AID personnel in the field who have questions concerning their privileges and immunities are advised to consult their AID mission for guidance, specifically, the regional legal advisor or the executive officer.[47]

---

[45] Reproduced in facsimile as T.I.A.S. 9481 in U.S. Department of State, *United States Treaties and Other International Agreements* (cited as T.I.A.S.), Vol. 30, part 4, 1978–79 (Washington: U.S. Government Printing Office, continuous series), pp. 4610–21.

[46] Ibid., p. 4612.

[47] "Privileges and Immunities," *What Do I Do Now?: A Soucebook on Regulations, Allowances, and Finances*, Overseas Briefing Center Supplement, Feb. 1986, Dept. of State Publication 9296, p. 1.

The Military. Members of military forces abroad, the members' dependents, the civilian employees accompanying the forces, and those employees' dependents often enjoy a status of partial exemption from local jurisdictions, and certain privileges and rights, provided they are not nationals of the territorial state. This situation had grown up in customary international law; but after World War II, when numerous forces were stationed abroad for long periods in time of peace, multilateral and bilateral agreements were felt to be needed to clarify their status.

The NATO Status of Forces Agreement of 19 June 1951[48] is the best guide to the system that has emerged. Several works explaining it and describing practice under it are given in the suggested reading list. An excellent brief account is contained in Derek W. Bowett's article, "Military Forces Abroad," in the *Encyclopedia of Public International Law.*[49] The following three paragraphs are derived from that article.

The 1951 NATO Status of Forces Agreement required all persons covered by it to abstain from political activity and to observe local laws. They are under the jurisdiction of the sending state if they commit an offense "against the property or security of that State; or . . . against the person or property of another member of the force or its civilian component or a dependent"; or if the offense is committed "in the performance of an official duty." Other offenses are tried in the territorial courts. Persons tried for an offense in the territorial state are entitled to a fair trial.

The agreement covers rights "to purchase goods and to enjoy medical, travel and communications facilities" (article IX); "exempts the members of the force from acquiring a tax domicile, and exempts their salaries from taxation by the territorial State" (article X); and exempts them "from import duties on their personal property" (article XI).

Interestingly, the Warsaw Pact has some analogous agreements, namely, bilateral treaties between the Soviet Union and Poland, East Germany, and Hungary respectively. When the Arab League sent an Arab League Security Force to Kuwait in 1961–63 to counter a possible Iraqi threat, the League and Kuwait concluded an agreement on 12 August 1961 which "provided for the exclusive criminal jurisdiction of the contributing or sending State over members of its contingent, conceding no criminal jurisdiction to Kuwait."

Serge Lazareff in *Status of Military Forces under Current*

---

48 T.I.A.S. No.2846, often cited as NATO SOFA.
49 R. Bernhardt (ed.), Instalment 3 (1981), pp. 266–69.

International Law[50] gives a list of bilateral status of forces agreements and their dates. Most numerous were those of the United States, which had concluded such agreements with Australia, the Bahamas, Belgium, Canada, Denmark, the Dominican Republic, Ethiopia, France, Greece, Iceland, and Japan. But there are many more. In the introduction to his work, Lazareff notes that "the United States, as an example, has entered into bilateral agreements on the status of its forces with more than fifty States, the classified agreements not being mentioned."

The scale of operations under the system of status of forces agreements is impressive and seems to be far larger than that involving diplomatic immunity. A study by Larry Renner published in 1984 gives some indication.[51] Renner notes that although other NATO nations have not published statistics on offenses by members of their forces, the U.S. Department of Defense did so on the U.S. forces for the year 1 December 1980 to 30 November 1981. According to that report, "United States military forces stationed worldwide were involved in 64,101 offenses subject to primary or exclusive jurisdiction of foreign tribunals. Of these cases, 38,237 involved traffic offenses including drunken and reckless driving and fleeing the scene of an accident. The report indicates that 24,955 of the cases worldwide involved concurrent jurisdiction. Of these cases a waiver of local jurisdiction was obtained by the United States in 21,521 (86.1%) of the cases where the host nation had primary jurisdiction."[52] It would be interesting to know what the number of cases was for other NATO nations' forces during the same twelve-month period. Presumably it would amount to many thousands.

The immunities and privileges of forces abroad are a separate system, distinct from that for diplomatic and consular personnel. Lazareff puts it clearly: "Only military personnel enjoying diplomatic immunities (and therefore not coming under SOFA) have been given immunities similar to those of diplomatic personnel of equivalent rank," such as senior officers of the U.S. Military Assistance Advisory Groups.[53]

To this writer, the distinction seems functional. The immunities of military forces and their dependents abroad are sought by the sending state and granted by the receiving state in order to make the forces abroad have better discipline and morale and therefore

---

[50] (Leyden: Sijthoff, 1971), pp. 457–58.

[51] Larry E. Renner, "International Law and Criminal Jurisdiction over Visiting Armed Forces: Reconciling the Concurrent Jurisdiction Discontinuity," *California Western International Law Journal*, Vol. 14, Number 2 (Spring 1984), pp. 351–81.

[52] Ibid., p. 374.

[53] Lazareff, *Status of Military Forces*, p. 345.

greater effectiveness in achieving the goals of an alliance or a bilateral, shared strategic relationship.[54] The immunities of diplomats, as we have seen, exist to make the whole system of relations between sovereign states function. This is obviously a longer-range goal and a broader one. In practice, every national government wants its diplomats to have immunity on a reciprocal basis. In contrast, the majority of governments see no general need to station their armed forces abroad, and few relish the idea of having foreign forces stationed in their own territory, with or without special rights and privileges.

In general, diplomatic immunities and privileges under the Vienna Convention are enjoyed only by those military personnel attached to diplomatic missions. In practice, foreign military and associated civilian personnel may in special situations be given immunities and privileges comparable to diplomatic ones under a bilateral agreement. This has been the case, for example, in U.S.-Israel relations, though without the concept of reciprocity. Israel agreed that U.S. Department of Defense personnel – military and civilian and their dependents – connected with an airfield construction project should "be accorded privileges and immunities no less than those accorded to members of the administrative and technical staff of the United States Diplomatic Mission."[55] Many specific stipulations of that agreement concerning immunity from taxes, prevention of abuses, the availability of tax-exempt fuel for vehicles, and other matters seem to reflect limitations that are stricter in practice than those on immunities customarily accorded to diplomats.[56]

The Peace Corps. U.S. Peace Corps volunteers work abroad under bilateral agreements that determine their status. The Peace Corps has issued an official book as a guide to its regulations and policies.[57] The legal status of Peace Corps Volunteers is described (p. 33), with emphasis on their lack of immunity:

Volunteers are not officers or employees of the United States Government, except for limited purposes, and do not have diplomatic immunity. Their legal liability usually does not change as a result of registration as trainees or

---

[54] Cf. G.I.A.D. Draper, *Civilians and the NATO Status of Forces Agreement* (Leyden: A.W. Sijthoff, 1966), pp. 16–17.

[55] Article 11, "Privileges and Immunities," in the US-Israel Agreement of 6 April 1979 on Airbase Construction, T.I.A.S. 9450, published in *T.I.A.S.* Vol. 30, part 4, pp. 4107–33.

[56] Ibid., pp. 4127–31.

[57] *Peace Corps: The Peace Corps Handbook* (Washington: U.S. Government Printing Office, 1978).

enrollment as Volunteers. Thus, they generally are subject to state and federal laws while in the United States and to host country laws while overseas. This can have serious ramifications for Volunteers overseas who might become involved in such situations as automobile accidents or paternity suits, or who might be imprisoned for possession of drugs. It cannot be emphasized too strongly that while American Embassy officials have diplomatic immunity overseas, Peace Corps Volunteers and staff members do not [and] will be treated in accordance with the local laws.

The Peace Corps Country Director, who provides guidance to the volunteers from a country headquarters, also lacks diplomatic immunity (p. 62):

Like Volunteers, Country Directors and other staff members have no diplomatic privileges or immunities, no PX or commissary privileges. They do not draw hardship pay in places where other American officials do. They may not use the diplomatic pouch or the Army Post Office for personal mail and are expected to live modestly.

International Immunities

As noted in chapter 1, the privileges and immunities of international organizations and officials are defined in a set of treaties separate from the Vienna conventions. There was little precedent for such organizations until the creation of the League of Nations after World War I. The practices that have grown up under the separate treaties and headquarters agreements, the national laws implementing them, and municipal court rulings on cases are now, especially in the period since World War II, a major challenge to describe.

There has been a natural tendency for international immunity to follow the experience of diplomatic immunity, but there are many important particular differences. There is also no general agreement on international immunities that has achieved the universality and "codifying" status of the Vienna Conventions of 1961 and 1963, nor does one seem likely to emerge in the foreseeable future.

The 1946 UN Convention and 1947 Headquarters Agreement. In 1945, long before the Vienna conventions, the intention expressed in the UN Charter was that the new organization should have "such privileges and immunities as are necessary for the fulfillment of its purposes" and that representatives of UN member states and UN officials "shall similarly enjoy such privileges and immunities as are necessary for the independent exercise of their functions" (article 105).

To these ends, the General Convention on the Privileges and

Immunities of the United Nations was adopted by the General Assembly on 13 February 1946.[58] Its provisions with respect to privileges and immunities of members of delegations and of experts on UN missions seem adequate and even liberal (articles IV, V, and VI). The organization also was given generous immunities for its premises, property, and funds (article II). Article VII even required that UN *laissez passer* (i.e., the practical equivalent of national passports) should be accepted as valid and that their holders, when documented as travelling on official business, should have their visa applications "dealt with as speedily as possible" and that "such persons shall be granted facilities for speedy travel." (One may fairly wonder what effect article VII has had in practice and how much time its privileged beneficiaries may have saved as compared with ordinary travelers.)

The 1946 Convention was to come into force for each member upon accession (final article, section 32), and it was readily accepted. By 1949, at least twenty-one members had acceded, including Britain, France, India, Poland, Egypt, and states from all regions of the world.[59] However, the most significantly relevant member, the United States, did not at first accede and was therefore not bound by the convention. Instead, the United States negotiated the Headquarters of the United Nations Agreement, which was signed on 26 June 1947 and has remained in force since 21 November 1947.[60] The coming into effect of the agreement was authorized by a Joint Resolution of the U.S. Congress of 4 August 1947.

Article III of the Headquarters Agreement does state that "the headquarters district shall be inviolable." Article V gives resident representatives of member nations "the same privileges and immunities, subject to corresponding conditions and obligations" as are accorded to diplomatic envoys accredited to the United States. However, if the United States does not recognize the representative's government, then "such privileges and immunities need be extended . . . only within the headquarters district, at their residences and offices outside the district, in transit between the district and such offices, and in transit on official business to or from foreign countries."

The immunities of personnel in the secretariat of the United Nations are governed generally by the 1946 Convention, to which

---

58 TIAS 6900; 1 UNTS 16; text in *American Journal of International Law*, Vol. 43 (1949), Supplement, pp. 1–7. As noted earlier, a corresponding convention covering the UN Specialized Agencies was adopted in 1947.

59 Ibid., p. 1.

60 Text in ibid., pp. 8–17. The Headquarters Agreement is divided into 28 consecutively numbered sections, grouped under 9 articles.

121 member states had acceded as of June 1988, including the United States in April 1970.[61] Briefly, the secretary-general and all assistant secretaries-general have immunities similar to those of diplomatic agents. In the United States, other personnel of the UN Secretariat have immunity only for their official actions, as provided in the International Organizations Immunities Act (22 U.S.C. 288), but not personal inviolability.[62]

State Department practice with respect to the recognition and administration of immunity in the United States for members of permanent missions to the United Nations, for the UN secretary-general, and for the assistant secretaries-general has developed under section 15 of the 1947 Headquarters Agreement and section 19 of the 1946 Convention on the Privileges and Immunities of the United Nations. A State Department study and report to Congress of 18 March 1988 described the arrangements.[63]

The Office of Host Country Affairs (OHCA) in the U.S. delegation to the United Nations (USUN) has responsibility for registering and documenting the persons entitled to immunity. The process differs from the regular system for diplomats and consuls in the United States in that OHCA "performs a ministerial rather than a discretionary function," since the United Nations is the accrediting agency for UN permanent missions, which must notify the UN Protocol Office about new mission members. That office makes accreditation decisions and transcribes the necessary data onto its own forms, with copies sent to OHCA "for entry into the [State] Department's records system and the issuance of credentials." The UN Protocol Office also notifies OHCA twice monthly of the departures of diplomatic personnel. Every six months, USUN publishes *Permanent Missions to the United Nations*, listing officers of missions who are entitled to diplomatic immunity. It also keeps a current record of changes in the list between published issues.

Around early 1988, the State Department began to issue to members of the diplomatic communities in New York and Washington new photographic identification cards, "with distinctive color-coded borders and language indicating the level of immunity of the bearer," as well as 24-hour telephone contact numbers for inquiries

---

[61] U.S. Department of State, *Treaties in Force*, DOS Publication 9433, 1 Jan. 1987, p. 321; and UN Information Centre, Washington, DC, 14 June 1988.

[62] Department of State, Office of Protocol/Office of Foreign Missions, *Guidance for Law Enforcement Officers*, March 1987, p. 9.

[63] U.S. Department of State, *Study and Report Concerning the Status of Individuals with Diplomatic Immunity in the United States*, prepared in pursuance of *Foreign Relations Act, Fiscal Years 1988 and 1989, P.L. 100–204, Section 137*, presented 18 March 1988, pp. 28–31.

by local authorities and others. This is a tightening up of the regulatory process, part of a trend in U.S. practice discussed in chapter 4 below. As of early 1988, however, local authorities still needed to call the State Department to verify the status of nondiplomatic mission employees, who had not yet been issued any kind of identification cards.

The status of American citizens at the U.S. delegation to the United Nations and its organizations in the United States, unlike delegates from other member states, is that they have no diplomatic privileges and immunities. For, as Satow notes, "States are not obliged to accord any privileges or immunities to their own representatives."[64]

Satow points out an important difference between UN Secretariat officials and diplomats with respect to waivers of immunity; namely, that the secretary-general must "waive the immunity of an official where in his opinion immunity would impede the course of justice" and waiving it would not be harmful to UN interests. In contrast, states are not required to waive any diplomatic or consular immunities.[65]

When diplomats serving in national delegations at the UN join the secretariat, they lose their status as diplomats and have only official function immunity. This fact was made clear by several court cases. Soviet citizens who had held diplomatic positions in the Soviet Foreign Ministry or its delegation to the General Assembly sought to retain diplomatic immunities when they became secretariat employees. Their claims were denied by U.S. courts.[66]

THE QUESTION OF SOVEREIGNTY. Is the United Nations Headquarters District, under the Headquarters Agreement and joint resolution, the UN Charter, and the General Convention on the Privileges and Immunities of the United Nations, in any way a sovereign territory? Or, as a layman might say, a secular Vatican or a Principality of Monaco on the East River? The Headquarters Agreement does not say flatly that it is not, but the answer is certainly in the negative.

The question was answered unequivocally by Ernest A. Gross, Legal Adviser of the Department of State, in an article published in 1949, "Operation of the Legal Adviser's Office."[67] He recognized that the agreement had "presented novel problems" and that its negotiation involved not only infrequently arising constitutional

---

[64] Satow, 5th ed., p. 370.
[65] Ibid.
[66] Theodor Meron, "Staff of the United Nations Secretariat: Problems and Directions," *A.J.I.L.*, Vol. 70 (1976), No. 4, pp. 674–75, where cases are cited.
[67] *A.J.I.L.*, Vol, 43 (1949), No. 2, pp. 122–27.

problems, but "completely new" constitutional problems. One of these was that the area of the Headquarters District was inviolable and that specifically "federal, state, or local officers or officials" cannot enter it to perform official duties "except with the consent and under conditions agreed to by the Secretary General." However, he said, "making the Headquarters District of the United Nations inviolable does not, of course, amount to transferring sovereignty over the area to the United Nations." The reason was that section 7 of the agreement provided that federal, state, and local law "shall apply within the Headquarters District," and U.S. courts "shall have jurisdiction over acts done and transactions taking place in the Headquarters District." The only exception was that the United Nations would have power to make regulations "necessary for the full execution of its functions." Thus no illegal business could be set up there nor contracts made "outside the effect of the law of New York."

HOT PURSUIT. On the potentially delicate question of a person trying to evade hot pursuit by the New York City police by rushing into the United Nations, Gross was confident that the United Nations could work out "an arrangement with the state and local authorities whereby the hypothetical case of 'hot pursuit' could be settled in the best interest of all – except the pursued." Gross also cited section 13 as providing a necessary safeguard for the United States, namely, that "if a person gains access to the United States by reason of the fact that he is an employee of the United Nations and, after arrival, engages in activities which are outside the scope of his official activities and which would render him liable to deportation, Section 13 makes it clear that he has no immunity from our deportation laws."[68]

Similarities and differences between diplomatic missions and the UN. The ability of the U.S. government to require the departure from the United States of UN diplomats who commit serious offenses against U.S. laws was demonstrated in late 1987 by the case of Floyd Karamba, an administrative attaché at the Zimbabwean mission to the United Nations. New York City authorities found on 11 December 1987 that Karamba's nine-year-old son Terence had been abused and beaten by his father. On December 21, the State Department ordered Floyd Karamba to leave the United States within twenty-four hours on the grounds that his conduct was unacceptable.[69]

Karamba left his wife, his son Terence, and two other children in the United States, resulting in a troubling aftermath. The case of Terence Karamba did not involve the question of international

---

[68] Ibid., pp. 126–27.
[69] *Washington Post*, 30 Dec. 1987, and 6 Jan. 1988.

immunity but rather questions of asylum (for the boy) and considerations of reciprocity and possible countermeasures by the Zimbabwean government against Americans in Zimbabwe. After brief but intensive legal struggles and public concern, the U.S. Supreme Court on 15 January 1988, without comment or dissent, lifted a stay of execution granted earlier, thus freeing the State Department to follow the requirements of international law and, after several additional weeks, turn the boy over to Zimbabwe for placement in a foster home there.[70]

Young Terence departed for Zimbabwe on 28 February 1988. The State Department had arranged for a psychiatric consultant to accompany him and for a law firm in Harare to follow up on the case, if necessary. A social worker who had been Terence's New York foster father said the boy had reached a point of trust for adults that enabled him to say he was ready to return to his own country, where his father was understood to be in counseling under government and church auspices.[71]

The contrast between the inviolability of the UN Headquarters area under the UN secretary-general and the inviolable status of even a large diplomatic mission under its ambassador stems from functional differences. The internal situations arising within the two must be very different in practice. Unlike an embassy, the UN Headquarters is the workplace of over a hundred often rival national groups. An ambassador in an embassy presides over his mission's fairly diverse "country team," but their diversity is quite unlike that of the UN member nations.

The following incident illustrates the sort of event that can happen in the UN's premises involving UN diplomats. In early November 1986, on the third floor of the UN Secretariat building, three diplomats from the UN delegation of Afghanistan (a first secretary and two second secretaries) physically attacked, punching and shoving, two representatives of the Afghan resistance forces. The two Afghans were the invited guests of the UN Correspondents' Association, and they were en route to a press conference approved by the secretary-general.[72] It would be difficult to conceive of a comparable attack in an embassy.

A second illustration: A member of the UN Development Program staff was speaking one late October to a group from the union of UN employees, convened to discuss the need for an independent international civil service. The staff member, Alice

[70] *Washington Post*, 16 Jan. and 1 Mar. 1988.
[71] *Washington Post*, 1 Mar. 1988.
[72] *Washington Times*, 10 Nov. 1986.

Wesolawska, was to speak on the plight of about sixty UN employees imprisoned in different countries. Her own experience was that she had been imprisoned in Poland for four years on a charge of spying. A moment before she began to speak, the microphones were ordered removed from the stage. This action was taken by the UN Department of Conference Services on the grounds that it had not authorized the meeting. The head of the department was a former Polish chief UN delegate who was on loan to the UN Secretariat by the Polish government.[73]

Clearly privileges and immunities, inviolability of premises and residences, applying the principles of functionalism and reciprocity, and the protection of diplomats' security and dignity are likely to operate quite differently in the international immunity context from the way they do in the long tradition of interstate diplomacy.

The 1975 Vienna conference and beyond. A serious new attempt to achieve an authoritative convention covering questions of international immunities began as early as 1958 when the International Law Commission (I.L.C.) of the United Nations took up the matter. In 1963, a specially appointed rapporteur, Abdullah El-Erian of Egypt, submitted a proposed text with commentaries, which was circulated to governments for their comments. In 1971, the I.L.C. prepared a revised draft, and government comments were again solicited. The General Assembly in a resolution of 14 December 1972 voted to convene a conference to discuss the subject and embody its conclusions in an international convention.

Such a conference was convened in Vienna from 4 February to 14 March 1975. Though the conference adopted a draft convention by a vote of 57 to one (Belgium), there were 15 abstentions and these included the major host countries of international organizations, namely, the United States (host to the U.N.), Switzerland (I.L.O., W.H.O., and the U.P.U.), Austria (I.A.E.A. and U.N.I.D.O.), Canada (I.C.A.O.), France (U.N.E.S.C.O.), and Britain (I.M.O.).[74]

The text of the 1975 Convention is conveniently published in the *American Journal of International Law*, Volume 69, July 1975, pages 730–58. In general, its arrangement of topics, concepts of immunity and privilege, and in many cases actual wordings are similar to the Vienna Conventions of 1961 and 1963.

In a thoughtful review of the conference and the resulting conven-

73 *New York Times*, 26 Oct. 1986.
74 J.G. Fennessy, "The 1975 Vienna Convention on the Representation of States in Their Relations with International Organizations of a Universal Character," *American Journal of International Law* Vol. 70, January 1976, pp. 62–72.

tion, J.G. Fennessy, who attended the conference, expresses the personal opinion that the majority of states at the conference, who were from sending countries, sought to give too high a level of privileges to the representatives of states. The host countries, who naturally wished to keep privileges down to essentials, were outvoted on such questions as the host's right to declare delegates *persona non grata*. Without the major host countries' adherence, the convention will have little effect on practice. That will continue to be governed mainly by the various headquarters agreements, which were already in place in 1975, and by national legislation of the host countries. Fennessy thus concludes that "the practice of states will probably not be sufficiently uniform to justify an assertion that the 1975 Vienna Convention represents the law which should be applied in this field. As an exercise in the codification and progressive development of international law, therefore, the 1975 Vienna Convention is likely, it must be feared, to be classed as a regrettable failure."[75]

The absence of an accepted equivalent to the diplomatic and consular conventions covering the same questions for international organizations and personnel leaves the whole subject of international immunities less manageable. The level of immunity of an international organization and its representatives, officials, "experts," and their dependents can best be determined by consulting the many, often overlapping, agreements applicable to that organization. Some guidance may be derived from the works listed under suggested reading. Specific questions of international immunity are likely to require expert advice.

Historically, diplomatic immunity, which is the subject of this work, has been used as a practical precedent for some types of international immunity. Apparently, the future of international immunity will also hold problems analogous to the problems of diplomats. Paul C. Szasz in 1983 concluded an evaluation of international immunity with this sobering thought:

In the long run the increasing resistance towards immunities of all kinds, including those deriving from inter-State relations, and the pressures resulting from the significant increase in the number of these [international] organizations, their activities and their staffs, are likely to lead to substantial clashes involving and possibly significantly diminishing even the functional immunities of [intergovernmental organizations].[76]

[75] Ibid., p. 72.
[76] Paul C. Szasz, "International Organizations, Privileges and Immunities," in Bernhardt (ed.), *Encyclopedia of Public International Law*, Instalment 5 (1983), p. 159.

4

ADMINISTRATION AND ADJUDICATION: TRADITIONS AND INNOVATIONS

Responsibility for handling diplomatic immunity is usually lodged in the protocol office of a government's foreign affairs ministry. The legal department of that ministry is also directly involved because the language of treaties and conventions must be interpreted and legal precedents considered. Because individual cases of abuse of immunity can sometimes have political repercussions, the appropriate geographic office of the ministry and a particular country director in that office are often drawn into the decision making.

In the U.S. Department of State, a new Office of Foreign Missions (OFM) was created in 1982. Its statutory responsibility is to administer the many benefits enjoyed by foreign missions accredited in the United States and to promote the security and effectiveness of U.S. missions abroad by a more calculated application of the ancient and familiar principle of reciprocity. Relatively new on the American scene, OFM's existence and emerging role illustrate one of the more significant trends in the field of diplomatic privileges and immunities and in U.S. official attitudes toward foreign governments.

Outside the foreign ministries, many other agencies and authorities are frequently involved in administering the rules of diplomatic immunity. We need to look at least briefly, for example, at the roles of the dean of the diplomatic corps, the police, the tax authorities, and the courts. Court rulings with respect to diplomatic immunity, and especially on the question of who is accredited, are often guided by the executive. In the United States, however, the federal courts are an independent branch of government under the Constitution, and in practice they can be fully independent of the executive in their judgments. In many other countries also, courts are jealous of their status and their right to have the last word on cases brought before them.

The Protocol Office

In a modern foreign ministry there is almost always a protocol section in charge of relations with the heads of foreign diplomatic missions on such subjects as formalities, ceremonies, privileges and immunities.[1] The protocol office is headed by a chief of high rank, generally at the level just below the permanent undersecretary. (See, for example, the charts of the British, German, French, Italian and other foreign ministries in the 1982 *Times Survey of Foreign Ministries of the World.*) The U.S. State Department has a branch protocol office in New York City. Among the many other responsibilities of protocol offices are state visits and official guests of the head of state and head of government, the organization of conferences, preparing the diplomatic list, and advising other government agencies on questions of precedence and appropriate ceremonies involving foreign officials and political leaders.[2]

The protocol office and the foreign ministry as a whole have a large stake in the institution of diplomatic immunity. As Richard Gookin, associate chief of protocol of the Department of State, said in a speech on 19 July 1985, they are aware that "the basis for immunity is to protect the channels of diplomatic business by exempting diplomatic representatives from local jurisdiction so that they can perform their official functions with complete freedom, independence and security. It is the State Department's job to uphold the principle of diplomatic immunity and to win acceptance of it. There are, of course, mutual advantages. . . . Immunity is essential to the United States in shielding its diplomats serving abroad from arbitrary or cumbersome legal processes."[3]

Law enforcement. The State Department's Office of Protocol prepares and transmits guidelines to law enforcement officers on the handling of incidents where diplomatic immunity of premises or persons must be recognized. A 25-page booklet, for example, describes diplomatic immunity and consular immunity and distinguishes between the degrees of immunity accorded career and honorary consuls.[4] It describes methods of handling incidents and minor offenses, especially traffic violations. It concludes with a request for reports of serious actions taken and lists the telephone numbers in the Protocol Office to call for verifying identification or requesting advice. Portions of the February 1988 guidelines are reproduced as appendix D.

---

[1] Feltham, *Diplomatic Handbook*, p. 10.

[2] J.R. Wood and J. Serres, *Diplomatic Ceremonial and Protocol* (New York: Columbia University Press, 1979).

[3] Richard Gookin, "Remarks on the Protocol Function in the Conduct of Foreign Relations," Leesburg, Virginia, 19 July 1985 (unpublished).

[4] *Guidance for Law Enforcement Officers: Personal Rights and Immunities of Foreign Diplomatic and Consular Personnel*, Office of Protocol and Office of Foreign Missions, U.S. Department of State, Publication 9533, February 1988.

When a serious incident occurs, the protocol office may be required to testify in court. Where a citizen or a company has suffered damages and cannot get redress through litigation because of diplomatic immunity, the protocol office makes itself available to both sides to seek a resolution of the problem. Sometimes this can result in at least an *ex gratia* payment by the diplomat or his government to the injured party.[5]

The Diplomatic List. In many capitals, the protocol office of the foreign ministry periodically issues a diplomatic list. This can be a useful guide on questions of who is entitled to diplomatic immunity, though in a court of law it may be only *prima facie* evidence, not decisive, and may require supporting testimony from the foreign ministry.

Diplomatic lists are in various forms and may be supplemented, as in the United States, by consular lists. The lists are distributed to foreign missions and to local authorities, such as mayors' offices, the customs service, and the police. In Washington, they are on sale by the Government Printing Office. A page from the London list is reproduced as figure 1.

The list is not normally a classified document, but in some countries, including the United Kingdom, it is not readily available to the public, perhaps for reasons of security. The listing for diplomats from a government that is particularly security conscious may, at the embassy's request, include less than the normal information. For example, in the Washington Diplomatic List of August 1987, the listings for Israel, Turkey, and many Arab states give only the office address of each diplomat, whereas most other states' listings include individual residential addresses and telephone numbers. (See, for example, figure 2.)

The diplomatic list records the name and official designation of the head of each diplomatic mission, followed by the names and diplomatic rank of the members of his staff. The addresses and telephone numbers of the mission and of its officials are given and the names of their spouses at the post. If the mission has separate buildings for certain sections, such as military or commercial, those addresses are also included. In the same publication, there is another list giving the order of precedence and date of presentation of credentials of the heads of mission, starting with the dean and running chronologically to the most recent arrival, as shown in figure 3. Often the diplomatic list also has the national holiday of each nation. The Washington list gives the names of diplomats of

5 Gookin, op. cit., p. 13.

The London Diplomatic List

*Alphabetical List of the representatives of Foreign States
and Commonwealth Countries in London with the names
and designations of the persons returned as composing their
Diplomatic Staff*

June 1985

m. *Married*
* *Married but not accompanied by wife or husband*

AFGHANISTAN
Embassy of the Democratic Republic of Afghanistan:
31 Prince's Gate, SW7 1QQ.   01-589 8891
(Vacant.) *Ambassador Extraordinary and Plenipotentiary.*
31 Prince's Gate, SW7 1QQ.   01-589 8891
Mr. Mohammad Homayon Mokammil. m. *2nd Secretary (Chargé d'Affaires).*
31 Prince's Gate, SW7 1QQ.   01-589 8891
Mr. Abdul Habib Majid. m. *2nd Secretary.*   Flat 6, 31 Putney Hill, S.W.15

ALGERIA
Algerian Embassy: 54 Holland Park, W11 3RS.   01-221 7800
  Consular Section: 6 Hyde Park Gate, S.W.7.   01-221 7800
  Cultural Section: 6 Hyde Park Gate, S.W.7.   01-221 7800
  Military Section: 54 Holland Park, W11 3RS.   01-221 7800
HIS EXCELLENCY MR. AHMED LAÏDI. m.
Ambassador Extraordinary and Plenipotentiary (since 14 September 1984).

	c/o Embassy
Madame Aïcha Laïdi	
Mr. Abdel Halim Hammat. m. *Minister Plenipotentiary.*	c/o Embassy
Mr. Abdelkader Djouti. m. *Minister Plenipotentiary.*	c/o Embassy
Mr. Mohammed Larabi Si Ahmed. m. *Counsellor.*	c/o Embassy
Mr. Bellahsene Bouyakoub. m. *Counsellor.*	c/o Embassy
Mr. Hadj Osman Bencherif. m. *Counsellor (Cultural Affairs).*	c/o Embassy
Mr. Smail Allaoua. *1st Secretary.*	c/o Embassy
Mrs. Zahra Bendib. m. *1st Secretary.*	c/o Embassy
Lieutenant-Colonel Bachir Taouti. m. *Defence Attaché*	c/o Embassy
Commandant Salah Bedoud. m. *Military Attaché.*	c/o Embassy
Commandant Zemri Benheddi. m. *Naval Attaché.*	c/o Embassy
Mr. Abdelkrim Senouci. m. *Attaché.*	c/o Embassy
Mr. Mohamed Ksouri. m. *Attaché.*	c/o Embassy
Mr. Bachir Bentayeb. *Attaché.*	c/o Embassy
Mr. Abdelatif Rabai. *Attaché.*	c/o Embassy
Mrs. Fatima El Aziza Senouci. m. *Attaché.*	c/o Embassy
Mr. Abderrezak Bouali. m. *Attaché.*	c/o Embassy
Mr. Ahmed Benzina. m. *Attaché.*	c/o Embassy
Mr. Abdelkrim Boukhors. m. *Attaché.*	c/o Embassy
Mr. Youssef Adrai. m. *Attaché.*	c/o Embassy
Mr. Mohamed Alami. m. *Attaché.*	c/o Embassy
Mr. Maamar Meraghni. m. *Attaché.*	c/o Embassy

Fig. 1.   Page from the London Diplomatic List.

AFGHANISTAN—Embassy of the Democratic Republic of Afghanistan

Chancery: 2341 Wyoming Ave. N.W. 20008 (234-3770, 3771).
National Holiday: Anniversary of the Saur Revolution, April 27.

Mr. Abdul Samad KUSHAN; Mrs. Rahima Kushan
Second Secretary, Chargé d'Affaires ad interim (August 10, 1987)
2341 Wyoming Ave. NW. 20008

Mr. M. Ashraf SAMIMI; Mrs. Fauzia Samimi
Second Secretary
2341 Wyoming Ave. NW. 20008

Mr. Mohammad Sharif YAQUOBI; Mrs. Sidiqa Yaquobi
Third Secretary
2341 Wyoming Ave. NW. 20008

ALGERIA—Embassy of the Democratic and Popular Republic of Algeria

Chancery: 2118 Kalorama Rd. NW. 20008 (328-5300).
National Holiday: Anniversary of the Revolution, November 1.

His Excellency Mohamed SAHNOUN; Mrs. Sahnoun
Ambassador E. and P.
2118 Kalorama Rd. NW. 20008   Tel. 328-5300

Mr. Mahieddine ABED; Mrs. Abed

Mr. Mohamed AOUNI
Administrative Attaché
2118 Kalorama Rd. NW. 20008   Tel. 328-5300

Mr. Abdelkader BOUAKKAZ
Administrative Attaché
2118 Kalorama Rd. NW. 20008   Tel. 328-5300

Mr. Omar BOUKKAZOULA
Administrative Attaché
2118 Kalorama Rd. NW. 20008

Consular Section and Cultural Affairs Office
2137 Wyoming Ave. NW. 20008.

Iranian Interests Section
2209 Wisconsin Ave. NW. 20007 (965-4990).

ANTIGUA AND BARBUDA—Embassy of Antigua and Barbuda

Chancery: 3400 International Dr. NW., Suite 2H. 20008 (362-5211, 5166, 5122, 5225)
National Holiday: November 1.

His Excellency Edmund Hawkins LAKE; Mrs. Lorna M. Lake
Ambassador E. and P.
919 - 6th St. SW. 20024   Tel. 484-3190

Mr. Paul O. SPENCER; Mrs. Edel Spencer

Fig. 2.   Page from the Washington Diplomatic List (excerpt).

Dean of the Diplomatic Corps (Since April 12, 1986)

SWEDEN
H. E. Count Wilhelm Wachtmeister .... 5 June 1974

WESTERN SAMOA
H. E. Maiava Iulai Toma .... 15 February 1978

TUVALU
H. E. Ionatana Ionatana .... 10 May 1979

CYPRUS
H. E. Andrew J. Jacovides .... 24 July 1979

TURKEY
H. E. Dr. Sukru Elekdag .... 13 August 1979

NAURU
H. E. T. W. Star.......................... 6 June 1980

CAPE VERDE
H. E. Jose Luis Fernandes Lopes .... 22 August 1980

BULGARIA
H. E. Stoyan Iliev Zhulev .... 24 November 1980

MAURITANIA
H. E. Abdellah Ould Daddah .... 24 November 1980

JAMAICA
H. E. Keith Johnson .... 24 February 1981

NIGER
H. E. Joseph Diatta .... 22 November 1982

GHANA
H. E. Eric Kwamena Otoo .... 17 March 1983

EQUATORIAL GUINEA
H. E. Florencio Maye Ela .... 17 March 1983

MEXICO
H. E. Jorge Espinosa de los Reyes.......... 17 March 1983

TRINIDAD AND TOBAGO
H. E. Dr. James O'Neil-Lewis .... 7 April 1983

OMAN
H. E. Ali Salim Bader Al-Hinai............. 7 April 1983

LEBANON
H. E. Abdallah Bouhabib............... 16 June 1983

GERMAN DEMOCRATIC REPUBLIC
H. E. Dr. Gerhard Herder............... 12 July 1983

TOGO
H. E. Ellom-Kodjo Schuppius ....13 October 1983

HUNGARY
H. E. Dr. Vencel Hazi.................. 13 October 1983

GREECE
H.E. George D. Papoulias.............. 24 October 1983

SAUDI ARABIA

Fig. 3.   Order of Precedence (excerpt), Washington Diplomatic List.

countries with whom relations have been severed (Cuba and Iran, as of 1988) under the embassy of the protecting power (Czechoslovakia and Algeria, respectively).

In a preface, the Washington list also gives the text of the Vienna Convention's articles 29, 31, and 38 on diplomatic immunity, together with a note that names on the list should be verified with the Office of Protocol because "changes occur daily." At the end of article 31, a note explains: "A diplomatic agent's family members are entitled to the same immunities unless they are United States nationals," and adds (in capital letters): "ASTERISKS (**) IDENTIFY UNITED STATES NATIONALS." In 1987, there were a number of these, including the spouses of chiefs of mission of at least two Mediterranean countries.

The list also includes heads of mission who are accredited to but not located in Washington. In August 1987 three of these were very high in the order of precedence within the diplomatic corps of 152 missions. One, the ambassador of Western Samoa, whose chancery was in New York at the United Nations, was second only to the dean of the corps, the ambassador of Sweden. Immediately behind him was his colleague of Tuvalu, who resides in Tuvalu (formerly the Ellice Islands, near Fiji), and the sixth in precedence was the ambassador of Nauru, who resides in Melbourne, Australia.

The State Department issues twice a year a separate list, *Foreign Consular Offices in the United States*, covering locations throughout the nation and including the numerous honorary consuls. Other nations often include the consular officers in the diplomatic list.

The Office of Protocol in the Department of State periodically publishes a list titled *Employees of Diplomatic Missions*, which is available for sale by the Superintendent of Documents, U.S. Government Printing Office. Its preface explains that it "contains the names of alien members of the administrative and technical staffs as well as service staffs of the diplomatic missions who are not permanent residents of the United States and who enjoy immunity under provisions of the Vienna Convention on Diplomatic Relations." An asterisk identifies service staff members. The February 1987 edition listed approximately 3500 names, most of which were followed by a position – clerk, driver, interpreter, maid, tutor, social secretary, assistant to attaché, gardener, and a host of others – a few with their nationality in parentheses, and all followed by an address. A few missions, including Israel, South Africa, and Britain, gave no addresses, and a few, including Britain, the Soviet Union, and South Africa, gave all positions simply as "employee." The Soviet Union listed the seventeen members of its trade representation with no indication of either position held or address. As in the Diplomatic List, there is a caveat that changes occur daily and that the status of persons on the list should be verified with the Protocol Office.

The chief advantages of a diplomatic list include its convenience as a reference for diplomats and local businesses, as a guide to correct addresses for correspondence, and as possible evidence of diplomatic immunity. Both the embassies who assemble the data and the protocol offices who arrange and edit it have a strong interest in keeping it accurate and up-to-date. The U.S. Protocol Office in 1988 was entering all successions and terminations into its computer database, with weekly printouts for the use of its duty officers. These officers are available round-the-clock by telephone to answer questions on the status of diplomats, consuls, and employees, and their dependents.[6]

Circular notes. The State Department's Office of Protocol administers many aspects of diplomatic immunity by sending circular notes to the chiefs of mission to inform the diplomatic corps of U.S. policies and practices. This is a dignified and discreet procedure. The notes are on long sheets of high-quality paper with the State Department seal embossed at the upper left of the opening page. In recent years they have opened with the courteous formula: "The Secretary of State presents his compliments to Their Excellencies and Messieurs and Mesdames the Chiefs of Mission and has the honor . . ." The note then may invite their attention to some new legislation or policy or bring to their attention a matter of concern to the department, such as evidence of some abuses of immunity. An example of a circular note is shown in figure 4.

This series of notes was the channel to inform the missions, on 31 October 1978, of the enactment on 30 September 1978 of the Diplomatic Relations Act, of its effective date, December 29, and of the new and generally more restrictive practices on diplomatic immunity that would be resulting from the new act.

On 1 October 1982, a note informed the missions of the Foreign Missions Act, enacted on August 24, to take effect on October 1. This important act reformed the system of regulating foreign missions and established an Office of Foreign Missions in the State Department to implement new lines of policy emphasizing U.S. national security and the principle of reciprocity in granting benefits to foreign missions, but with the Office of Protocol to continue performing its traditional functions involving foreign missions.

A note of 3 February 1983 exemplified the use of circular notes to

---

[6] Department of State, *Study and Report* of 18 March 1988, op. cit., p. 27.

The Secretary of State presents his compliments to Their Excellencies and Messieurs and Mesdames the Chiefs of Mission and has the honor to bring to their attention the policy of the Department of State regarding the carrying of firearms in the United States.

The Chiefs of Mission are informed that the granting of permission to carry a firearm falls under the jurisdiction of local authorities and is not a matter under the control of the Federal Government. Any request to carry a firearm must, therefore, be forwarded to the appropriate authority in the local jurisdiction in which the affected person resides or in which he proposes to carry such a weapon.

As a matter of policy, the Department will generally not intervene in a decision regarding issuance by local authorities of permits to carry firearms.

Department of State,
       Washington, February 3, 1983.

Fig. 4.   Circular Note, U.S. Department of State.

express concern. Stating that permits to carry firearms must be requested from local jurisdictions, not the federal government, the note pointed out that the State Department's policy was generally not to intervene in such decisions. Another example was the 21 March 1984 note on policy with respect to the serious matter of "allegations of criminal activity on the part of a few members of the missions or family members." In such cases, although the department might ensure immunity, it would expel the person concerned and take precautions so that if in future he were to reenter the United States, his serious crime would be on record and he could be arrested and prosecuted in the normal manner, unless his crime "related to the exercise of official functions, or the statute of limitations barred prosecution."

A note of 17 December 1984 reminded the missions that it is State Department policy for its representatives abroad to pay fines for traffic violations, that missions in the United States have for many years been expected to adopt a similar policy, that the Office of Foreign Missions would review the extent of violations by individuals, and the Department of State would judge whether such individuals would be permitted to operate an automobile.

These are only a partial selection of the kinds of business relating to diplomatic immunity covered in the series of circulars. The texts of the notes are available at the State Department for scholarly or other use. Many of them are summarized, quoted, and discussed by experts in the *American Journal of International Law*'s regular feature on "contemporary practice of the United States." The circular notes provide a useful guide to American policy on many aspects of diplomatic and consular immunity and may well exert a wide influence on opinion in this field. The United States has a very large number of diplomatic missions in its capital; American policy has historically been liberal in its interpretations of immunity; and the contemporary problems of abuse of privileges have all had to be faced by Washington policymakers in the full light of media publicity and legislative concern.[7] A sophisticated Viennese once remarked that it is impossible for a government anywhere in the world to think up an economic policy which has not already been tried and failed in Austria. Presumably it could also be said that there are very few modern problems of diplomatic immunity which have not

---

[7] According to the *New York Times* of 18 February 1987, there were 139 diplomatic missions in Washington (up from 94 in 1960), and they occupied "more than 320 separate buildings, some of which serve as residences, some as offices, and some as both residences and offices." In his speech on 19 July 1985, Richard Gookin gave round totals of "about 2500 diplomatic officers and nearly 5000 embassy employees," not including families and dependents.

already had to be tackled in Washington, successfully or otherwise.

The British Foreign and Commonwealth Office (FCO) and probably many other foreign ministries issue an analogous series of circular notes to diplomatic missions. A number of the FCO circulars on the subject of firearm regulations, for example, are reproduced in the 1984 Report of the House of Commons Foreign Affairs Committee on the abuse of diplomatic immunities. In 1976, these FCO circulars seem to have come from "the Head of Protocol and Conference Department of the Foreign and Commonwealth Office," who presented "his compliments to Their Excellencies [the heads] of Diplomatic Missions and International Organizations in London." As of January 1980, the source was "the Vice-Marshal of the Diplomatic Corps," who presented his compliments to the same addressees. The contents of these British official circulars are also of general interest as a guide to contemporary good practice in matters of diplomatic privileges and immunities.

The U.S. Office of Foreign Missions

Toward the end of 1982, a new Office of Foreign Missions (OFM) was established in the Department of State as directed by the Foreign Missions Act (FMA) of August 1982.[8] The purpose of the Act, as explained in the 30 November 1981 report of the Senate Foreign Relations Committee, was to meet "a serious and growing imbalance between the treatment accorded . . . to official missions of the United States and that made available to foreign government missions in the United States." The Department of State lacked authority "to enforce reciprocity in an appropriate manner." The Act would provide "mechanisms whereby the operations of foreign missions . . . and the benefits available to them from Federal, State and local authorities, public utilities and private persons may be cleared through the Federal Government and adjusted *according to United States needs abroad as well as national security interests here at home*" (emphasis added). Foreign governments "will have an incentive to provide fair, equitable and nondiscriminatory treatment to U.S. missions and personnel in their territory, thus contributing to significant savings in the costs of operating U.S. missions, improved working conditions for U.S. personnel, and mutual respect in our foreign relations."[9]

---

[8] Title II of the Department of State Authorization Act, Fiscal Years 1982 and 1983 (22 U.S. Code §4301) *et seq.*

[9] U.S. Senate, Committee on Foreign Relations, *The Foreign Missions Act of 1982, Report*, 30 Nov. 1981, 97th Cong., 1st Sess. (Washington: Government Printing Office, 1981), pp. 1-2.

It seemed clear from this 1981 report and from the favorable vote on the Act in 1982 that Congress had studied the situation, held hearings, asked questions, and ended in a mood to which parallels could be found in a number of other American foreign policy fields at this time – an attitude of "No more Mr. Nice Guy!" This attitude reflected the desire to negotiate on a basis of strict reciprocity, but with an undertone of reciprocity with a vengeance.

A few of the kinds of unbalanced treatment to be countered were specified. They included the fact that in the Soviet Union and Eastern Europe the United States is barred from purchasing residences or offices and must obtain them through government-controlled sources, although in Washington the Soviets and East European governments have purchased and own both kinds of property. Another imbalance was that in Kuwait, Bahrain, and the United Arab Emirates, the United States may not purchase staff housing sites but must pay "exorbitant short-term lease charges." In the Washington area, these same states own residences. In Indonesia, the government is converting the U.S. tenure of properties from ownership to long-term leaseholds with considerable ground rents. In the United States, Indonesia is free to buy, sell, or lease property.

In countries with state-directed economies, including the Soviet Union and its allies, the U.S. embassies must go through designated foreign ministry offices for such administrative services as travel, employees, housing maintenance, utilities, and admission tickets. Often a fee is added for these unwanted services. In India, the U.S. embassy's administrative and specialized staff do not receive duty-free import privileges. In Mexico, Venezuela, the Near East, and elsewhere, the U.S. government's employees face far greater restrictions on importing vehicles and other personal effects than are imposed on these countries' employees in the United States. The Department of State was found to lack authority to impose countervailing restrictions and conditions and had only such crude and extreme options as declaring some persons *non grata* or barring a government from using property it had acquired.

Under the Foreign Missions Act, the OFM would be able, under the secretary of state's supervision, to deny benefits to a foreign mission or impose conditions on them. The purposes to be served by these actions include facilitating relations between the United States and the sending state, protecting U.S. interests, adjusting for costs of obtaining benefits for U.S. missions, and assisting in resolving disputes involving a foreign mission.[10]

10 Ibid., pp. 2-3.

The approach is not just legally but psychologically and ideologically different from the past. The Vienna Convention accepted the idea that the functions of diplomats were essential to intergovernmental relations and that immunities for diplomats were required so that they could carry out these functions in an unhampered, efficient manner. In contrast, the Foreign Missions Act emphasizes that diplomatic missions and diplomats receive benefits from the receiving state. These benefits are not to be regarded as a sort of entitlement that the representatives of sovereign states by their nature can automatically expect to enjoy, but rather a kind of payment from the United States which they ought to stay on their toes and work hard to deserve, a payment that needs to be rationed by the United States and distributed only in return for proven service to the interests of the United States.

The implications for international diplomatic law of the United States' harsh mood and toughened stance on withholding benefits were viewed with concern by J.L. Hargrove, executive director of the American Society of International Law. "The primary, and quite legitimate, purpose of [the Foreign Missions Act] is to enable the United States to enforce reciprocity. . . . But in an excess of zeal perhaps stimulated by the trauma of the Iranian hostage crisis, it goes beyond this purpose and quite probably authorizes a violation of the Vienna Convention by a kind of harassment of diplomats as a means of accomplishing policy objectives extraneous to the maintenance of diplomatic relations themselves." In contrast, the 1978 Diplomatic Relations Act "had scrupulously respected the obligations of the receiving state" under the Vienna Convention.[11]

"Benefits" are a key idea, recurring frequently in the Foreign Missions Act and in the Senate Committee's report on its purposes. Some are listed in the Act itself ("Definitions," sec. 202): acquisitions by a foreign mission of real property in any form of tenure; "public services, including services relating to customs, importation, and utilities, and the processing of applications or requests relating to public services; supplies, maintenance, and transportation; locally engaged staff . . . ; travel and related services; and protective services." In addition to this impressive array, "benefits" may include "such other benefits as the Secretary may designate."

As one legal officer in the Department of State in 1986 tersely described the new situation, " 'Benefits' are what we say they

---

[11] John Lawrence Hargrove, "Security of Diplomats as a Problem of International Community Policy," in N.K. Hevener, ed., *Diplomacy in a Dangerous World* (Boulder, CO: Westview Press, 1986), p. 19.

are. . . . The reach of the Foreign Missions Act is farther than that of the Vienna Convention." As an illustration he gave the subject of housing, on which the Vienna Convention only touches in article 21, saying the receiving state shall, "where necessary, assist missions in obtaining suitable accommodations for their members." The FMA permits the State Department to define housing as a "benefit" far more precisely.

The Office of Foreign Missions is staffed with Foreign Service officers, other government employees, and experts and consultants. It operates from an office suite in the main Department of State building, with branches elsewhere, including offices located in the former premises of the Iranian embassy.

The Congress intended, as the Senate committee report explains, that the OFM should have a particular organizational structure. The director is appointed by the secretary of state and performs under the secretary's supervision and direction. However, unlike the situation regarding other office directors, "the Secretary is prohibited from delegating supervisory authority over the Director to any official below the rank of Under Secretary."[12]

The Senate committee's view was that the OFM would thus be separated from the operating bureaux, "which deal with foreign missions on substantive issues on a day-to-day basis." The responsibility for regulating foreign missions is to be discharged by the OFM, "precluding its exercise by the operating bureaus." The committee decided against using the term "independent" as a description of the OFM, indicating instead that OFM is "to operate as an adjunct of the Department of State, not affected by the day-to-day operations of the Department."[13]

Whenever a new office or agency is established in the federal government, its turf or area of responsibility turns out to have been at least loosely occupied already. It is a bit like the American West, where new settlers entering an area generally found Indian tribes, prospectors, Spanish missions, or other territorial claims to complicate life and require discussion and agreement. The congressional creators of the OFM identified several such existing organizational interests.

One of them was the Treasury Department's Secret Service, the historic agency whose responsibilities include protecting the life of the President. At the request of the Treasury Department, the Senate committee inserted language in the Act to specify that "the

---

[12] Senate Committee on Foreign Relations, *Foreign Missions Act of 1982*, p. 7.
[13] Ibid., pp. 7, 8, and 15.

concept of providing benefits on the basis of reciprocity does not extend to those protective services provided by the U.S. Secret Service . . . with respect to foreign diplomatic missions, or . . . with respect to a visiting head of a foreign state or government or certain distinguished foreign visitors''; nor is the Act intended to affect the authority or procedures of the Secret Service or to influence its policy of providing protection at a level commensurate with protective requirements.[14] This seems to mean that the Secret Service will continue to decide policy about the kind and amount of protection it will provide (e.g., through its Uniformed Division) without necessarily applying reciprocity as a test or a way to put pressure on a foreign government, as the OFM may do in other spheres of "benefits."

Another aspect of regulating the privileges and immunities of foreign missions in the Washington area concerns the location and extent of their premises in the District of Columbia. Washington, D.C., proper, with a 1987 population of about 620,000, is not a huge city like London, Paris, Tokyo, or Cairo, but has as many embassies as they do or more. Foreign chanceries therefore make a proportionately larger impact on Washington. For an American city, Washington has an unusually elaborate set of building controls due to its historic origins, having been planned from the start, nearly two hundred years ago, to be a city of dignity and beauty, worthy of symbolizing the greatness of an important nation and latterly of attracting and satisfying American visitors and foreign tourists.

The question of who shall control the right to build offices, including chanceries, in Washington is also politically loaded. For many years, a movement among the residents has been seeking full local self-government and even eventually statehood. Implicit in this movement is increasing devolution of responsibility for District of Columbia affairs from the federal government to the District government. One obvious area for such devolution is the power to decide whether a foreign chancery can be built in the District or established in an existing District residence. Before the Foreign Missions Act of 1982, there were existing mechanisms for handling these questions. The federal government was represented on planning bodies, but the trend, strongly supported in the District and broadly accepted in Congress, was toward greater and greater decision-making power by District representatives.

The Foreign Missions Act goes against this trend. In testimony to the Senate committee, D.C. Mayor Marion Barry objected to the draft bill's language on this question. Two minority members of the

---

[14] Ibid., pp. 9–10.

committee, senators from states neighboring the District, signed a statement, annexed to the report, opposing the creation of a presidentially appointed commission to handle questions of the location, replacement, or expansion of chanceries, considering it a retrogressive step away from democratic home rule.[15] In rejecting this minority position, the committee said that the Act "will provide for significant District participation in the decision-making process regarding the location of foreign chanceries, consistent with the important federal interests involved."[16] Certainly the Act leaves room for the federal interest to be paramount.

Within the State Department, the office most directly affected by the creation of the OFM was the Office of Protocol. The Senate committee's report recognized this and offered clear views on the matter. The committee saw a logical division between "protocol duties and those duties involving regulation of foreign mission activities." Its intent was to separate out the regulatory responsibilities from the Office of Protocol and assign them to the OFM. Although there might be certain areas where the secretary of state might consider it appropriate for the two offices to share responsibilities, in general, they should be separate, and "appropriate liaison between the offices should assure that conflicts are minimized."

The Senate committee thought it would be sensible to move the following responsibilities from the Protocol Office to the OFM:

(1) The determination of eligibility and issuance of credentials of diplomatic, consular, and other foreign government officers and employees with respect to rights, privileges, and immunities; (2) advising and acting as liaison to state and local government authorities on diplomatic privileges and immunities and related matters; (3) providing certifications of the immunity status of individuals for use in court cases; (4) requesting waiver of immunity in appropriate cases; (5) assisting in the negotiation of consular conventions and other treaties and agreements involving rights, privileges, and immunities of foreign government missions and personnel; and (6) providing advice and assistance to diplomatic missions.[17]

The Foreign Missions Act (section 203) itself lists the second and sixth responsibilities, with other functions to be determined by the secretary of state as they may be necessary to further the policy of the act.

The creation and mission of the OFM demonstrate the mood of Congress in the aftermath of the Tehran hostages crisis and reflect a worldwide trend toward restricting diplomatic privileges and immunities. The act establishing the OFM gives it the power to charge fees ("surcharges") for many of its services and allows

---

[15] Ibid., pp. 35–37.
[16] Ibid., p. 11.
[17] Ibid., pp. 7–8.

the secretary of state to decide what constitutes a "benefit." In October 1985, for example, the State Department ruled that the requisition of telecommunications goods and services by the Soviet and Soviet bloc missions was a benefit that must be obtained through the OFM.

The act requires an annual report from the OFM on its operations, to include an evaluation of "the effectiveness of the operations . . . in achieving diplomatic reciprocity and enhancing national security." The report also provides an opportunity for the OFM to "make recommendations for changes in existing procedures, regulations or law, where warranted."[18]

Armed with its formidable set of statutory powers and backed by such an unusual (for the State Department) degree of declared congressional support, the OFM achieved a great deal in its first five years. In its March 1986 report to Congress, the OFM reviewed progress in eleven different areas of regulation. Several new programs had been introduced in 1985, and further expansion of the OFM's role was foreseen.

In general, the impact of the OFM's regulatory innovations has been, as Congress no doubt intended, to restrict the previous liberality of U.S. policies on privileges, immunities, and exemptions for foreign missions.[19] However, the OFM's report realistically acknowledges that the news is not all good, or at least not all that simple. As the experts at OFM study ways to reduce unfavorable imbalances in conditions abroad versus those in the United States, they have found that "in certain countries U.S. missions receive benefits which are not routinely duplicated here." In such cases reciprocity, one of the key principles of the Foreign Missions Act, "is a two-edged sword." There are, it appears, among the benefits enjoyed by foreign missions, which in general need to be pruned back from their present luxuriant growth, a few which need to be cultivated. The OFM report identifies some of these: "Particularly with regard to zoning, taxation and other property rights, the Department must move to protect and expand benefits *which serve the national interests*" (emphasis added).[20] This statement recognizes that in some countries zoning and other restrictions are less burdensome than in the United States.

In these areas, conflicts may arise between the OFM, representing national interests, and local jurisdictions, such as the District of Columbia, as seen in the testimony on the Foreign Missions Act. If so, the State Department would seek to "achieve mutually accept-

18 OFM Annual Report, March 1986, p. 1.
19 See, for example, a 26 August 1986 *Washington Post* interview with OFM Director James Nolan headlined, "The 'Secretary of Retribution': Tit-for-Tat Diplomacy."
20 OFM Annual Report, March 1986, p. 2.

able solutions whenever possible." However, the department would always "uphold its commitment to reciprocity and equality" even if that involved "legal or other alternatives. . . . The possibility of contentious litigation cannot be ignored."[21] In such litigation, the OFM would be assisting a foreign mission to secure something it wanted that local U.S. persons or interests were resisting.

The State Department finds itself having to exercise patience when citizens accuse the department's officers of falling over backwards to do the bidding of foreign governments and of showing no interest in local residents' feelings. Ronald Mlotek, OFM Chief Counsel, has reminded residents of the District of Columbia that Washington's status as the federal city confronts them with the constant "possibility that a federal or civilian or military [facility] or a foreign mission may be located near [a resident's] property. This is not rural Virginia."[22]

Anyone who has been a country desk officer in a foreign affairs ministry will recall that when a fellow national, whether it be a small caterer or the representative of a huge oil company, has a business complaint against a foreign embassy, he is likely to suspect that the desk officer, the protocol office, or the whole foreign ministry is entirely too unhelpful and that any claim that such alleged unhelpfulness is based on the broader national interest must surely be exaggerated. It is always a personally uncomfortable position.

Real property. The OFM receives requests from foreign missions to acquire, dispose of, or alter real property, and acts on them within sixty days. There were 277 such requests in 1985 and all but 18 were approved. In 1986, there were 307 requests, and only 22 were denied. The properties concerned are mainly in the Washington area. Since consulates are included, they also come from many other cities and from Puerto Rico. Denials may be on the basis of national security, reciprocity, or potential violation of local zoning and land use laws or regulations.

A handsomely illustrated 48-page handbook titled *Foreign Missions and International Organizations: Real Property Manual*, published in July 1987, was a joint product of the National Capital Planning Commission, the District of Columbia government, and the State Department. Its purpose was to guide foreign missions, international organizations, government agencies, and others through the required steps and procedures "to acquire, locate, relocate, replace, expand, and improve embassies, chanceries, and office space in the District of Columbia." Particular attention is paid to the requirements laid down by the Foreign Missions Act of 1982.

21 Ibid., p. 3.
22 *Washington Post*, 25 Oct. 1986.

The manual includes a map of the District, with shadings to indicate locations permitted for chancery facilities. In those areas requiring a review by the D.C. Board of Zoning Adjustment, chanceries are to give preference to sites in areas that are (1) earmarked and developed by the U.S. government for such purposes, (2) designated as historic districts and special streets, or (3) being assisted by government renewal programs. The manual's appendices provide such practical information as short descriptions of the roles of the U.S. agencies involved, their addresses, and telephone numbers.

Copies of the *Real Property Manual* are freely available to foreign missions. State Department officers also distribute them when briefing neighborhood councils on issues raised by the presence or expansion of foreign missions.

In 1985, OFM commenced a housing program under which it can exercise reciprocal control on the housing of missions, such as Bulgaria, whose governments control U.S. diplomats' housing in their countries. In the case of Bulgaria, the results have been positive from the U.S. standpoint.

There was considerable discussion with the People's Republic of China in 1986 on the application of the principle of reciprocity. The U.S. side withheld approval for a number of PRC residential facilities, and OFM representatives traveled to China to study the basis for housing reciprocity. In 1986, the OFM for the first time extended its housing requirements to personnel of a foreign commercial entity, in this case Aeroflot Soviet Airlines personnel. In spite of the atmosphere of tension in U.S.-Nicaraguan relations in 1986, OFM approved five Nicaraguan lease requests, including one for an ambassador's residence in Scarsdale, New York, although four other residences for Nicaragua were denied in the Washington area.

Another ruling in 1985 was that the New China News Agency was a foreign mission under the Foreign Missions Act and must have OFM approval for acquiring real property.

In several real property issues the OFM in 1985 was working to assist a foreign mission to achieve something that a local authority had turned down. These included the Italian, Ethiopian, and Benin embassies.

Travel. A travel program, in operation since the OFM's first year, 1983, requires fifteen countries and the Palestine Liberation Organization (PLO) to obtain tickets and reservations through the OFM. Starting in September 1985, UN employees who are nationals of those countries became subject to the same requirement. In January 1986, four additional countries were added. The aim is to

enhance U.S national security in some cases and, in others, to produce liberalization for U.S. diplomats abroad. Though no positive
results on liberalization seem to have occurred, the OFM judged
that the requirements had proven "an effective tool in curbing and
monitoring activities of mission personnel."[23] In 1986, there was an
extension or tightening generally of the travel program, based on
further applications of the principle of reciprocity. For example, at
the end of 1986 Soviet news media personnel in the United States
were put under the requirement, already applied to Soviet diplomatic and consular personnel, that they and their dependents give
advance notice to OFM for both official and private travel.

Taxation. The tax program begun in late 1984 seeks to use reciprocity to reduce the taxing of U.S.missions and employees abroad
and/or to increase the collection of taxes on missions and their
personnel in the United States. The OFM issues cards to persons
eligible for exemption from sales tax anywhere in the United States.
In early 1986, a total of 14,000 such cards had been issued. The OFM
report on 1985 states, significantly, that "because the cards are
issued on the basis of reciprocity and because there are 29 countries
that deny U.S. diplomatic and consular personnel tax exemption,
there are approximately 8,400 fewer eligible recipients than had
been the case when exemptions were granted by the individual
states, thus increasing sales tax revenues and reducing administrative costs to state and local jurisdictions."[24]

The OFM can vary the level of exemption from sales tax to match
the treatment accorded U.S. personnel by foreign governments.
This is achieved by issuing cards at six different levels of exemption.
The most valuable are blue-striped, which entitle the bearer to
exemption from all sales taxes. Green-striped give exemption from
all but hotel room taxes. Red-striped cards give exemption from
sales taxes on purchases totaling over $50, $100, $150, or $200, as
indicated on the card. The OFM can also, on the basis of reciprocity,
withhold cards from certain categories, such as consuls. With a
number of countries this leverage has enabled OFM to increase tax
exemptions granted to U.S. personnel. In 1986, the OFM began
using an information system, "OFMIS," which reduced by 80 percent the time needed for issuance of cards and gave the OFM capa-
bility to produce card reports rapidly for itself or for tax authorities.

---

[23] "1986 Annual Report on the Implementation of the Foreign Missions Act of
1982, As Amended (P.L. 97–241)," Department of State, Office of Foreign Missions, April 1987, p. 7.
[24] OFM Annual Report, March 1986, p. 8.

An ingenious new program, which seems unlikely to be duplicated in the smaller developing countries of the world for some time, is the reciprocal gasoline and motor fuel tax exemption program. Launched in 1985 in the Washington metropolitan area, it was expanded to New York State in 1986 and is to be gradually extended to the other states. Eligible individuals use an oil company credit card. No tax exemptions are allowed at the pump, but upon certification by the OFM to the oil company involved, a tax-free account is established and sales taxes charged by the distributor are removed at billing time. While futurologists dream of an age in which credit cards would make possible a cashless economy, the OFM system enables diplomats to glimpse a bright utopia.

Motor vehicles. The motor vehicle program administered by OFM builds on a great deal of earlier work by its predecessors. The subject is extremely important for the physical safety of individuals, the efficiency of urban traffic circulation, and the reputation of diplomats as a profession. The number of cars in cities, the number of diplomats in capitals, and the number of cars per diplomat had all increased dramatically since the two Vienna Conventions of 1961 and 1963. Eileen Denza has observed that the immunities of diplomats with respect to their cars would have been less liberally conceded if a few more years had passed before the 1961 convention was agreed. By 1963 the concept of limiting immunity in this field had hardened.[25]

The OFM has taken a firm hold on U.S. government practice and made solid improvements, providing an example that could have beneficial effects worldwide. The insurance program was tightened in 1985 to enable OFM to track the status of individual diplomats, inform their missions, and prevent any who are not insured adequately (including minimum third-party liability of $300,000) from operating a vehicle. OFM now registers titles and issues license plates for all diplomatic and consular vehicles. The number of such vehicles had been reduced by about 30 percent that year, and local authorities reported improvement in payments by diplomats for parking violations.

Also in 1985, the State Department commenced a new practice of issuing country-coded license plates for foreign diplomats' cars. The red-white-and-blue plates, which are manufactured at the District of Columbia's Lorton Reformatory, are attached to both the front and back of the vehicle. They carry three elements of identification: First, the letter D for diplomat, C for consul, S for staff member, or

---

[25] Denza, *Diplomatic Law*, pp. 151–52.

A for United Nations. Next comes a country code of two capital letters, apparently chosen to avoid direct connection with the country's name (e.g., QW is Poland, GP is Albania, and ND is Romania), followed by three digits in a series commencing with 001, 002, etc. "Issued by the United States Department of State" appears in small lettering along the bottom.

The system was accepted by the diplomatic corps and is applied nationwide. In 1987, several countries asked that their coded letters be changed, and the State Department complied, although the plates apparently cost the U.S. government, which supplies them, about ten dollars apiece. Those embassies requesting and receiving a change (for example, the Soviet Union from SX to FC and South Africa from FY to BL) may sometimes be those of countries experiencing periods of unpopularity in the United States.

Many other governments supply license plates to the diplomats accredited in their capitals, and sometimes the numbers are country-coded. For example, the license plates of U.S. diplomats in the Soviet Union carry the number "04" to indicate their country.[26]

Not everyone is convinced of the value of this system. An unnamed State Department official, for one, reportedly expressed concern that possible publicity about the country designators would "invite harassment of U.S. diplomats abroad or pressure from foreign embassies to have the new system scrapped." He added that repeated requests for changes (there were more than 200 Soviet cars) would be an expense the department would rather avoid.[27]

The OFM in 1985 made preparations to issue State Department driver's licenses to embassy, consular, and UN personnel. Driving privileges were to be more tightly controlled in the interests of both reciprocity and public safety. Implementation began on 1 April 1986, when newly designed licenses were issued to personnel and their family members at selected missions. By the end of the year, OFM had issued 2,247 permanent licenses and 1,645 temporary ones for use during transition. Procedural arrangements had been concluded with individual state licensing authorities and with the American Association of Motor Vehicle Administrators.

The OFM's Diplomatic Motor Vehicle Office has established a traffic violation tracking program which includes a weighted point system. When the total goes above a certain number, the individual's driving record is reviewed. If it is one of serious disregard for

[26] *The Times* of London on 18 Aug. 1987 mentioned the Soviet system: "Cars belonging to foreign residents in Moscow carry special license plates: D for diplomat, K for correspondent and so on, followed by a number which identifies the country. Britain is 001 - of course."

[27] *Washington Post*, 21 Feb. 1986.

safety, driving privileges can be revoked. There were nine such revocations in 1985 for reckless or drunken driving. By 1987, OFM had succeeded in "securing financial restitution for parking violations that had been previously disregarded by mission personnel."[28] In one serious traffic accident involving a diplomat and damage to property in Montgomery County, Maryland, OFM intervention resulted in the diplomat's embassy paying the county for the damage.

The aim is to have a licensing program that enables the OFM to control "which diplomats may drive, how they obtain their licenses and insurance, how their cars are registered and, most importantly, how well they obey driving laws and regulations."[29]

Accreditation. The OFM and the Office of Protocol co-chair an important body, the Accreditation Review Panel (ARP), established in late 1984. The ARP generally meets weekly, or more frequently when necessary. Members include representatives of the Legal Adviser's Office, the Bureau of International Organization Affairs, the Under Secretary for Political Affairs, and, since 1986, the Bureau of Diplomatic Security. When visa issues are to be discussed, the Visa Office also participates.

This body aims "to tighten the standards and procedures by which the many foreign government representatives and installations in this country are granted legal recognition, privileges, immunities, and consent to undertake various activities requiring U.S. government approval."[30] The ARP's functions may be summarized as: (1) reviewing current policies on accreditation of persons and property and instituting changes where needed; (2) looking at instances of abuse by foreign officials to see what U.S. response is warranted and whether a general policy statement would help deter such an abuse in the future; (3) reviewing foreign mission activities to see if they endanger security, threaten public safety, or prejudice legal rights of U.S. citizens and implementing policy rules on such problems, for example, by limiting the number of persons entitled to immunities in certain missions (Cuba was a case in point); and (4) insuring, in some cases, that U.S. rules on accreditation and the scope of mission activity are reciprocated.

The report on the OFM for 1986[31] mentioned several examples of ARP's work that affect U.S. practice with respect to diplomatic

---

28 OFM Annual Report, April 1987, p. 13.
29 OFM Annual Report, March 1986, p. 12.
30 Ibid., p. 14.
31 Sec. VII, "Accreditation," pp. 15–18.

immunity, most notably "insuring respect for U.S. laws." A major policy goal of the panel is to see that foreign officials act in conformity with the laws, and especially with laws "whose violation would injure the safety, welfare or property interests of Americans." The panel noted that the United States is host to a far larger diplomatic presence than any other nation, so misconduct by diplomats "is occasionally bound to occur." ARP aims to deter such misconduct and insure that "when it does take place, the offending individual does not escape all consequences of his acts by virtue of diplomatic immunities he may possess – immunities which the United States remains deeply committed to respect."

After careful study, ARP has come up with "a more refined view of the principle of diplomatic immunity which, while not violating that essential rule, would nevertheless provide for the imposition of certain punitive measures against diplomats who commit crimes." These views have been publicized by the ARP "among both the diplomatic community and law enforcement authorities."

One specific refinement of practice turned out to be directly relevant to the case of a Papuan ambassador's automobile accident in Washington in February 1987, as described in chapter 5 below. This was that "immunity from criminal prosecution for other than official acts dissolves once an individual ceases to be a diplomat," and that "accordingly, an arrest warrant or indictment issued against a diplomat, though not immediately enforceable, could legally remain in effect even after the offender departed the United States. This, in turn, would confront the individual with two highly effective sanctions: either, be forever barred from returning to the United States; or, be subject to arrest and prosecution upon return."

A second illustration of the Accreditation Review Panel's activity was the tightening of standards for approving the opening of new consulates in the United States. The motives were to keep the number of consular personnel entitled to immunities to a reasonable level and to hold down the cost of providing security for consulates "at a time of general budget austerity." Past practice had been to grant requests for new consulates "almost invariably" and "as a matter of course." Commencing in 1985, the Department of State "for the first time instituted the requirement that foreign governments support their requests for new consulates with detailed justifications of the objective need for consular presence in the city concerned." The result of the new standards was that the total of consulates declined from 1,549 in 1984 to 1,481 in 1986.

A third type of ARP action mentioned in the OFM's report on 1986 was that of barring business and commercial activities by diplomats. All foreign embassies were notified that U.S. law prohibits foreign diplomats from "pursuing outside employment or commercial activities." The embassies were requested to inform their respective diplomatic and consular personnel of this rule. The notice emphasized that individuals who violated the rule "lack immunity from civil legal proceedings arising out of their business activities" and that "any income produced from such activities would be fully subject to applicable federal, state and local income taxes." In 1986, when a number of violations were discovered, the embassy concerned in each case "was informed that the offending . . . employee was abusing his or her privileges and immunities. Such notice effectively means that continued violation . . . would subject the offender to the withdrawal of diplomatic status and expulsion from the United States, with the possibility of being permanently ineligible for re-entry in the future."

Customs. Since the customs program was transferred to the OFM from the Office of Protocol in 1985, the OFM has surveyed the situation of customs practices affecting diplomatic missions and diplomats worldwide. The office works closely with U.S.Customs and briefs U.S.Customs attachés posted abroad. An aim is to reduce fees and simplify procedures that U.S. diplomatic cargoes encounter abroad.

One current problem is that some governments try to impound U.S. diplomatic pouches, subject them to X-ray examination, or separate them from couriers. The tactic of simply enforcing reciprocity would not be productive in several such cases because the governments concerned ship fewer and smaller pouches than the United States does.[32] In time the OFM plans to assemble enough data to develop a "baseline" code of minimally acceptable customs practice and seek to achieve it in more areas.

A new obstacle to the OFM's effort to prevent the scanning of U.S. diplomatic pouches appeared in September 1986. The Italian government at cabinet level announced that diplomatic luggage and pouches would be subjected to metal detection and X-ray scanning as an antiterrorist measure. Though the intent may be to focus on the diplomats of such states as Libya, who are regarded as particularly dangerous, the press quoted Italian police officials as saying, "It's a blanket control. Not even the ambassadors of powerful countries will be exempt anymore." The measure apparently will

32 OFM Annual Report, March 1986, p. 16.

apply even on internal flights; at least one ambassador has submitted to screening upon arrival in Rome from Venice. The British Foreign Office indicated initial concern that the scanning of diplomatic bags "could threaten the integrity of cypher equipment."[33]

In 1986, a "banner year" for its customs program, the OFM worked with the Customs Service to design, coordinate, and implement "reciprocity packages" for three foreign missions and had four more under way. Several actions affected U.S. practice vis-à-vis the Soviet Union. One was to require, on grounds of reciprocity, inventory lists of incoming and outgoing household effects of Soviet personnel assigned to the United States. OFM and the Customs Service cooperated in efforts to reduce "the flow of critical technology to the Soviet Bloc." At the request of the Customs Service, the State Department had the main customs vehicular crossing point for Soviet officials on the New York–Canadian border shifted to Champlain, New York.

The OFM helped, through improved computer use, to integrate customs processing of duty-free requests from foreign missions and UN Secretariat employees in New York with Washington operations. A Customs Service inspector was assigned to work with the U.S. Mission to the United Nations. These measures aimed to assist the monitoring and timely processing of foreign mission requests for duty-free imports.

Banking. Since February 1985, the State Department has ruled that banking by foreign missions is one of the benefits to be regulated by the OFM. Moves by the OFM in this area involve consultation with such powerful agencies as the Treasury Department, the Federal Reserve Bank, the Comptroller of the Currency, and the Federal Deposit Insurance Corporation. The ticklishness of the banking issue was reflected by an OFM representative, who said in an interview: "We don't want to alarm the U.S. banking system, or upset the arrangement Treasury and the Federal Reserve have with the central banks of the various countries. However, we view this as an area where the United States is operating at a severe disadvantage, and we have the mandate to investigate it. We will be proceeding, albeit fairly slowly."[34]

Some of the problems OFM sees as in need of solution because of the trouble they can cause for U.S. missions abroad include: delayed crediting of currency purchases and other deposits; interest on credit balances not allowed, although minimum balances are required;

[33] *Daily Telegraph* (London), 11 Sept. 1986.
[34] *Foreign Service Journal*, April 1986, p. 44.

imposition of taxes on U.S. government accounts and on currency purchases; and unreasonable ledger fees.

The OFM report on 1986 (p. 20) noted that a banking operations officer had been designated, and OFM had made direct contact with the State Department's Regional Administrative Management Center in Paris to discuss reciprocity issues. The office had also worked with the State Department Office of the Comptroller "to review host government currency exchange markets and controls to determine if the Department can obtain its foreign currency requirements under more favorable terms." For example, "in those countries where parallel or off-shore exchange markets offer more attractive rates, it is hoped that savings under departmental budget restraints" may be possible.

Construction and properties. The Office of Foreign Missions has three programs concerning construction and properties. The Custodial Properties Program has custody of Iranian, Cambodian and Vietnamese properties in the United States. A total of over thirteen different properties of these governments, which have no diplomatic missions, are managed by OFM, usually by renovation and leasing, with the income of about $1 million annually going mainly into maintenance. In 1987, the Iranian and Vietnamese chanceries continued to be used by State Department offices.

The Construction Program in 1986 was engaged in design, construction, and procurement management for five projects with an estimated value of $4.3 million. Some of these were for the mission of the People's Republic of China, others for the Soviet mission, and one to assist the South African embassy's external physical security.

The OFM's International Center Properties Program leases space to foreign missions in Northwest Washington, D.C., in a tract designated the International Center. This is a parcel of federal government land divided into lots that are available to foreign governments for diplomatic missions. There are twenty-two lots that may be leased for this purpose for ninety-nine years, with an extension clause for an additional ninety-nine years. No one government may lease more than one lot. The Department of State negotiates the terms of the leases on the basis of reciprocity. The aim of the program is to provide suitable and convenient land for embassies, thus facilitating security arrangements and taking some of the pressure off land in other residential areas of Washington. The limit of one lot per country is to prevent a rich country from leasing several contiguous lots on favorable terms and using some of the scarce space for gardens.[35]

By the end of 1986, nine leases at the International Center had been signed, and several more were expected soon thereafter. The countries with leases were Israel, Kuwait, Bahrain, Jordan, Yemen Arab Republic, Qatar, Bangladesh, and Ghana.

Protection. The security of diplomatic mission premises and personnel is another area in which OFM helps foreign missions in the United States. The OFM's assistance is intended partly to stimulate efforts of other governments to provide effective security services to U.S. posts and government personnel. This requires coordination within the Department of State with the Bureau of Diplomatic Security. The OFM also works with police forces in Washington (the Metropolitan Police, the Uniformed Division of the Secret Service, and the U.S. Park Police) and in other U.S. localities. Some diplomatic missions and consulates in the United States have a problem of threats of harassment, and the OFM does what it can to facilitate the short-range protection measures they may need.

The Department of State's long-standing practice is to insist that if a foreign government wishes to have a diplomatic mission in the United States, it should be located in the District of Columbia. Among other reasons this is intended to simplify arrangements for protecting the missions.[36] A partial exception to this practice is the location of the office that performs official functions for the governing authority of Taiwan. The premises of that agency are in Bethesda, Maryland, just across the District line.

In the words of its April 1987 report (p. 24), the OFM seeks "through fast, reasoned reaction to the legitimate security needs" of the Washington diplomatic community to encourage "similar responsiveness to U.S. Embassy requirements on the part of host governments abroad." An additional position staffed by a professional officer from the Bureau of Diplomatic Security was established to assist the department to respond quickly and effectively to security needs and "when appropriate, to identify similar security-related requirements affecting U.S. establishments overseas."

The Diplomatic Corps and Its Dean

In each capital the body of diplomats, including all the attachés, constitutes the diplomatic corps. The most convenient method of

---

[35] Talk given at Kalorama neighborhood council meeting by Richard Massey of OFM, 5 May 1987.
[36] Ibid.

determining who the members are is to look at an officially published *Diplomatic List*.

The dean, or *doyen*, of the diplomatic corps is the senior head of mission in terms of the date of official arrival, although in some predominantly Catholic countries the Apostolic Nuncio may be recognized as the dean *ex officio*.[37]

While the dean's functions are mostly ceremonial, he is also traditionally the watchdog and spokesman for the protection of the privileges and immunities of the corps against any infringement by the host government. His usual contact for this function would normally be the foreign minister or the chief of protocol.

The dean's assistance may also be requested by the host government if it thinks members of the diplomatic corps are abusing their privileges, for example, to circumvent customs restrictions or disregard parking rules. He may then circulate a note to heads of mission asking them to assist on the matter and to take it up with members of their staffs.[38] This procedure sounds a little too gentlemanly to be effective if the abuses are serious.

No function of a dean is mentioned in the Vienna Convention of 1961, nor in fact is the office of dean itself, except indirectly in article 16, where the custom of according precedence to the Holy See's representative is accepted.

In practice, the dean might propose to convene a meeting of his colleagues on some subject, but if so, each of them would consult his home government before agreeing to attend. If the meeting saw fit to take any action, they would then seek authorization from home and probably need clearance to accept the particular wording of the dean's proposed message.[39] The reception the dean would have at the foreign ministry on such business might well be correct but chilly, which would further inhibit his government and him personally from orally reinforcing his démarche.

In spite of the painful delicacy inherent in this process, the existence of a strong customary basis for the dean's role is a useful deterrent to extreme actions by inexperienced or volatile national leaderships encroaching on diplomatic privileges and immunities. The world may yet see the appearance of additional regimes such as Idi Amin's Uganda, Khomeini's Iran, and Qadhafi's Libya.

An example of what seems to have been an historically justified use of the dean's role as the spokesman for the protection of diplomats occurred in 1906 in Caracas, Venezuela, and involved the

[37] Feltham, *Diplomatic Handbook*, p. 13; Satow, 5th ed., p. 161.
[38] Satow, 5th ed., p. 162.
[39] Ibid.

French minister. The diplomatic corps protested twice, through the dean, against the contention of the host government that "a diplomat lost his immunity the moment his mission terminated."[40] The custom at that time, now codified by the Vienna Convention of 1961 (article 39), was that immunity ceased only when he left the country or after a reasonable time in which to leave had expired. The practical effect on an individual diplomat who may be ending his mission because of strained relations is obvious.

This writer can remember the alarming thoughts engendered in one's mind by the threat of an unreasonably early termination of diplomatic immunity at a time of political crisis. To continue briefly in the first person: In June 1967 when the Six-day War broke out, I happened to be head of the political section in the American embassy in Baghdad. With our ambassador away on home leave, his deputy was chargé d'affaires and I was the deputy's deputy. On the third day of the conflict, the chargé called at the Foreign Ministry and was given the only formal notice we ever received of the break in relations and the deadline for our expulsion. This important communication was handed to him as a single, indistinct ozalid copy of two pages typed in Arabic. It had no heading, no signature, and no date except, as I recall, at the bottom of the second page "0800," presumably of the day on which the chargé received it in the afternoon. The requirement for our withdrawal stated that the head of the mission must leave Iraq within three days and the rest of the personnel within about a week longer. The chargé decided, wisely, that we would close out our work, hand over American interests, and have all the Americans at the embassy out of Iraq by his own required time of three days. This firm, sensible position was mainly based, the chargé told me, on the fact that the diplomatic immunity of our American staff and their families was a priceless asset under the circumstances, and we must not let it expire while any of us were in Iraqi territory.[41] I thought at that time and in the years afterward that he was completely right.

If the circumstances had been different, this might possibly have been a case where the diplomatic corps, after consultation and through its dean, might have protested that three days was not a "reasonable time" for the ultimatum's deadline for departure, especially since evacuation by air was not feasible. In addition, the

---

[40] O'Connell, *International Law*, p. 907; see also Satow, 5th ed., p. 182.

[41] This incident is recounted in detail in the author's chapter entitled, "Evacuation and Hand-over to a Protecting Power: The Baghdad Embassy in 1967," in David D. Newsom, ed., *Diplomacy Under a Foreign Flag: The Protecting Power and the Interests Section* (Washington: Institute for the Study of Diplomacy, Georgetown University, 1989).

protest might have extended to the implied discourtesy of the form in which the ultimatum was delivered. The possibility of such an old-fashioned démarche was never even considered. By a curious coincidence, the transfer of the office and functions of dean of the corps in this instance would have been awkward at best. Our own ambassador happened to be the current dean, and he was in Washington. Our chargé had the official files of the dean's office, but his status as chargé would not have been satisfactory for such an important piece of diplomatic business. The next in line in seniority among the heads of mission in Baghdad happened to be the ambassador of the People's Republic of China. U.S. policy at that time was one of nonrecognition and even a measure of hostility toward his government, and he himself may have been preoccupied by the Cultural Revolution then underway at home and within his own embassy. All in all, it was not a time to test the ability of a dean of the corps to stand up to the host government on behalf of a diplomatic colleague.

The Police

Police forces in every country have the delicate responsibility of enforcing the law when diplomats are the offenders, most frequently in capitals where diplomatic missions are located and in cities where international organizations have their headquarters. New York is a prime example of the latter.

To minimize incidents and friction, the usual arrangement is for the foreign ministry to prepare written guidelines on diplomatic and consular immunity. Appendix D contains an example of such guidelines. These documents, updated as necessary, can be circulated to police headquarters, local stations, and even individual officers, and filed in police offices along with their own regulations, where they can be readily accessible. Such guidelines can include a telephone number in the foreign ministry to which calls can be made for advice or to check statements made by a diplomat in police custody.

The most specific guidance to police, in practice, is likely to be on traffic violations. For example, the State Department's guidance on this subject states that if a diplomat commits a moving traffic violation, he or she may be given a citation or warning, for this does not constitute an arrest or detention. If he has been stopped for driving while intoxicated, he may be taken to the station to permit him to recover, provided with an opportunity to telephone a relative or friend, put in a taxi, or provided with transportation to his home. He should not be handcuffed or subjected to a sobriety test. Only a minimum of force may be used, with discretion, to prevent injury to the diplomat or others.

In June 1984, the British Home Office submitted a memorandum on diplomatic immunities and privileges to the House of Commons Foreign Affairs Committee.[42] The committee had asked, "What problems are caused to the Home Office and the police in their work by the operation of, and actual or potential abuse of, the Vienna Convention?" The response is significant as a summary of diplomatic immunity not as viewed by foreign ministries or diplomats or national governments or the public, nor by editorialists and journalists, but rather as it reflects the experience of policemen and public security officers. It is perhaps a specially valuable indication of police practice because of London's situation as both a great urban center and a national capital.

Drawing on the advice of the Commissioner of Police, the Home Office memorandum opened by noting the inherent difficulties posed for the police in both protecting diplomats and preventing them from abusing their privileges and immunities in breach of the law. In carrying out the protective duties required of the receiving state, for which they must depend on the willing cooperation of the diplomatic missions, the police and the Home Office maintain close reporting links with the Foreign and Commonwealth Office. After these introductory generalities, the Home Office memorandum took up, article by article, those provisions of the Vienna Convention particularly relevant to the police in their work. There were several of these.

First was the *inviolability* of diplomatic premises outlined under article 22 of the 1961 convention. The inability of the police to enter and search the premises of a mission for evidence "of actual or potential criminal offences" or to deal with "breaches of public order" was cited as a hindrance to effective police action, particularly in "preventing and responding to acts of terrorism." Citing a specific example, the report recalled that, in April 1984, constables were refused access to the Iranian embassy for several hours after the consular staff had detained a group of demonstrators who had entered the premises.

While expected not to violate a mission's premises, the police were also expected to protect them. Article 30 requires police to "provide routine security cover," and increased cover when there is a terrorist threat or other special circumstance. This duty was not considered

---

[42] Appendix 2, "Diplomatic Immunities and Privileges (DIP 12)," memorandum by the Home Office, 19 June 1984, House of Commons Report, 1984, Appendices to the Minutes of Evidence Taken before the Foreign Affairs Committee, pp. 56–59.

much of a "problem" since it falls within the general duty of the police to prevent any disorders and threats to security within their jurisdiction. Nevertheless, the Home Office observed, the "special duty of protection" sometimes encouraged missions to be lax in providing for their own security, thus putting a greater burden on the police.

The Home Office then turned to article 29, which provides for personal inviolability of diplomats and their families and the mission's technical and administrative staff, and for their immunity from arrest. These provisions, which prevent the police from detaining a diplomat suspected of offences under general criminal law or suspected of being involved in "acts of terrorism under the prevention of terrorism legislation," may also inhibit the police in preventing further offences by that person or another person. The inviolability provision also bars the police from searching diplomats for weapons or explosives they may be carrying, though they may "stop a person to establish whether he is a bona fide diplomat." The police may "in exceptional circumstances . . . take measures to prevent further offences" and request that a claimant to diplomatic immunity accompany them to a police station to properly establish his identity. Further, the requirement to provide physical protection to diplomats, families, and staff "makes demands on police manpower," although not to the same extent as protecting premises.

The diplomatic bag, under article 27, "shall not be opened or detained." The Home Office had "grounds for concern" that this article "is in a few cases seriously abused" in disregard of the requirement that the bag "may contain only diplomatic documents or articles intended for official use." But article 27 prevents the police from opening and searching the bag or "requiring that it be returned to the country of origin." Home Office practice, like that of "nearly all states," is to forego electronic scanning of diplomatic bags. Though "not expressly covered by the Convention," it is arguable whether it is permitted. In any case, the memorandum noted, such scanning was ineffective in detecting prohibited articles which can "be disguised to appear wholly innocuous on an X-ray screen." Successful scanning would require the ability to open bags.

On the immunities of consular premises and bags, under articles 31 and 35 of the 1963 Vienna Convention, the Home Office observed, the police have "more scope to deal with threats to public order or safety" at consular premises than at diplomatic premises. This is because, as noted in chapter 3 of this work, the inviolability of consulates only covers "that part of the consular premises which is used exclusively for the work of the consular post" and, moreover, consent to enter even that area is assumed in the event of fire or other equivalent disaster.

The police have somewhat greater latitude in preventing abuse of consular bags than is the case with diplomatic bags. This is because requests can be made to open consular bags if they are believed to contain prohibited articles. The bag must be returned to its place of origin if the request is refused. Diplomatic baggage, in contrast, is exempt from inspection unless "serious grounds [exist] for presuming that the baggage contains prohibited items." The troublesome question of what constitutes such grounds is answered in British practice by allowing the police to act on "specific information that a diplomat's personal baggage was likely to contain weapons or explosives."

The Home Office memorandum then took up the immunity of diplomats and consuls from criminal jurisdiction (articles 31 and 37 of the diplomatic convention, article 43 of the consular). "In practice" this immunity "is most frequently invoked in relation to traffic offences and in particular illegal parking where the provisions . . . prevent prosecution or the enforcement of fees payable." Additionally, "the means of transport of a mission shall be immune from search, requisition, attachment or execution." This also covers "the private transport of diplomatic agents, administrative and technical staff, and their families" (articles 22, 30, and 37). The practice of the British police is based on the view that these convention articles preclude "action against diplomatic vehicles which is penal in intent and effect. The removal of vehicles which are causing an obstruction is permitted but not wheel-clamping."

Finally, the Home Office reviewed the question of waivers of immunity as they affect police practice. The 1961 Vienna Convention's requirement (article 32) that "the waiver must always be express . . . means that the agreement of the sending State has to be obtained specifically for each stage of the criminal process." Since these are at least three – the police interview and taking of statements, the trial, and the sentence – an initial waiver covering all stages, "successfully sought in few serious cases, . . . is rarely a practical course." Sending state cooperation is unlikely, while delays in sending requests through diplomatic channels hamper police operations and "prejudice the chance of a successful prosecution." Since diplomats are not exempt from their sending state's jurisdiction (article 31), home governments that refuse to waive immunity sometimes agree to "consider prosecution on receipt of the available evidence."

Even when immunity is not waived nor sending state jurisdiction assumed, the FCO may, where warranted, "take a range of actions which can result in the recall of the diplomat or a warning [that] further infringement of the law" will not be tolerated. The problem then lies in ensuring "that the evidence is sound and cannot be discredited." Evidence is often deficient, however, especially in drunken driving cases, where the British practice is that a diplomat "can be breath-tested only with his head of mission's consent."

It is clearly important for police authorities routinely to keep in touch with the foreign ministry when police actions involve a diplomat. In the same 19 June 1984 memorandum, the British Home Office detailed its arrangements for coordination with the FCO: "The Police are under instruction to report to the Home Office the facts of any case where it has been established that a person who has been reported for an offence is entitled to immunity." In considering such reports, the Home Office may consult the police in determining that the evidence is adequate to conclude that "in the absence of immunity, criminal proceedings would have been instituted." The "best possible" evidence is then transmitted to the Foreign Office "for appropriate action." Always there is close consultation between Home Office and Foreign Office officials on what action to take, for example, a request for a waiver or for withdrawal. "Arrangements for swift contact out of office hours exist [using] Home Office duty officers and FCO Resident Clerks, who are able in emergencies to contact appropriate officials at their homes. These arrangements are kept under close review and are examined carefully in the light of particular incidents," such as the shooting from the Libyan embassy.[43]

As in Britain, the police elsewhere play a direct and essential role in the task of assuring the protection and inviolability of diplomatic and consular missions. Some capitals have a special unit or a specially trained group within the police force. The work of protecting an embassy can be tedious or dangerous or both intermittently. The situation of the special Iraqi guards sent to protect the inviolability of the American embassy in Baghdad after the outbreak of the June 1967 war, for example, was one of long hours of duty over several days, though the one brief stone-throwing demonstration had occurred before their arrival. No food or water had been planned for them by their own organization, and they were grateful to be sustained from the dwindling stocks of cooked food in the embassy's small commissary. The men on duty stood at attention and saluted the chargé on the afternoon he departed, and shook hands warmly with the officers who drove off later that night to the Iraq-Iran frontier, expelled by the guards' own government.

---

[43] Summary points and quotations from the Home Office memorandum are all from the December 1984 House of Commons Report, loc. cit.

In Washington, the Metropolitan Police Force of about 3,800 members[44] has the normal responsibilities of a large municipal police department. Its traffic and other police units have instructions and training in the special subject of the status of diplomats.

For many years, the Secret Service of the Department of the Treasury has been assigned the heavy national responsibility of protecting the life of the president. In 1970, a Uniformed Division of the Secret Service was created to meet the expanded demands of security for the missions of new countries.[45] By 1987, it had grown to a force of nine hundred. The duties of the force include the protection of the immediate surroundings of the president and vice president and of the embassies in Washington.[46] They wear a distinctive police uniform and have vehicles with special insignia. When an embassy requires an around-the-clock police guard, as did the Turkish embassy near Dupont Circle during 1986, 1987, and 1988, due to the threat of Armenian terrorist attacks, this was the force assigned.

An example of the practical need to coordinate and exchange information among the various separate police forces that operate in Washington in the vicinity of embassies is a program of the National Park Service of the Department of the Interior. Since 1983, biologists of the Park Service have studied the habits and movements of raccoons in the Washington area because of public health concern to prevent the spread of rabies. The scientists initially anesthetized about thirty raccoons, immunized them against rabies, and fitted them with little collars carrying radio transmitters and flexible antennae. Thus the raccoons' movements could be traced. Raccoons move mainly at night, so the scientists parked their van in the dark of night in Rock Creek Park and moved about with large directional antennae. To avoid suspicions that they might be surreptitiously monitoring human communications rather than doing research on animal life-styles, the Park Service notified the embassies in the area, the D.C. police, the Park Police, and the Uniformed Secret Service.[47]

The police in a capital need to guard an embassy when intelligence information indicates that the embassy is in danger from terrorists. They also need to be there to keep hostile demonstrations at a safe distance and to prevent demonstrators from using violence. In the United States, a 1937 law prohibited hostile placards and

---

[44] Final Report of the Metropolitan Police Force (Washington, DC: Metropolitan Police Force, 1986), p. 9.

[45] The Uniformed Division has also been called the Executive Protective Service.

[46] *Washington Post*, 11 March 1987.

[47] *Washington Post*, 30 April 1987.

demonstrations closer than 500 feet from an embassy. This 1937 law had become controversial in recent years, with accusations of "selective prosecution" of demonstrators against the Soviet embassy, but not of the thousands of persons protesting near the South African embassy.[48] In a case involving the arrest of two protesters in September 1983 who breached the 500-foot limit near the Soviet embassy during a demonstration protesting the Soviet downing of a Korean airliner, the Court of Appeals upheld the law.

In March 1988, however, the U.S. Supreme Court ruled (5-3) in *Boos* v. *Barry* that protesters might demonstrate immediately outside foreign missions in the District of Columbia provided that the demonstration did not interfere with a mission's normal activities nor become a threat to its security. The case had been viewed as pitting the requirements of international law against the protection of individual rights. The decision was thus welcomed by both conservative and liberal activist organizations as upholding their First Amendment rights to freedom of speech and assembly.[49]

The protest demonstrations at embassies in Washington in the late 1980s have been directed mainly against the South African and Soviet missions, but there have also been arrests for breaking the 500-foot rule at the Israeli, South Korean, and Vatican embassies. Under the new rule, protest groups can carry their messages closer to their target. On the other hand, the groups have lost the publicity potential of mass arrests achieved by merely walking toward an embassy, as in the dramatic media coverage of the arrest of a group of rabbis outside the Soviet embassy in 1986.[50]

On balance the protest groups welcomed the court's decision, as did the American Civil Liberties Union. An editorial in the *Washington Post* summed up the widespread mood of the American public regarding diplomatic immunity in practice by trumpeting, "The First Amendment has come to Embassy Row."[51]

The agencies and persons concerned with the conduct of foreign relations and with the protection of diplomats and missions were not pleased by the practical effects of the new rule, however. Almost immediately, protest groups deliberately and publicly tested the limits of the new legal situation to see what practices the police would permit. One of the first of these demonstrations took place outside the Soviet embassy on the afternoon of March 23 (the day after the Supreme Court decision), when twelve representatives of Jewish

---

48 *Washington Post*, 24 Feb. 1987.
49 *New York Times* and *Washington Post*, 23 Mar. 1988.
50 *Washington Post*, 23 Mar. 1988.
51 Ibid.

groups and two U.S. senators, observed by twenty-six reporters and photographers, protested against human rights abuses in the Soviet Union. The police permitted the demonstrators to sit on the sidewalk in front of the embassy, read prayers and speeches, sing, chant, and hand out leaflets to passersby and Soviet embassy personnel. Only when a rabbi tried to block the path of a group of Soviet diplomats did the police step in, explaining that it was illegal to interfere with anyone's movements.[52]

Protest demonstrations during the first week after the new Supreme Court ruling also occurred at the Iraqi and Somali embassies and during an important reception at the residence of the Korean ambassador Kim Kyung-won in an affluent Washington neighborhood. Angry Korean protesters gathered at the gates of the compound, and some of them pelted the limousine carrying Secretary of State Shultz and his wife with eggs, rice, and other objects. Under the new ruling, the demonstrators were allowed to stand immediately outside the residence gates, within a few feet of entering automobiles.[53]

Meanwhile, the D.C. police, the U.S. attorney's office for the District, the U.S. Secret Service, and the Department of State convened meetings of officials to discuss the impact of the Supreme Court's ruling. The State Department expressed its concern that the level of protection provided to foreign officials and embassies in Washington was "significantly reduced by the ruling." Officials at the State Department were apprehensive that unruly demonstrations might appear to be provocative and might provide an excuse to limit the protection of U.S. embassies. Assistant D.C. Chief of Police I.M. Fulwood explained that the elimination of the 500-foot zone meant that police must react more swiftly to events during a demonstration and must be present in larger numbers. Fulwood also mentioned the danger that diplomats inside an embassy might panic and react wildly, and referred to the incident outside the Libyan embassy in London in which a policewoman was killed during a protest demonstration by gunfire from within the building. The Secret Service spokesman, William Corbett, said the Supreme Court's ruling put the Uniformed Division of the Secret Service in a difficult position. Without the 500-foot buffer zone, an officer "finds himself with foreign soil behind him and a potentially hostile group in front of him."[54]

In the 1980s, organized street demonstrations have become

52 *Washington Post*, 24 Mar. 1988.
53 *Washington Post*, 26 Mar. 1988.
54 Ibid.

frequent events in many countries, most of which have laws requiring advance permission for such demonstrations. Even in democratic countries, where to demonstrate is a civil right, the laws may require that these permits stipulate the time and place and the route, in the case of a procession, and they may require a week or more of advance notification by the organizers.

Article 22 of the Vienna Convention of 1961 does not mention demonstrations in front of embassies, but it does require the receiving state "to protect the premises of the mission against any intrusion or damage and to prevent any disturbance of the peace of the mission or impairment of its dignity." *Satow's Guide* observes that although states are not obliged to legislate "especially severe penalties for attack or trespass on embassy premises, or to make mere insult to the premises or the flag of the embassy a criminal offence," such provisions "have been very common."[55]

G.I.A.D. Draper, an expert witness before the House of Commons Foreign Affairs Committee, proposed that the United Kingdom might need "legislation specifically framed to . . . [satisfy] obligations in respect of mission premises." This might be done, he said, by amendments to the Public Order Act, 1936, to "give power to the police to route a demonstration away from the mission premises against which it is organised, and to disperse it if carrying out certain activities before such premises." He mentioned that such a proposal had already been made in an official report by Lord Scarman in 1975 (Command Paper 5919) on earlier disorders.[56]

The South African embassy in London presents a special problem in this regard. It is the general policy of the police there to keep demonstrators on the pavement, or sidewalk, on the opposite side of the road from a target embassy. Trafalgar Square, the site of the South African embassy, has no such opposite pavement, however, only the square itself. A decision to move demonstrations out of the square and around the corner to the street on the side of the embassy was "primarily a matter for the Home Office and the Police," with no participation by the FCO, based on articles 22 (2) and 29 of the Vienna Convention.[57]

---

[55] Satow, 5th ed., p. 111.

[56] Appendix 6, "Diplomatic Privileges and Immunities (DIP 18)," Memorandum by Col. Prof. G.I.A.D. Draper, 6 July 1984, House of Commons Report, 1984, p. 75.

[57] "Copy of a letter to the Chairman from the Secretary of State for Foreign and Commonwealth Affairs (DIP 22)," 25 July 1984, in House of Commons Report, December 1984, p. 41.

It is understandable that governments and their foreign ministries and even their interior ministries will leave to the police as much as possible this sensitive political question of exactly what practice to follow in protecting a foreign embassy against what may be a popular hostile demonstration. Nevertheless, from the personal standpoint of the diplomats inside an embassy during a hostile demonstration, no doubt the ideal distance to be required between the demonstrators and their target would be several miles, or as a minimum more than "a stone's throw"! In developing countries with authoritarian governments, a hostile demonstration may be tolerated or even tacitly sponsored by the regime. In such cases, the police may not be present, or may be too few, or may melt away. Subsequent complaints to the foreign ministry about damages after the dust has settled may be met with brief, evasive defenses or expressions of such hedged apology that they amount to only a regret that the spontaneous demonstrators exceeded their instructions.

The Taxation Authorities

The general principle that the premises of a diplomatic mission and the diplomats themselves should be exempt from taxation in the receiving state has been a part of customary international law for centuries. The 1961 Vienna Convention's articles 23 and 34 express this principle for embassies and diplomats respectively and set out a short list of exceptions, as discussed in chapter 3.

However, both before and after the Vienna Conventions the practice of different states with respect to the exceptions has varied considerably. A sovereign state is historically insistent on its right to its own system of taxation. With the growth in government expenditures, standardizing practice regarding taxes – the source of most government income – is not easily accomplished by international treaty.

The American government's practice, affirmed on 21 July 1986, is that "property owned by diplomatic missions and used to house the staff of those missions is exempt from general property taxes." This policy was published in the Federal Register as Public Notice 975 and came after several years of arguments in the courts.[58] The notice, prepared by Michael G. Kozak, principal deputy legal adviser of the State Department, describes some of the steps through which the policy emerged, as follows.

---

[58] *Federal Register*, vol. 51, No. 146, Wednesday, 30 July 1986, pp. 27303–4, appended to the April 1987 Annual Report of the Office of Foreign Missions.

The Vienna Convention of 1961 came into force in the United States on 13 December 1972. The convention exempted premises of a diplomatic mission from general property taxes, i.e., those taxes that do not have the character of payment for specific services, such as water and sewerage. However, neither the convention itself nor its legislative history made clear whether staff housing owned by the mission was covered. The U.S. government, prior to 1980, took the narrow interpretation that only the residence of the chief of mission was exempt from general taxes. In 1980, the U.S. government concluded that staff housing was also exempt on the basis of customary international law.

This reconsideration arose out of litigation between the German Democratic Republic (GDR) and Arlington County, Virginia. The GDR had purchased an apartment building in 1976 for use as staff housing. Arlington County brought suit in 1978 to collect 1977 taxes and to impose a lien on the property. The Department of State at that time agreed with Arlington, as did the Federal District Court that heard the case and ruled in favor of the county. The GDR protested the court's verdict, and the U.S. government and the GDR made a bilateral agreement in 1979 specifically exempting government-owned property. The U.S. government filed an action to have the Arlington taxation set aside. The District Court then concluded the property was exempt, but only since the 1979 bilateral agreement. Following further appeals and counterappeals in 1982 and 1983, the Court of Appeals in 1983 upheld a pre-1979 exemption. The State Department Legal Adviser's Office and the Office of Foreign Missions subsequently carried out a detailed, comprehensive survey of international practice, which led to a reaffirmation of the 1980 legal opinion that staff housing is exempt.

The input of the OFM and the hardening impact of recent events between 1980 and 1986, such as the Tehran hostage crisis, seem to be reflected in the final clause of the July 1986 Department of State Public Notice 975, namely, that the exemption is "subject to reciprocal treatment of comparable property owned by the United States abroad."

A statement of the particular taxes and customs duties to be collected from diplomats by the receiving state is usually communicated to the foreign missions by the foreign ministry. The statement will probably have been drafted and will certainly have been cleared with the tax authorities in the treasury ministry. The sums involved are not large, however, in the government's total tax take. Since the principle of reciprocity and provisions of pertinent treaties need to be weighed, the foreign ministry may well have had a large say in the policy.

The Courts

The courts' role in relation to questions of diplomatic immunity has been clarified and simplified by the guidance on the law provided by the Vienna Conventions. It is still the courts of a country that have the final word in many cases on who and what are entitled to diplomatic immunity. For example, a plaintiff might be maintaining before a court that a diplomat was engaging in a commercial activity for private profit or that he was really a permanent resident of the receiving state. Such questions would be decided by the courts on the basis of domestic law and practice.[59] In the case of consular immunities, the courts are also the source of decision on whether an officer's action was covered by immunity as part of his official functions.

For many years after the Act of 1790 in the United States, an ambassador or his servants could not be sued by a citizen except before the Supreme Court. This archaic arrangement, which was tested only once in the course of 180 years,[60] has now been superseded, and cases against diplomats can be tried at the district court level.[61] The foreign missions in Washington were notified of this change by the State Department circular note of 31 October 1978.

[59] Satow, 5th ed., p. 128.

[60] Department of State internal memorandum, April 1977, in author's files. The single instance occurred in 1971 in the case of *Founding Church of Scientology* v. *Lord Cromer, et al.,* when the Supreme Court denied a "motion for leave to file a bill of complaint."

[61] Section 8 of the Diplomatic Relations Act of 1978.

5
LIMITS AND CONTROLS

Diplomats and consuls enjoy their privileges and immunities within the limits of applicable law, customary practices, and considerations of reciprocity. In practice, they are limited also by the receiving government's level of tolerance or suspicion.

Persona Grata Requirement

In the first place, the individual officer, as well as the embassy or consulate in which he or she works, must be acceptable to the host government if the officer is to have any official status at all. This is assured by the procedures known as *agréation* in the case of a head of mission, acceptance as *persona grata* in the case of other officers, and the issuance of a written authorization known as an exequatur for the head of a consular post and sometimes for other consular officers. Consular officers whose arrival for duty has been notified to the receiving government's authorities are assumed to have the status of being accepted unless the receiving government indicates they are not acceptable.

The workings of these procedures therefore have the possibility of a limiting effect on privileges, because no person can enjoy diplomatic or consular immunities if the receiving state believes that person is likely seriously to abuse them.

The Vienna Convention of 1961 (article 4) stipulates that before a head of mission has been accredited, *agrément* (the traditional term for acceptance of this kind) must be sought. The receiving state is under no obligation to give reasons for a refusal. There have been cases where a proposed ambassador was rejected because he was thought to have engaged during his career in intelligence or political activities of which the receiving state disapproved. In most cases, because of the delicacy of the subject, no official information about negative reactions is likely to be available.

In recent decades, the practice of seeking *agrément* and of responding has been done in confidence. The name can be submitted through the ambassador who is departing or the chargé *ad interim*. If the two countries are establishing relations for the first time, they can use their missions at the United Nations or in a third capital.[1] In any case, before the proposed candidate is accepted, the receiving

---

[1] Satow, 5th ed., p. 89.

state can decide whether it wishes to accord him the great dignity and considerable privileges of an ambassador in their country. The response of the receiving government may be given in writing or orally, or it may be delayed for so long that it has the effect of a tacit request for a substitute nomination. This last runs the risk of giving some impression of discourtesy by the receiving government.

An unusual twist in the *agréation* process occurred in April 1988, when the Swiss government accepted the appointment of Seyeb Mohammed Malaek to be Iranian ambassador in Bern. On April 22, the U.S. Department of State expressed its concern and displeasure at this action, saying it considered Malaek's accreditation "entirely inappropriate" because he had been a leader of the hostage-taking at the U.S. embassy in Tehran. Four other nations had declined to accept Malaek as ambassador.[2]

The names and functions of mission staff members are notified to the receiving government, but the 1961 convention (article 7) stipulates no requirement for *agrément*. The possibility for such a requirement is, however, latent in article 9's statement that "a person may be declared *non grata* or not acceptable before arriving in the territory of the receiving State." In such a case, no explanation for the decision need be given.

"In the case of military, naval or air attachés," states article 7, "the receiving State may require their names to be submitted beforehand for its approval," in view of the possible risks posed by their work to the security of the receiving state. There is no reference to a requirement of explanations for refusals, so the analogy of heads of mission would presumably be followed.

In her 1976 monograph on the diplomatic convention, Denza takes up the question of what should happen when a receiving state, upon learning of the appointment of a diplomatic agent to a mission in its capital, immediately refuses to accept him and declares him *persona non grata*. If already arrived, is he still entitled to diplomatic immunity until a reasonable period for his departure from the receiving state has elapsed? The receiving state might feel that his enjoyment of privileges and immunities was sure to be abused. For example, he might be "a person against whom serious civil proceedings or even criminal proceedings are pending." Denza concludes that the best tactic in such a case would be for the receiving state to "explain the circumstances to the sending State and ask it to treat the appointment and notification as never having been made." Should the sending state decline, the receiving state can point out that it is not a *"normal"* situation when "the receiving state

2 *Washington Post*, 23 April 1988.

immediately on receiving notification of an appointment refuses to accept it."[3]

The Vienna Conference considered the inclusion of language that would limit the duration of immunity to the time when the receiving state expressly or tacitly accepted the person's appointment. The United States, France, and Italy supported an amendment to that effect, but it did not carry.

Limiting Abuses of Immunity

Another facet of the *persona grata* limitation on immunity is that a diplomat who misuses his privileges either for his own personal advantage or to do things inimical to the security and welfare of the host country can be declared *persona non grata* and ultimately, if necessary, detained and expelled.

What limits the scope of a diplomat to perform criminal acts? Like any other person guilty of a crime, he must first be detected. Moreover, because of the inviolability of his person and premises, detection is especially difficult.

The 1961 Vienna Convention, article 31, in one sentence tersely codified the theory and practice of more than two centuries: "A diplomatic agent shall enjoy immunity from the criminal jurisdiction of the receiving State." Here the functional consideration, the need for governments to communicate with each other, prevails. Hence, as Satow explains, "If a diplomatic agent commits a crime in the country to which he is accredited, he cannot be tried or punished by the local courts." Satow further noted that no cases could be cited where such a trial or punishment had occurred without the offending diplomat's consent or that of his government.[4]

There are in practice some curbs on the necessarily ominous implications of this legal situation. If a diplomatic agent's criminal offense is minor but repeated, such as a parking or traffic violation, notification can be made to the head of the mission, who may reprimand the offender. If the crime is serious (and diplomats have been known to steal from shops, rape women, and assault police), the receiving state can ask that the perpetrator's immunity be waived so that he can stand trial. Although this waiver may be refused, the offender is likely to be transferred out of the country. If not, he can be declared *persona non grata*, and his right to immunity then soon ceases to exist.

This is a logical sequence of steps and may sound like a course of

---

[3] Denza, *Diplomatic Law*, pp. 34 and 245.
[4] Satow, 5th ed., p. 124.

escalating pressures on which a protocol office could embark with confidence. However, the many protocol officers, desk officers, and office directors who must be kept informed know that such cases are nearly always delicate and time-consuming. As the 1985 British white paper on diplomatic immunities and privileges explained, after listing the categories of offenses by diplomats which could cause them to be declared *persona non grata*, "The criteria for dealing with alleged offenses are applied with both firmness and discretion, but not automatically. Full account is taken of the nature and seriousness of the offence and any inadequacies in the evidence."[5] Similarly, Satow notes that "states do not have set rules as to when they will ask for a waiver of immunity or declare an offender *persona non grata*. . . . All the circumstances will be considered by both governments in each case."[6]

In its March 1988 "Study and Report" to the Congress, the U.S. Department of State proposed that it report annually on "serious criminal offenses committed in the United States by individuals entitled to immunity" from U.S. criminal jurisdiction, and on debts delinquent over six months owed to U.S. creditors by foreign missions and covered individuals. The department admonished, however, that "no useful purpose is served" by making public such details as the names of the individuals or missions involved. The annual reports should assist in resolving such cases, in the department's view, but should avoid gratuitously impairing friendly relations.[7]

Some abuses of immunity arise under article 33 of the 1961 convention, which states that a diplomat is exempt from social security provisions of the receiving state with respect to private servants in his sole employ, provided they are not nationals of nor permanent residents in the receiving state, but is required to observe the social security laws of "the sending State or a third State." Occasionally, some diplomats of developing countries bring in as private servants poor, sometimes illiterate girls from their countries. In some cases, they pay them little or nothing and may treat them harshly. The victims seldom know their rights and are fearful of asserting them when they do.

Such a case was reported in the Washington area in October 1986.[8] A Somali maid, Isha Aden Mudey, aged 21, ran away from

---

[5] Cmmnd. 9497, April 1985, p. 25.

[6] Satow, 5th ed., p. 125.

[7] U.S. Department of State, *Study and Report Concerning the Status of Individuals with Diplomatic Immunity in the United States* . . . , 18 March 1988, op cit., p. 10. This document is discussed at length in chapter 7.

[8] *Washington Post*, 25 Oct. 1986.

employment in the home of the Somali embassy's counselor for consular affairs, Abdullahi Said Hersi. She said she had worked for him for well over a year without being paid or given a holiday. Hersi's version of her status was that she was not entitled to wages because he had arranged with her parents in Somalia that she would work for him in America, and his brother in Somalia would pay her parents the equivalent of $150 per month. Ms. Mudey was seeking to recover her passport from her employer and to remain in the United States. She was being assisted by a local private group of Somalis, the Organization for Somali Affairs.

The practice in such cases is for the individual domestic worker to make a complaint to the State Department's Protocol Office, which "is eager for foreign workers to know that the office offers some recourse." Their approach is one of conciliation, i.e., "Once a complaint is filed, the office meets with the ambassador or deputy chief of mission to sort out the charges." The *Washington Post* story on the Mudey case reported that the Protocol Office receives about four such complaints a year, but believes there are far more cases unreported because its service is not widely known and the often uneducated workers are reluctant to seek help.

Exceptions to Immunity

The diplomat's immunity from civil and administrative jurisdiction is limited by three specific exceptions, as given in article 31 of the 1961 Vienna Convention.

The first concerns any action to settle claims involving ownership or possession of private immovable property in the receiving state, unless the diplomat "holds it on behalf of the sending State for the purposes of the Mission."

The second exception concerns "an action relating to succession in which the diplomatic agent is involved as executor, administrator, heir or legatee as a private person and not on behalf of the sending State." The exception is thus worded so that when a diplomat as a private person is involved in a succession to property, he becomes under the jurisdiction of the receiving state and must therefore satisfy the tax and other authorities just like anyone else. Death and taxes have their proverbial link of certainty, even for diplomats.

The third exception concerns actions "relating to any professional or commercial activity exercised by the diplomatic agent in the receiving State outside his official functions." Though the 1961 convention (article 42) prohibits diplomats from engaging for personal profit in professional or commercial activities, this third exception covers the few cases where a diplomat's own government and the receiving government waive objections to his or her doing so. More significantly, the exception would also prevent the diplomat's spouse or other family members from claiming immunity from civil jurisdiction in connection with professional or commercial work they may be doing for profit in the receiving state.

There are increasing numbers of career wives and at least a few career husbands in the American and many other diplomatic services. Perhaps a few employers engaged in legally or morally dubious commercial activities would hire such diplomatic family members on a preferred basis if they had immunity on the job. However, the absence of any right to such immunity may be an advantage to them, on balance, for it removes one very likely objection by receiving countries to issuing them work permits. The U.S. State Department has been working to expand the number of states covered under bilateral agreements on spouse and dependent employment. At this writing, the United States had concluded bilateral treaties on the subject with twenty-two states and maintained *de facto* reciprocal arrangements with sixty-four others.[9]

Setting Administrative Limits on Immunity

The greatest potential for limiting the scope of diplomatic privileges and immunities may lie not only in the ancient principle of reciprocity, but in the newer, indirect means of administrative regulation. In the preceding chapter, we have described the major emphasis placed on this strategy by the U.S. government and given a picture of some of the specific programs through which the State Department keeps a sharper eye on the uses of immunity by diplomats, seeking to prune out excesses and prevent abuses.

This process of administrative regulation has been underway for many years. An early example in the United States and the United Kingdom was to require diplomats who operate automobiles to carry third party insurance. As a result of this practice, victims of diplomatic drivers have a better chance of receiving compensation, although the diplomats' immunity under the Vienna Convention remains intact and its functional purpose continues to be recognized.

In the United States, under a 1984 State Department regulation, diplomats are required to carry at least $300,000 in liability insurance.[10] Though this is considerably more than is required by any

[9] U.S. Department of State, unclassified airgram A-599 of 21 Aug. 1985 to all diplomatic and consular posts concerning local employment of dependents of U.S. and foreign diplomatic and consular personnel.

[10] *Washington Post*, 14 Feb. 1987.

U.S. state, some people argue that minimum coverage should be raised, perhaps as high as $3 million, either by congressional legislation or by the State Department acting under the authority granted it by the Diplomatic Relations Act of 1978.[11]

In Britain, a 1930 court case established that an insurance company could not take advantage of an insured diplomat's immunity to refuse to pay damages. The Foreign Office followed up by obtaining assurances from all authorized motor insurers "that they would not attempt to rely on the privileged position of their diplomatic clients." In 1958, the Foreign Office reminded all diplomatic missions of their obligation to carry insurance before driving. In 1984, the Foreign Office said in a published letter that it would "take a serious view of any diplomat driving without third party insurance and would probably request his removal from the UK if such conduct came to our knowledge."[12]

This sort of tightening administrative action to limit diplomatic immunity has been, as we have seen, intensified in the United States by the operations of the Office of Foreign Missions since its establishment in 1983. An incident in Washington on 13 February 1987 illustrated how much and how little can currently be done to limit the sometimes tragic effects of misbehavior by diplomats entitled to immunity. It also marked a new step in a program of the U.S. government to penalize diplomats when they are guilty of serious criminal actions while engaged in private, unofficial actions.

About 12:15 a.m. that morning, Ambassador Kiatro Abisinito of Papua New Guinea, aged 32, was driving his car on Wisconsin Avenue in a condition later described in a police report as "had been drinking" and "obviously drunk." The ambassador's car crashed into the rear of a parked car in which Stephen Hagan and Martha Clement were sitting. The ambassador must have been traveling with considerable momentum for his car then caromed off two empty cars on the opposite side of the avenue, jumped a sidewalk, hit another car waiting at an intersection, and bounded back across the avenue until it was stopped by a small brick wall. Hagan and Clement were both injured, Hagan critically with head and other injuries. Abisinito was also apparently slightly injured and was released from hospital the following day.[13]

The police charged the ambassador with failing to pay full time and attention to driving, for which the fine can be as much as one

---

[11] *Washington Post*, 21 Feb. 1987, and idem., Letters, 22 Feb., 1 Mar., and 8 Mar. 1987.
[12] House of Commons Report, 1984, p. 94.
[13] *Washington Post*, 14 Feb. 1987.

hundred dollars, but police and State Department officials agreed he could not be prosecuted because of diplomatic immunity.[14]

What significant measures could be taken? The head of the Office of Foreign Missions, James E. Nolan, said Abisinito's driving permit was revoked on the day of the accident and the ambassador was so informed by diplomatic note. Ten embassy-connected persons had lost their driving privileges in the previous year. While "it is quite rare for an ambassador," said Nolan, "we are trying to protect U.S. citizens and we don't make distinctions because of the grade of the man."[15]

On the day of the accident, the State Department asked U.S. Attorney Joseph E. diGenova to prepare a criminal case against Ambassador Abisinito in the event Hagan were to die, "the first time the State Department had ever made such a request," according to diGenova. The State Department's "very pointed and direct request" had come from the Office of Foreign Missions.[16]

DiGenova spelled out the implications of the new legal tactic. While the ambassador could not be prosecuted at the time, a criminal charge against him would bar his later reentry to the United States. Thus, diplomats facing such charges who decided to return to the United States would no longer be protected by diplomatic immunity. They "not only could be prosecuted, but would be prosecuted," declared diGenova. The motive of the government's action was "to serve as a warning to members of the diplomatic community who choose not to obey the laws in the nation's capital," diGenova said, adding, "This incident culminates a series of such incidents over the years," resulting in a decision "to investigate and, if appropriate, charge persons covered by diplomatic immunity."[17]

This particular incident wound down in a few days. On February 16, Ambassador Abisinito released a statement of regret, offering sympathy to Mr. Hagan and his relatives and friends and full cooperation with the authorities. Abisinito's government recalled him, and he announced he would be going home by February 24. He informed the State Department that he had sent letters to Hagan, expressing regret and offering assistance, and to other Americans who incurred damage. Hagan on February 20 was reportedly improving under hospital care and had a favorable prognosis. On February 25, it was reported that he had filed a $7.5 million suit

---

14 Ibid., 14 and 15 Feb. 1987.
15 *Washington Post*, 20 Feb. 1987.
16 *Washington Post*, 15 Feb. 1987.
17 Ibid.

against Abisinito's insurance company, State Farm Insurance. Clement had filed one also for unspecified damages.[18]

About ten months later, some significant additional information about the implications of the Abisinito case appeared in an article by Marian Nash Leich of the Legal Adviser's Office, headed "Prosecution of Former Diplomats for Unofficial Acts."[19] Summoned to the Department of State, the ambassador had declared his imminent return to Papua New Guinea. Thereafter, following press reports on the department's request for an investigation of the accident by the police and district attorney, the Papuan embassy "conveyed its Government's request for assurances that any criminal investigation or indictment of the former ambassador . . . would be quashed." The Papuan note referred to the Vienna Convention of 1961, Article 31, paragraph 1 on a diplomat's immunity from criminal jurisdiction and to a part of the International Court of Justice decision of 24 May 1980 on the Tehran hostages.

The State Department rejected the embassy's representations in a note on 22 June 1987. The department cited article 39, paragraph 2, of the 1961 Convention, which states that a diplomat's immunity ceases when he leaves the country, but "with respect to the acts performed by such a person in the exercise of his functions . . . immunity shall continue to subsist." The Department stated that "the Vienna Convention thus makes clear that the immunities of former diplomats do not subsist in respect of acts that, during the period of performance of diplomatic functions, were not performed in the exercise of functions as a member of the mission." The department recalled that it had transmitted a circular note on 21 March 1984 to all diplomatic missions which highlighted "this aspect of the applicable international law."

As for the case of the American hostages in Tehran, the department did not consider that Ambassador Abisinito's case in any way paralleled theirs. They were diplomatic agents who had neither been expelled nor withdrawn, and their imprisonment precluded any departure within a reasonable time.

In the department's view, "the concept of total exoneration or pardon for acts committed while in a status affording the individual criminal immunity is unknown in international law." The department did not "consider that, under the circumstances, Ambassador Abisinito's driving at the time of the accident may be characterized as 'an act performed . . . in the exercise of his functions as a member of the mission.' " The United States therefore rejected the contention that international law precluded his prosecution.

[18] *Washington Post*, 17, 21, and 25 Feb. 1987.
[19] Contemporary Practice of the United States section, *AJIL*, vol. 81, no. 3 (Oct. 1987), pp. 937–39.

This exchange of notes, taken together with the speedy public reaction and firm tone of the OFM and the district attorney, suggest that if Ambassador Abisinito were to return to the United States from Papua New Guinea and wished to avoid prosecution, he would need iron-clad proof that his early morning drive that unlucky Friday the 13th was on official business for his government in Port Moresby.

Public and press comment on the Abisinito incident typifies the intensity of reaction that occurs when diplomats commit serious offenses against local laws. An editorial in the *Washington Post* on February 18 noted the importance, "however symbolic," of the "reportedly unprecedented" State Department request to prepare criminal charges for a possible second-degree murder. The *Post* also published conflicting letters on the issue of whether a diplomat can be prosecuted for unofficial actions after his immunity has ceased. A letter from Washington lawyer Peter D. Trooboff on February 22 commended the strengthened State Department policy under which "the U.S. attorney and other local law enforcement authorities will investigate and charge serious crimes committed while driving. State should make absolutely clear that it will declare *persona non grata* a diplomat charged with a serious driving offense who asserts his immunity," and subject him to arrest should he return.

On March 1, a letter from Bennett Caplan, another Washington attorney, argued that Trooboff's position had "emotional appeal," but was "bad policy," on the grounds that it ignored the principle of reciprocity and that there was no international or U.S. legal requirement to "subject a diplomat to local laws." In the absence of any precedent "in which a country has brought criminal charges against an ambassador and held its enforcement jurisdiction in abeyance until he lost his diplomatic immunity," Caplan asserted, the State Department would be in violation of "customary international law."

A week later, in the March 8 edition of the *Post*, Trooboff replied "that the strength of international law rests in its capacity to respond with solutions to today's problems." He distinguished between the immunity of official and nonofficial actions by diplomats; noted that "after their service, immunity attaches only to performance of their prior *official* duties;" protested that "a diplomat's driving violations before recall should not fall within the Vienna Convention's protection for prior official conduct;" and hoped that the U.S. position would be adopted by the world community.

As the case eventually turned out, Mr. Hagan and the Papua New Guinea government reached a negotiated, out-of-court settlement. In a picturesque spear-breaking ceremony on 29 July 1988, as reported in the next day's *Washington Post*, the new ambassador, Renagi R. Lohia, presented Hagan with his government's cheque for an undisclosed amount in excess of $200,000. Though Hagan's lawyer found the Papuans "remarkably understanding, compassionate, and forthcoming," Ambassador Lohia observed that the American "legal system makes it all very complicated and difficult."

The incident of Ambassador Abisinito's car crash seems unlikely to produce the full clarification that an actual court case might have done. However, it has created a precedent for future State Department actions. The department's intervention in this case was the first following its policy decision in mid-1986 "to notify local law enforcement officials of government interest in a thorough investigation in case of 'possible serious violations' of U.S. law by foreign diplomats." In the past, police had often reacted with "instant paralysis" upon learning of a suspect's diplomatic status. They have now been informed that "obtaining an indictment, information or arrest warrant, even though they would be without immediate legal effect, would lay the basis for a prosecution at a later date."[20]

Sending State Jurisdiction over Its Own Diplomats

A limitation on diplomatic immunity, or at least on its exploitation by individuals for private profit, lies in the lack of immunity of all diplomats from the jurisdiction and laws of their own governments. In cases where the sending government is mindful of its reputation for lawful behavior, as many governments are (reinforced by publicity in the media), the diplomat's knowledge of possible prosecution by his own government can be an effective deterrent. A sending government may well invoke its jurisdiction when its diplomat's abuse of his immunity has harmed its own interests, as well as those of his host government. The forgery of currency, for example, is an activity objectionable to all established governments (except as a wartime device against an enemy belligerent).

In the U.S. Foreign Service, among others, it would be extremely damaging to an individual's career, to put it mildly, if he were found to have used his diplomatic immunity as a shelter for illegal or even improper activities. British diplomats overseas are expected to respect the laws of receiving states and to pay fines for parking offenses. In 1985, the Foreign Office went so far as to say that "the Government would not maintain diplomatic immunity from criminal jurisdiction in cases where a waiver would be without prejudice to the work of the mission and the fair treatment of the individual."[21] Unfortunately, this does not seem to be the situation in the case of many other countries, especially those of the Eastern bloc and some of the less experienced new countries.

20 OFM Director James Nolan, quoted in the *Washington Post*, 21 Feb. 1987.
21 Command Paper 9497, April 1985, pp. 25–26.

An illustration of applicable U.S. policy occurred in 1960, when seven Marines at the embassy in London were found to have been selling substantial amounts of cigarettes and liquor that had been imported free of duty under the embassy's exemptions. A Netherlands citizen who had bought some of these goods was apprehended by the British authorities, tried, and convicted in a British court. The Marines avoided similar treatment because of their diplomatic immunity. It was a situation with sordid aspects. The writer, serving in the political section of the embassy at the time, recalls unofficial talk that some of the Marines had taken advantage of their function of checking the security of embassy offices after hours to see that no classified documents were left unsecured. In desk drawers they had sometimes found "ration cards" for the embassy's duty-free goods commissary and made unauthorized use of them. These Marines were later tried by U.S. court martial, convicted, fined, demoted, and transferred.[22]

The Waiving of Immunity

As noted in chapter 3, any right to immunity from local jurisdiction may be waived (1961:article 32, 1963:article 45). To recapitulate briefly, the terms are similar in both Vienna Conventions. The waiver must be express ("in writing," for consuls). A waiver in respect of court proceedings, however, does not imply a waiver for execution of judgment. That requires a separate waiver. In addition, if the diplomat or consul has initiated the proceedings, he thereby, in effect, waives his immunity in regard to any directly related counterclaims.

In practice, a waiver of immunity is very unlikely to be made, especially in a criminal case, for either court proceedings or the execution of judgment. A situation where it might be waived at the request of the receiving government would be one in which the diplomat had been a crucial witness of a crime. His ambassador might decide that it was in the interest of the sending state's good relations to allow his officer to further the cause of justice. Even then, some ambassadors, including those of the United Kingdom and the United States, are required to seek instructions from their own foreign ministry.

An illustration of the U.S. government's recent practice and policy on waiving immunity involved an incident in London in December 1985 that came to light in the press only in January 1987, when it was extensively reported in the British press.[23] The inci-

---

[22] *New York Times*, 2 Feb. 1960, p. 3, and Ashman and Trescott, *Outrage*, p. 111.
[23] See, for example, "Fury over Sex Scandal Immunity," *Daily Mail*, 21 Jan. 1987.

dent involved James Myers Ingely, a clergyman whose wife was a diplomat at the American embassy. In December 1985, he was to be charged with "gross indecency" with a minor girl, reportedly under thirteen. This is a crime in Britain punishable by up to five years in prison.

According to the *New York Times* of 23 January 1987, "the American Embassy issued a statement denying that rape had been involved, as some reports said. The statement confirmed that the embassy had refused to waive diplomatic immunity and that the man and the diplomat had left the country immediately. The embassy declined to identify either the man or his wife." When parliamentary questions were raised, "Prime Minister Thatcher responded with a statement that the offense was not rape." The Foreign Office was asked if the United States refusal to waive diplomatic immunity in this case in effect constituted rejection of the Government's request for help by diplomatic missions in the prosecution of employees accused of serious crimes, which request had resulted from the 1984 killing of Policewoman Fletcher outside the Libyan embassy. In reply, the Foreign Office made clear that its "grave concern" had been expressed and that "the U.S. Embassy could have been in no doubt" about how seriously the Foreign Office viewed the incident.

The American embassy had declined to waive diplomatic immunity "after due consideration of the case and consistent with the long-standing U.S. government policy on such issues," expressed its deep regrets, and noted that the individual involved had been returned to Washington for medical treatment. "Under provisions of the U.S. Privacy Act," the embassy stated, no further information could be released. The U.S. ambassador at the time, Charles H. Price 2d, did not comment on the case.

The practice of the State Department in this incident indicates that even when there is little question of the fact of a serious crime having been committed, of the probable fairness of the courts, or of the treatment that would be accorded the accused if detained, other considerations may be of sufficient weight to cause refusal of a waiver of immunity.

A February 1986 Department of State guidance to the Foreign Service on the subject of privileges and immunities discussed the question of waivers, emphasizing that the right to waive immunities belongs to the sending state government.

The individual who ultimately benefits from the immunity has no power to waive such immunity even in cases where he or she believes that it would be in his or her personal or commercial interest to do so. Rather the sending State may waive immunity when it judges that to do so is in the national interest. An individual whose immunity is waived has no standing to protest this determination. While the power to waive immunity is always available, it is the usual practice of the Department of State to waive only in benign circumstances (e.g., to permit an employee or dependent to testify in court).

No doubt on the basis of experience, the department thought it necessary to caution against the independent exercise of the "good Samaritan" instincts and impulses characteristic of many Americans abroad:

Even in a case where everyone agrees that it would be in the interest of the U.S. Government for a certain immunity to be waived (e.g., an embassy employee is the sole, disinterested witness to the commission of a crime and as a "good citizen" wishes to testify as a witness at the trial), authorization for a limited waiver of immunity must be sought from the Department of State by the embassy. If granted, it must be expressly communicated to the foreign ministry of the receiving State before the employee takes any action. (A limited waiver might, for example, be devised to permit a diplomat to testify regarding an automobile accident which he or she witnessed, but leave completely protected the diplomat's immunity from the jurisdiction of the receiving State in all other respects.)[24]

There are at least two situations in which a request for a waiver of immunity might be requested as an appropriate way of limiting the exemption of a diplomat or consul from local jurisdiction. A landlord might understandably require that a diplomat should have a clause in his lease waiving immunity if disputes arise under the lease. Though such clauses might be valid, there must be prior authorization by the sending state.[25]

The second situation might be a waiver request by a foreign ministry before declaring a diplomat *persona non grata*. When a diplomat has become unacceptable because of some offense, the ministry might orally suggest to his head of mission that he be transferred for the sake of good relations. If that suggestion is refused or ignored, the ministry might request that the diplomat's immunity be waived so that he can be indicted for his offense. If this request is in turn declined, then *the persona non grata* declaration could be made, followed in a reasonable time, if necessary, by his expulsion.

An illustration of a reasonable standard of practice with respect to the expulsion of erring diplomats is the policy of the British government, as stated in the Foreign Office Command Paper 9497 of April 1985:

---

[24] "Privileges and Immunities," *What Do I Do Now?* Overseas Briefing Center Supplement, Feb. 1986, op. cit. (see ch. 3, note 47).

[25] Satow, 5th ed., p. 129.

As a general rule espionage and incitement to or advocacy of violence require an immediate declaration of *persona non grata*. Those involved in violent crime or drug trafficking are also declared *persona non grata* unless a waiver of immunity is granted. In addition, the followirg categories of offence normally lead to a request for withdrawal in the absence of a waiver:

(*a*) firearms offences;
(*b*) rape, incest, serious cases of indecent assault and other serious sexual offences;
(*c*) fraud;
(*d*) second drink/driving offence (or first if aggravated by violence or injury to a third party);
(*e*) other traffic offences involving death or serious injury;
(*f*) driving without third party insurance;
(*g*) theft including large scale shoplifting (first case);
(*h*) lesser scale shoplifting (second case);
(*i*) any other offence normally carrying a prison sentence of more than 12 months.

We shall see in the following chapter that a head of state, President Kenneth Kaunda of Zambia, a few years ago speedily and publicly waived the diplomatic immunity of one of his officials. His action had few precedents or emulators, but it dramatized effectively the need for governments of new nations as well as old to require their diplomats to obey local laws and use their privileges only for official purposes.

6
RECENT TRENDS AND PROBLEMS

The Increasing Number of Embassies and Diplomats

When the United Nations was first established at the San Francisco Conference of 1945 and began its work with a temporary headquarters at Lake Success in New York, it had 51 members. This was approximately the number of sovereign states at that time, for although the defeated Axis powers (Germany, Italy, and Japan) were not yet included, members did include Byelorussia and the Ukraine, whose sovereign independence can hardly be taken seriously.[1] Subsequently, a few independent states having diplomatic establishments, such as Switzerland and the Vatican, have chosen not to join the United Nations. By the middle of 1962, however, about 60 more states had become members, including such diplomatically significant states as Israel, Spain, Pakistan and Japan.[2] By 1982 there were 170 states, though not all were UN members.[3] As of July 1988, the total number of UN member states was 159.

Almost every UN member has diplomatic missions abroad. Some of the major ones, such as the United States, the Soviet Union, the United Kingdom, France, Japan, and India, may have over a hundred embassies plus numerous consulates. The Soviet Union in 1982 had 113 diplomatic missions (twice as many as in 1960) and an expanded number of consulates.[4]

It is difficult to make even a round estimate of the total number of diplomatic and consular officers in the world, but it may be over 100,000. The 1986/87 *World Guide to Foreign Services* documents 18,400 diplomatic and consular services, or missions, of 170 states, with staffs of widely varying numbers.[5] The number of their dependents (families and personal servants) entitled to complete or partial diplomatic immunity may be at least twice their number. The global total, therefore, might be 300,000 to 400,000.

[1] Bland, ed., *Satow's Guide to Diplomatic Practice*, 4th ed., p. 408.
[2] Ibid, pp. 409–10.
[3] Feltham, *Diplomatic Handbook*, p. 1. The 1985 *Encyclopedia Britannica Book of the Year* lists 197 "nations of the world."
[4] Steiner, *Times Survey of Foreign Ministries*, p. 534. The Soviets were conducting relations with 119 countries through 114 embassies and 16 consulates, according to the 1986/87 *World Guide to Foreign Services*, A Directory of Ministries of Foreign Affairs, Embassies, Consulates, High Commissioners, Missions, Legations, Delegations and Representations, 1st ed. 1986/87 (Weissenberg, Federal Republic of Germany: World Guides Internationale Publikationen, 1986), pp. 761–68.
[5] *World Guide*, p. I.

This vast postwar expansion of the mass of persons entitled to privileges and immunities, of the numbers of inviolable premises and dwellings, diplomatic and consular bags, official and private vehicles, of duty-free goods, special license plates and identity cards, reserved parking places and, often, priorities for housing, telephones, and various services – all this growth and proliferation have placed a heavy burden of responsibility on the agencies that administer the institution of diplomatic immunity.

To a certain extent, management reforms and improved technology, including the use of computers, electric typewriters, photocopying machines, automatic dialing, and recorded telephone messages, have been helpful to protocol offices, security forces, and police during the past thirty years. However, diplomatic immunity problems nearly always involve an individual diplomat, and even a minor crisis caused by his being the victim or perpetrator of an offense may involve hours of meetings, negotiations, and legal consultations. Administrators seek to have publicity minimized and each party's national ego and sensitivities considered. Cases drag on for years and even then may never reach a satisfactory conclusion. Of this, the Tehran hostage crisis is a clear illustration.

The pressure of increasing numbers of diplomats was one of the reasons the Vienna Conventions provided for new restrictions on both immunities themselves and the persons entitled to some of them. Subsequent administrative measures, for example withholding driving permission from offenders and limiting the importation of duty-free vehicles per diplomat, have been helpful in making the problem of control more manageable. However, most of those professionally concerned with diplomatic immunity, and certainly the general public, are generally convinced that there may be too many diplomats in the world, and in any case that some of their traditional immunities and privileges need to be further trimmed down to essentials, with tougher curbs applied to offenders.[6]

Blurring Diplomatic Traditions and Declining Standards of Diplomatic Courtesy

In the postwar period and especially since 1960, many of the nations that gained independence were former colonies in Africa, the Caribbean, or elsewhere. Their citizens and their governments had no previous direct experience of international relations. Sometimes their standards of living were relatively low and the educated

---

[6] Ashman and Trescott, *Outrage*, pp. 239–40, and editorials in *People* (London), 17 Aug. 1986, and the *Daily Telegraph* (London), 18 Aug. 1986.

proportion of the population was small. States that became independent in 1960, 1961, and 1962, for example, included (in alphabetical order as they were known at the time) Algeria, Burundi, Cameroon, Central African Republic, Chad, Congo (Brazzaville), Congo (Leopoldville), Cyprus, Dahomey, Gabon, Ivory Coast, Jamaica, Madagascar, Mali, Mauritania, Niger, Nigeria, Rwanda, Senegal, Sierra Leone, Somalia, Tanganyika, Trinidad and Tobago, Togo, Uganda and Upper Volta. Mongolia, though evidence of its effective independence at that time would have been difficult to discover, joined the United Nations in 1961.[7]

In many such cases, the new foreign ministries were modeled partly on those of the former ruling power, with the new diplomats trained at the time of independence in the metropolitan power's foreign ministry. Diplomatic procedures and sometimes French or English or some other generally serviceable language had to be learned. The new diplomats may have had some experience of consular immunity in their country's pre-independence days, but not of embassy premises and diplomatic immunity. Some of the rough treatment and even physical violence experienced by diplomats in the Congo in the early independence years may have been due to an insufficient grasp of the diplomats' right to personal inviolability.

Communist governments. Another relevant change in the postwar period has been the increased number of Communist governments. Soviet imposition or international Communist penetration has resulted in the appearance since 1945 of several communist-modeled governments – in Eastern Europe, Cuba, South Yemen, Ethiopia, Vietnam, North Korea, and, some would say, others like Nicaragua.

The Soviet approach to diplomacy and to diplomatic immunity is, to put it simply, "hard-line" rather than "liberal." Or rather, they are hardline within their own jurisdiction. The Soviet Union attended both the 1961 and 1963 Vienna conferences, signed both conventions, and in general, has strongly supported the principle of diplomatic immunity. It has concluded bilateral agreements, for example, with the United States and with Britain, extending the coverage of immunity to all embassy and consular personnel, well beyond the requirements of the Vienna Conventions. Nevertheless, the foreign diplomat in the Soviet Union is given a grudging minimum of privileges and immunities and a maximum of restrictions on free movement and normal contacts.

On the other hand, Soviet diplomats abroad can be equally assiduous in demanding all possible benefits and immunities, in other

---

[7] Satow, 4th ed., pp. 409–10.

words "liberal" treatment. It is Soviet practice regularly to over-staff their diplomatic missions and consulates with military and KGB officers. They have attempted to stretch the definition of a "diplomatic bag" to unprecedented limits. In July 1984, the Soviet Government sent a nine-ton Mercedes tractor-trailer into Switzerland, sealed against customs inspection. The three Soviet drivers said it was a diplomatic bag. This was too much for the Swiss customs to swallow. Their working rule was that a diplomatic bag ought not to exceed 450 pounds in weight. The Soviets moved their "diplomatic bag" across the frontier to Germany. The Germans pointed to another way in which the Soviets were claiming an exces-sively liberal interpretation. This "diplomatic bag" was motorized and capable of its own movement. Surely, they argued, that was not intended to be the meaning of the Vienna Conventions. In the end, the truck rolled back into Russia. This prolonged dispute illustrates that the Soviets do not hesitate, when it is in their own interest, to demand full diplomatic privileges and beyond.[8]

When a Soviet consular employee who was not carrying identifi-cation credentials was stopped for speeding on a California highway in 1983, the officer reportedly touched him on the arm. The Soviet employee subsequently said he had been struck in the face, and the Soviet government made a protest in Washington, charging he had been assaulted.[9] One is reminded of the touchiness of Peter the Great in 1708, or of Czar Paul when British ambassador Whitworth's coach went past the palace in St. Petersburg.[10] Soviet diplomats have also chalked up national records for the number of parking fines unpaid in Washington D.C.[11]

The combination of diplomatic restrictiveness at home and expec-tations of liberal treatment abroad also characterizes other Com-munist governments. It has, tended to make the delicate subject of diplomatic privileges even more complicated in the postwar period.

Revolutionary regimes. The behavior of revolutionary regimes in the past thirty years has also frequently failed to meet accepted standards of international behavior with respect to diplomatic immunity. It is probably inevitable for revolutionary leaders to be hasty and to feel insecure, and even illegitimate. In this mood they may take out their stresses and tensions on foreign diplomats and embassies. Perhaps the worst outlook for diplomatic immunity, an

---

[8] Ashman and Trescott, *Outrage*, pp. 107–8.
[9] Ibid, p. 227.
[10] As recounted in chap. 2.
[11] Ashman and Trescott, *Outrage*, table on p. 234

essentially civilized concept, occurs during civil wars, as in Uganda, the Sudan, and Lebanon in recent years. Still, a revolution and a revolutionary government can also be extremely bad news for diplomats and consuls.

United States diplomats have had more than their share of trouble. The notorious behavior of the Khomeini regime in Iran is the most serious case of flouting the rules of immunity. Interestingly, while the U.S. embassy hostages were undergoing their unprecedented ordeal, the other diplomatic missions in Tehran were almost entirely spared harassment or violence. Since that time, however, some of their diplomats have not fared so well.

A case in point was the May 1987 beating and 24-hour "arrest" of Edward Chaplin, Britain's second-ranking diplomat in Iran, by the "Central Komiteh" of the Iranian Revolutionary Guards on unspecified charges. The incident followed by one day the arrest of Ahmed Gassemi, an Iranian consular official in Manchester, England, on charges of shoplifting, reckless driving, and assaulting an officer. British officials insisted that Gassemi was entitled only to partial immunity under international conventions, limited to his official actions. Chaplin's ordeal and Tehran's refusal to explain or apologize for it provoked the British Foreign Office into closing down the Iranian consulate in Manchester and expelling the five Iranian officials working there, including Gassemi.[12]

The supporters of the Cultural Revolution in China, whose relation to official policy was tragically unclear, attacked the British embassy and severely mishandled diplomatic officers and others. On the night of 22 August 1967 a mob broke into the compound in Beijing, pillaged and burned the chancery building, and heavily damaged official motor vehicles and the residence of Chargé d'Affaires Donald Hobson. Hobson himself and his staff, including women, were attacked, and he was beaten black and blue.[13]

Qadhafi's regime in Libya, which came to power in a military coup in 1969 against the constitutional monarchy of King Idris, has gloried in revolutionary symbolism. Some Middle Eastern nations that had overthrown monarchies (e.g., Turkey, Egypt, Iraq, and Tunisia) styled their new regimes republics (in Arabic *jumhuriya*); but Libya invented a new Arabic term, *jamahiriya*, from *jamahir* ("mass"), for its revolutionary state creation.

Qadhafi renamed Libya's embassies "people's bureaus" and, as we have seen in London, tolerated their takeover by student revolutionary committees. There are about one hundred such Libyan

---

12 *Washington Post*, 30 May and 5 June 1987.
13 Satow, 5th ed., p. 196; also *Daily Telegraph* (London), 18 Aug. 1986.

missions, of which twenty-seven are in Western Europe and eight in Latin America.[14] Their actions and their style of public statements give diplomatic immunity a bad name. They have abused and exploited diplomatic immunities, stashing terrorist weapons in their inviolable premises and communicating plots of terrorist murders against Qadhafi's opponents through their diplomatic coded messages and their sealed diplomatic pouches.[15] When they were apprehended in 1986 using their diplomatic coded messages to relay instructions and reports between Tripoli and its terrorist agents in Europe, the Libyans did not curtail the practice. They simply arranged to purchase more advanced cryptographic equipment in Switzerland.[16]

The United States closed down the Libyan People's Bureau in Washington in May 1981 to put a stop to this hazard. More recently, France, Germany, and Italy have expelled Libyan diplomats who came under suspicion of fostering criminal activities.[17] The government of Mauritius in 1986 reportedly gave the Libyan ambassador and his staff a hasty send-off, almost a "bum's rush." Only half an hour elapsed between the knock on the ambassador's door and his boarding a plane at the airport.[18] In April 1986, the twelve European Community nations agreed to reduce the number of Libyan diplomats and consuls to the minimum required for official business and to restrict their movements to the cities of their assignments, except for travel with special permission.[19] These restrictions may be contrary to the spirit of the Vienna Conventions of 1961 and 1963, but they have clearly been provoked by persistent violent actions inspired by what the Libyans consider the ideology of Qadhafi's revolution.

Diplomats' Increased Need for Protection against Attacks

In the past twenty-five years, diplomats have been in greater physical danger than ever before. The public has often envied their privileges and immunities and deeply resented the abuses of their status by a few. However, the public has also lately become aware through the media that a diplomat's lot with respect to personal security is not a happy one.

Receiving states have a special responsibility under the Vienna Convention of 1961 (article 22, ¶2) "to take all appropriate steps to

---

14 *Washington Post*, 22 Apr. 1986.
15 Ibid.
16 *Boston Globe*, published in *Washington Post*, ibid.
17 Ibid.
18 *Times* (London), 27 Aug. 1986.
19 *Washington Post*, 22 Apr. 1986.

protect the premises of the mission against any intrusion or damage and to prevent any disturbance of the peace of the mission or impairment of its dignity.'' Receiving states are also admonished (article 29) that a diplomatic agent's person is inviolable, that he is not liable to arrest, and that the receiving state must "treat him with due respect" and "take all appropriate steps to prevent any attack on his person, freedom, or dignity.''

In line with these requirements, receiving states generally take such measures as stationing uniformed armed guards in front of embassy buildings and reinforcing them during periods of tension. Ironically, in Egypt in 1986, the part of the police force responsible for this rather tedious assignment mutinied, went on a rampage, and had to be disarmed. The diplomatic missions were thus left naked to their enemies, for a time. Such things can happen.

As was most apparent during 1980, the year of the Tehran hostages, U.S. diplomats have been among the most affected by the increasingly dangerous international environment. Since 1965, over seventy Americans attached to U.S. diplomatic missions have been killed, and others wounded, outside the United States.[20] Five American ambassadors have been murdered at their posts since 1968: John Mein in Guatemala in 1968; Cleo Noel in 1973 in the Sudan, along with Deputy Chief of Mission George Moore and the Chargé d'Affaires of Belgium, Guy Eid; Rodger Davies in Cyprus, 1974; Francis Meloy in Lebanon, 1976; and Adolph Dubs in Afghanistan, 1979.[21] A sixth U.S. ambassador, Arnold L. Raphel, was killed along with President Zia ul-Haq of Pakistan and others in a suspicious plane crash in August 1988.

Britain has had seven of its diplomats attacked by terrorists since 1976, four of them fatally: Ambassador Christopher Ewart-Biggs, killed by a car bomb in Ireland in 1976; Ambassador Sir Richard Sykes, murdered in 1978 in The Netherlands; Kenneth Whitty in Greece, 1984; and Perry Norris, in India, 1984.[22] The British honorary consul, Geoffrey Hutchinson, was shot dead by gunmen, motive unclear, in Colombia in 1986.

The three nonfatal attacks on British diplomats were the kidnapping of James Cross in Canada in 1970, the protracted kidnapping of Sir Geoffrey Jackson in Uruguay in 1971, and the wounding of Mrs. Nora Murray, whose hand was blown off by a letter bomb in the United States in 1973.[23]

Other diplomats, none of them ambassadors but all entitled to

---

[20] The names of those killed appear on a large plaque in the lobby of the Department of State main headquarters in Washington.

[21] *Parade*, 30 Mar. 1986; and contemporary news accounts.

[22] *Times* (London), 15 July 1986.

[23] *Times* (London), 12 July 1986.

inviolability and protection of their safety and dignity, have been killed in recent years. A partial representative list might be cited:

William Buckley was seized as a hostage in 1984 and was reportedly tortured and murdered by his captors in 1985. He was a political officer at the American embassy in Beirut and, according to the *Washington Post* of 14 December 1986, "the top CIA officer in Beirut and a specialist on terrorism."

Lieutenant Colonel Charles R. Ray, a defense attaché at the American embassy in Paris, was assassinated there by a Lebanese terrorist in January 1982. Georges Abdallah was convicted of complicity.[24]

Yacov Barsimantev, an Israeli diplomat, was assassinated in Paris in April 1982 with the same Czechoslovak pistol that killed Lieutenant Colonel Ray.[25]

Fyodor Gorenikov, Soviet naval attaché in Islamabad, Pakistan, was shot dead there on 16 September 1986 by Zafar Ahmedam, "said to be mentally deranged."[26]

Colonel Christian Gouttierre, military attaché at the French embassy in Beirut, was killed in front of the embassy by two shots in the head from an assailant armed with a gun with a silencer. Later a group calling itself "Revenge and Justice Front" claimed responsibility in a telephone call.[27]

Said Zaki, a first secretary of the Jordanian embassy in Turkey, was murdered in July 1985 in Ankara. On 10 November 1986, Turkish police accused Adnan Musa Suleiman Ameri, who confessed "he had been working on behalf of Islamic Holy War, a militant Shiite Islamic group based in Lebanon with close ties to Iran."[28]

These and the dozens of other violent attacks on diplomats in recent decades are the dark side of their special, official, privileged status. Their immunities, privileges, and rights to special protection for their security and dignity have been granted because they are persons doing essential business for their own governments and the receiving governments. Whatever incidents involve them are of immediate official concern and almost by definition newsworthy.

24 *Times* (London), 18 Sept. 1987.
25 Ibid.; and *New York Times*, 29 Jan. 1987.
26 *Times* (London), 17 Sept. 1986.
27 *Times* (London), 19 Sept. 1986.
28 *New York Times*, 11 Nov. 1986.

It is ironic that people engaged in diplomatic work are often criticized in the media as ineffective, preoccupied with mere protocol and ceremonial, wasting time at cocktail parties, and having little influence on important questions. Yet, unfortunately for diplomats, they and their offices and homes are regarded by terrorist groups and frustrated opposition elements as prime targets. To attack a diplomat is to make headlines. Desperate, violent organizations now believe that such attacks will serve two of their top objectives: to get publicity for themselves and their causes, and to put pressure on legitimate governments, for example to release their imprisoned comrades, to give them money, or to give a public hearing to their demands and programs.

Historically, violent actions have often dramatized and publicized eventually successful independence movements. From the Boston Tea Party through the Greek independence movement, Jomo Kenyatta's Mau Mau, and some of the exploits of Jewish organizations against the British Palestine Mandate authorities, violence and even terrorism have been later credited with the achievement of patriotic objectives.

It is surely a sad reflection on our times, however, that diplomats, whose work is essentially to seek to resolve conflicts through negotiation and to promote peace by official contacts and a patient search for understanding of other nations' points of view, should be the targets of politically inspired violence. Far from benefiting from a specially protected status, they have become poor insurance risks. They are entitled to the sympathy of the public for engaging in what is now as hazardous an occupation as those of firefighters, police, or the armed forces.

The picture is not entirely gloomy. Two lines of action are being taken, and a third would seem worth trying.

The first is to coordinate national policies and practices on the prevention and punishment of crimes against diplomats. An international convention against the hijacking of aircraft was signed in Tokyo in 1963 and came into force in 1969. Something analogous for diplomats was seen to be necessary.

The UN General Assembly in 1971 asked the International Law Commission to prepare the draft that became the Convention on the Prevention and Punishment of Crimes against Internationally Protected Persons, Including Diplomatic Agents.[29] It was adopted by the General Assembly in December 1973 and came into force in February 1977. The convention provides that persons charged with

---

[29] British Command Paper 6176, September 1975.

attacks against diplomatic agents should be either extradited or tried in the state where they are present. It also gives guidelines on intergovernmental cooperation, transmission of information, and the treatment of alleged offenders.[30] There are also the 1971 O.A.S. Convention to Prevent and Punish Acts of Terrorism Taking the Form of Crimes against Persons and Related Extortion That Are of International Significance, and the 1977 European Convention on the Suppression of Terrorism.[31] The latter stipulates that the offenses of hijacking, kidnapping, and certain crimes of violence should not be regarded as political offenses for the purpose of extradition.[32] One hopes such conventions help to prevent some attacks on diplomats and to punish them when they do occur.

The second positive line of action is one being taken by sending states. Almost all governments are rethinking and improving security arrangements for their diplomatic missions. In 1986, Secretary of State Shultz asked Congress for $4.4 billion to finance antiterrorist measures at U.S. foreign service posts, with $2 billion eventually being approved.[33] The training of diplomats now includes a much greater emphasis on security against terrorism. Such training teaches diplomats greater awareness of possible dangers not only in their offices but in their homes, on the way to and from work, and during holidays and leisure hours. They are warned that the threat extends not only to heads of mission and high-level officers but to all members of the mission, their wives and families.[34] In certain particularly hazardous areas, such as Beirut, Kabul, and Kampala, American Foreign Service officers have received a 25 percent or more salary bonus in recognition of the current problem of personal security.[35]

The receiving state is generally realistic enough to recognize that although it will try to do all in its power to protect embassies and diplomats in times of tension, its own security forces may be stretched to the limit. Therefore, they accept that it is reasonable for embassies to do what they can to protect themselves by walls and barriers and by keeping their personnel trained and alert against danger.[36]

[30] Satow, 5th ed., pp. 202–3.
[31] British Command Paper 7031, Dec. 1977.
[32] Satow, 5th ed., p. 203.
[33] *Times* (London), 28 Aug. 1986.
[34] Harold G. Bean, *Diplomats and Terrorists II – Overseas Security: Our People Are the Key* (Washington: Institute for the Study of Diplomacy, 1987), pp. 25–28; also *Washington Post*, 22 Apr. 1986.
[35] *Parade*, 30 Mar. 1986.
[36] Satow, 5th ed., p. 202.

Two examples of American security measures for embassies illustrate what receiving states have found to be acceptable. In Vienna, capital of a stable, officially neutral country that welcomes thousands of tourists and foreign businessmen, the American embassy chancery has the normal precautionary arrangement of a heavy steel protective door. Inside that door in late 1986, the visitor was assisted by an Austrian local employee and observed from a distance of several feet by the Marine guard in uniform behind another locked door and heavy glass panel. The *New York Times* correspondent thought this "stepped-up security" gave the embassy "an Alamo atmosphere." The ambassador told him there had been several threats during his first year. This ambassador, an affluent noncareer diplomat from New York, had hired nine private body-guards, of whom several were Germans, "to protect himself and his family" and moved around Vienna in two limousines with "his paramilitary escorts."[37]

In Lebanon, a country of frequent headline-making violence, where few tourists or foreign businessmen ventured in 1987, the receiving government had in practice turned over major respon-sibility for security to the sending governments. The situation made a grim impression on reporters from *Newsweek*.[38] They described the practical working and living conditions of the typical American diplomat as highly defensive.

Sometimes he packs a pistol. His apartment has steel-reinforced doors that would stop a small rocket, and his bedroom is like a vault. Typically, his office is in a trailer, with anti-grenade foils on the windows. Outside there are revetments filled with sandbags and lined with concertina wire.

At the embassy there were "scores of private guards," and the Lebanese army "seals all the neighboring roads with tanks and half-tracks." All of the approximately fifty Americans were volun-teers, without families at the post. They served one-year or two-year terms and received "what amounts to combat pay," a 50 percent premium. A normal procedure for a diplomat's getting to the office and back was as follows:

Every night before leaving work, he would notify the motor pool of a random pickup time between 5 a.m. and 8:30 a.m. the next day. Armed guards would arrive, search the neighborhood for car bombs or suspicious persons, then escort him to the embassy bunkers.

When Ambassador John Kelly went to call on Lebanese officials, it was "like an armed sortie, complete with a convoy of troop

37 *New York Times*, 23 Nov. 1986.
38 *Newsweek*, 9 Feb. 1987.

carriers." Can diplomacy be conducted under such siege conditions? Or is such an embassy only a symbolic presence, in danger of becoming itself a hostage?

A third positive contribution to the safety of diplomatic premises and persons would seem to be for the authorities, the judges and juries, to administer more severe penalties for the crime of assaulting a diplomat. One illustration of the depressing record is what happened to the murderers of U.S. diplomats Cleo Noel and George Moore and Belgian Chargé Guy Eid in Khartoum in 1973. Their murderers surrendered to the Sudanese government, were detained for a time, then handed over to the Egyptian government and eventually quietly released.

No one was ever penalized for seizing the American embassy in Tehran and holding over sixty persons in humiliating discomfort for over a year. In the view of Professor L.C. Green of the University of Alberta, the Iranian authorities completely disregarded the judgment of the International Court "while the world at large, which in the past took steps of a cooperative character to uphold the rights of diplomats, stood idly by."[39] Indeed, it appears that a student activist of the group that played a leading role in the embassy seizure was one of the Iranians who later met with Robert C. McFarlane when McFarlane and National Security Council staff member Oliver North visited Tehran in May and September 1986 bearing symbolic gifts. The Iranian, Hossein Sheikholeslam, had risen in the intervening years to be deputy foreign minister.[40] His subsequent career illustrates, not penalizing, but instead rewarding persons who have flagrantly terrorized diplomats.

Professor Green cites two additional examples of the treatment of perpetrators. In a case in Canada in which a diplomat was kidnapped, the kidnapper was sentenced to less than two years' imprisonment, served only six months, and was later employed by the government. In a 1975 case in Sweden, the German embassy was assaulted, hostages were held, and two of them were killed. The court sentenced the accused to fifteen years' imprisonment.[41]

It is hard to generalize about sentences for assaulting diplomats because, as Green notes, "in the majority of cases no prosecutions have ensued."[42] One would like to see the results of a systematic survey of the weight of penalties in such cases. On the whole, it may

[39] L.C. Green, "Trends in the Law Concerning Diplomats," *Canadian Yearbook of International Law*, Vol. XIX, 1981, pp. 132–55.
[40] *New York Times*, 28 Nov. 1986; and *The Independent* (London), 11 July 1987.
[41] Green, op. cit., pp. 139–40.
[42] Ibid., p. 140.

not be too cynical to observe that there is less risk to an assailant who commits a criminal assault on an "internationally protected" and "inviolable" diplomat than to one who commits the same crime against a member of the general public. Surely this situation needs to be corrected.

One should not leave the currently urgent topic of the physical security of diplomats without emphasizing an essential fact about their role. Subject to sensible security precautions, a diplomat must somehow have mobility in order to observe conditions. Equally important, he or she must maintain at least occasional contacts with citizens of the receiving country and access to key officials of its government. If diplomats are too securely hunkered down, the personal element in intergovernment relations for which they are uniquely qualified withers away, and it is hard to see why they have been sent out to their post.

Under the tense, dangerous conditions of a capital in turmoil and conflict, the diplomats need to follow expert advice on their physical security. But they must use their knowledge, ingenuity, and courage to keep up the essential function of diplomacy, which is to keep personal communications open and active between their own government and their host authorities. Like the couriers of the ancient Persian empire and like all the envoys and heralds of all the ages, they must somehow personally get their messages through. The tons of steel and bullet-proof glass and the millions of dollars' worth of sophisticated protective equipment are there to help them; but if diplomats cannot move or meet local contacts, they and the security apparatus are not of significant use to the government that provided them.[43]

State Security and Diplomatic Immunity

In the period since 1960, receiving states have often curtailed the diplomatic privileges of freedom to travel, observe, and have social contacts. In reaction, other more liberal states have imposed similar restrictions on a reciprocal basis.

The Vienna Convention of 1961 contemplated only a minimum of such restrictions. One of the express functions of a diplomatic mission, it states, is "ascertaining by all lawful means conditions and developments in the receiving State, and reporting thereon to the Government of the sending State" (article 3). The convention requires the receiving state to "accord full facilities for the

---

[43] Bean, *Overseas Security*, ch. 4, "The Great Fortress Embassy Debate," pp. 31–48, is a balanced discussion of this issue.

performance of the functions of the mission'' (article 25) and is even
more specific on what the mission may expect to be allowed: "Subject to its laws and regulations concerning zones entry into which is
prohibited or regulated for reasons of national security, the receiving State shall ensure to all members of the mission freedom of
movement and travel in its territory'' (article 26).

Governments in the postwar period have very frequently curtailed
the right of innocent travel by foreigners or even diplomats in vast
areas of their territory. Communist states and many Middle Eastern
states are particularly prone to require special permits without
explanation. In addition, any entry into military areas or any pho-
tography of military installations, airfields of any type, harbors, or
factories may be prohibited.

The restrictive policies of the Soviet Union, other Communist
states, and many Third World countries – requiring accredited diplomats to obtain permission to travel, restricting where they may go
and how they must move – are motivated by security or other reasons. Sometimes it is due to the shortage of accommodations or even
the sensitivity of the countries concerning their own local conditions.

On the whole, this practice of declaring no-entry zones, including
no entry by diplomats, seems to be increasing. There may, however,
be some significant exceptions. China's policy in recent years, for
example, is one of a cautious opening up of areas to travel by
accredited foreign visitors.

The gradual, intermittent normalization of Egyptian-Israeli relations, similarly, may make more areas open to innocent travel in
future. In 1985, one could take a commercial bus from Cairo to Tel
Aviv. One needed only a valid visa and a bus ticket. However, the
bus route was all the visitor was expected to visit. In Egyptian Sinai,
periodic road signs stated, "Welcome to Sinai, Land of Peace.
Foreigners may not leave the road." At the Israeli frontier, these
warnings ceased, but for many miles the bus route was lined by
well-maintained, stout steel fences, without gates and much too high
to climb. No doubt neither Egypt nor Israel would allow a diplomat
the freedom of movement mentioned in the Vienna Convention's
article 26 in these extensive parts of their territories.

Such freedom of movement and travel is clearly treated as a privilege or benefit by governments. The appropriate response by Western governments to Communist states' restrictions on diplomatic
travel has been to limit the movements of their diplomats to the
vicinity of the capital, a radius of twenty-five miles in the case of
Washington. Both the American and British governments apply
such a restriction, despite the obvious contrast with their generally
liberal policies in this field. The United States has imposed

restrictions of this kind reciprocally on numerous, mostly Communist, countries and extended them also to the same countries' nationals serving as diplomats or officials at the United Nations in New York.[44] Where such restrictions are imposed for security reasons, as on the representatives of the Palestine Liberation Organization at the United Nations, they are not on a basis of reciprocity.

Administrative limitations placed on contacts with dissidents or the spokesmen of ethnic minority groups constitute yet another curtailment of a diplomatic function permitted by the spirit of the Vienna Convention of 1961. The KGB keeps a more than watchful eye on Western diplomats who make contact with internal critics of Soviet policies or with Jewish citizens who would like to have greater freedom to travel or emigrate to Israel. In any of the world's numerous authoritarian countries, a diplomat risks being declared *persona non grata* if he has frequent social contacts with an activist political opposition group or a leader of a chronically dissatisfied ethnic minority (or majority in the case of some countries, such as South Africa). Any diplomat who has served in Eastern Europe or the Middle East knows that to ascertain "conditions and developments in the receiving State" and to "[report] thereon to the Government of the sending State" requires more than reading government speeches and the local press. One needs to invite an independent-minded academic to dinner or have a serious conversation with a representative leader of some restless linguistic minority, such as the Kurds of Iraq, Iran, or Turkey. Caution is necessary, however. In a period of tension, such contacts may become inadvisable, regardless of what international conventions have been signed.

Increasing Abuses of Immunity

An unfortunate trend of the past twenty years is an increase in abuses of the diplomatic pouch for smuggling and an increase in the abuse of the pouch and other diplomatic immunities for spying and state-sponsored terrorism. All such activities give diplomats in general and the whole idea of diplomatic immunity a bad name.

The extremely lucrative trade in drugs has drawn some diplomats into serious abuses. At times there have been indications that the sending government deliberately condoned the practice or was even using it to pay some of the expenses of the mission.[45] Usually, however, the offending diplomat, when caught, turns out to have

---

44 OFM Annual Report, March 1986, p. 7.
45 *Outrage*, pp. 94 and 111.

been operating on his own, or with the connivance of other individual diplomats, or with the assistance of a drug-smuggling organization that is bribing him to be their agent.

One such abuse of international immunity occurred in New York in March 1987. The chauffeur of the ambassador of Norway to the United Nations was arrested when he pulled up in the ambassador's official Lincoln Continental with two other men, allegedly to deliver a pound of cocaine. The recipients, to his surprise, turned out to be Federal undercover agents.[46]

When a diplomat is found to be smuggling drugs and claims immunity, the host foreign ministry is likely to request that diplomat's government to waive immunity in view of the particularly infamous nature of the offense. Although immunity is then waived in a few such cases, the waiver often comes after the criminal has had time to leave the country. The receiving government can then put him on their list of undesirables who will not be permitted to reenter, and the sending government, if it can apprehend him, may put him on trial. His career as a diplomat is presumably damaged.

President Kenneth Kaunda of Zambia has set an excellent example in this field. On 24 February 1985, the London police arrested a man in possession of about two kilograms of heroin who said he had obtained it from a house in London. The police went to the house and began a search, overriding the occupant's objections. After a quarter of an hour, the occupant claimed immunity as a third secretary of the Zambian mission and ordered the police to leave. When they checked and found his identity had been given correctly, they stopped their search and withdrew. The Zambian mission protested the following day, and the Foreign Office issued an apology, even though the police had stopped the search as soon as diplomatic immunity had been established. The police felt there were strong grounds for suspicion that the drugs had come in by diplomatic pouch, so the Foreign Office approached the Zambian head of mission and demanded that the third secretary's immunity be waived. The head of mission, reportedly displeased, undertook to consult President Kaunda, who swiftly waived immunity. The third secretary was arrested, and Kaunda's decision was conveyed in a letter, which was made public, saying:

Diplomatic immunity was never intended to prevent the investigation of serious crimes. I myself have a horror of all addictive drugs. It destroys human beings. . . . I feel I am acting to protect my people and also the people of Britain and indeed of the whole world.

When the request for the waiver of immunity reached me, I did not hesitate for a second. It was, I am told, an almost unprecedented action. But in this

46 *Washington Post*, 10 Mar. 1987.

fight we all must wage against this terrifying menace, I am convinced that I am right.[47]

One can only hope that President Kaunda's precedent will be followed in such cases in the future.

At Kennedy International Airport, the luggage is routinely sniffed by specially trained dogs to check for narcotic substances. Although diplomats' luggage is normally passed without being opened, if the dogs sense drugs, the diplomat is requested to open the suspicious baggage.[48] This practice is supported by the Vienna Convention, Article 36, which permits such challenges when "there are serious grounds for presuming" that luggage contains prohibited articles.

Another abuse of immunity for smuggling is in moving out small antiquities and works of art. This is a centuries-old practice, and it is stimulated by the immense increase in the prices of such objects in recent decades. No one now can use diplomatic immunity in this field on so grand a scale as in the "heroic" age of Lord Elgin in Constantinople, or of American Consul General Luigi di Cesnola in Cyprus, who transported over 35,000 pieces of Cypriot antiquities collected during his tour of duty from 1865 to 1876.[49]

There are also suspicions that many embassies have done what the Libyan embassy in London did: import, and perhaps export, firearms. In Britain it is illegal for a diplomat, or anyone else, to possess firearms without a police permit. The Foreign Office periodically reminds foreign missions of this rule and explains that if a permit is refused, the applicant may arrange for the firearm to be exported. However, the police doubt that this regulation is always followed by embassies. Members of Parliament have suggested that electronic surveillance of diplomatic bags would help to check the abuse.[50]

Two unrelated incidents in September 1988 involving gun-wielding diplomats in London – one Vietnamese, the other Cuban – renewed public attention to this problem. The Foreign Office expelled both diplomats after their ambassadors refused to waive their immunity, and in the Cuban case expelled the ambassador as well to demonstrate how seriously the incident was viewed, according to reports in the *Washington Post*, among others, of 14 and 15 September 1988.

The question of practice with regard to electronic surveillance of diplomatic pouches is one which smoulders as a current problem. In his 1986 article on couriers, Hans-Peter Kaul noted that alleged abuses of diplomatic bags "have often given rise to disputes among

---

[47] *Outrage*, pp. 55–56.
[48] Ibid., p. 96; and *New York Times*, 1 Aug. 1988.
[49] *Outrage*, p. 113, quoting *Newsweek*.
[50] Ibid., p. 124; and *Times* (London), 12 Sept. 1986.

States." Some, "stressing the notorious dangers, . . . seem to prefer in general the restriction under the 1963 Convention. However, recent practice . . . indicates a strong trend towards unconditional and complete inviolability of all kinds of bags. . . . The situation is similar," he says, on "the question whether the diplomatic bag may be examined by electronic or other mechanical devices." The Vienna Conventions leave the question open. "It has been argued that since such an inspection might involve neither opening nor manual search, electronic screening as used in airports would be admissible. In recent State practice, however, this view does not seem to have been generally accepted."[51]

Meanwhile the technology applied to security continues to become more and more powerful and sophisticated. Stephen Kindel has surveyed the state of the art of screening luggage.[52] One of the most effective methods, known as dielectric analysis, was worked out by William Gregory when he was professor of physics at Georgetown University. A simplified explanation is that Gregory exploited the fact "that every material has dielectric properties, numbers that reflect both its ability to store electric charge (the dielectric constant) and the ability to move the electric charge (the conductivity)." Their "characteristic curves . . . are as distinctive as fingerprints or signatures: no two are exactly alike." A machine can be trained to note without comment all "innocent" materials and sort out minute differences that indicate something anomalous. The bag containing the object would have to be hand-searched to identify the anomaly.

Gregory's method, dielectric analysis, "can be done easily and cheaply" and can be "effective against even very small quantities of explosives and incendiaries." In 1975–76, when there was a wave of letter bombs, mainly addressed to USIA, the Postal Service requested Gregory to install the device in the USIA mailroom in February 1977. "Out of more than 100,000 pieces of mail screened, Gregory's device caught each and every package and incendiary letter. More important, there were no false alarms other than packages that jammed the system."

Gregory's device languished when terrorism temporarily received diminished attention in the early 1980s. However, Kindel was confident it had further potential and reported that Gregory was in touch with Customs Canada and the U.S. Federal Aviation Administration. Customs hoped the device might be able to detect drugs in pouches or luggage.

Another security problem for scanning is the plastic pistol,

---

[51] In Bernhardt, *Encyclopedia of Public International Law*, Instalment 9, p. 51.
[52] "Catching Terrorists," *Science Digest*, September 1986, pp. 36–42.

Glock-17, which Kindel described as "moderately priced" at $444. Its Austrian maker "has a strong reputation for quality." When disassembled in a piece of luggage it would not be detected by X-rays. However, some device capable of picking up high-density plastic could presumably be developed.

Governments will need to continue watching for the possible abuse of the inviolability of diplomatic pouches for a long time. It is possible that technological methods may come increasingly into use.

Gravely harmful to the image of diplomacy is the abuse of diplomatic immunity that occurs when embassies and diplomats engage in the old practice of spying and the relatively new one of state-sponsored terrorism. Beginning in the late 1970s, Qadhafi's Libya has been the worst offender on the latter score. Other governments with a bad reputation are Khomeini's Iran and Ba'athist Syria. Bulgaria has also been suspected of practicing terrorism: the fatal poisoning of an expatriate Bulgarian by stabbing with an umbrella ferrule at a bus stop in London[53] and connivance in the attempted assassination of the Pope in Rome in 1981.

Nigerian officials in London in 1984 kidnapped an outspoken Nigerian opponent of their government, Mr. Umaru Dikko, and tried to ship him back from London to Nigeria in a crate labeled "diplomatic baggage," reportedly with some unofficial expert Israeli participation. Fortunately, they were forestalled by the British police at the airport.[54] Such actions emanating from diplomatic missions and deliberately threatening the lives of persons in the receiving country are a nightmare to international relations and a total contradiction of the functions of diplomatic missions under the Vienna Convention.

Embassy buildings have been used in recent decades for purposes not consistent with the spirit of the Vienna Convention. It is probable that most such cases are never detected, but the few that come to light illustrate the dangerous potential for using an embassy to provide inviolable security for terrorism or subversion.

One such case occurred in Pakistan in 1973. Early that year the Pakistani government suspected that arms were being imported and stored in the embassy of Iraq. They asked permission of the ambassador to make a search. Though he did not agree, the police proceeded to search and discovered a large quantity of illegally imported arms. Pakistan protested to Iraq, declared the Iraqi ambassador himself *persona non grata*, and recalled the Pakistani

[53] Graham Yost, *Spytech*, (London: Harrap; 1985), p. 261.
[54] *Keesing's Contemporary Archives* XXX, Dec. 1984, pp. 33529–61.
[55] Satow, 5th ed., p. 110, citing the *Observer* of 11 Feb. 1973.

head of mission from Baghdad.[55] Denza mentions this case as "virtually the only occasion when suspicion of abuse of the premises led to their search without permission."[56] When the Libyan embassy in London abused the inviolability of its premises, the British government, as recounted in chapter 1, did not follow the Pakistani example.

In Beirut, there was the mysterious case of the disappearance on 20 January 1987 of Terry Waite, the personal representative of the Archbishop of Canterbury. Waite was on a mission to seek the release of twenty-seven foreign hostages held in Lebanon. It appeared after a few weeks that Waite himself had been taken hostage by the pro-Iranian Hezbollah militia. In mid-March 1987, it was reported that the last sighting of Waite had been as he was "being hustled into the Iranian Embassy" the previous month.[57] In early May 1988, further reports from Beirut indicated that foreign hostages believed held in the Hujjaj section of the city's southern suburbs "had been removed in cars with Iranian diplomatic plates" shortly before Syrian troops moved into that area to take control.[58]

These and other incidents clearly contradict the intentions of Article 41 of the Vienna Convention of 1961, which states:

The premises of the mission must not be used in any manner incompatible with the functions of the mission as laid down in the present Convention or by other rules of general international law or by any special agreements in force between the sending and the receiving State.

Public resentment over these abuses runs high. In August 1986, for example, the mother of London Policewoman Yvonne Fletcher, who had been killed by gunfire from the Libyan embassy two years earlier, launched an international petition urging the British and other "civilized" governments to stop the abuse of diplomatic immunity. At a press conference, Mrs. Fletcher poignantly called for reforms, saying, "No one should be freed after committing a crime or violating another's property because he shoots from a foreign embassy or drives a car with a diplomatic licence plate." Among those signing the petition was Miss Charlotte Owen, who had been seriously injured when an attaché from the embassy of Kenya struck her motorcycle in a hit-and-run incident in London in January 1984. News accounts said the petition would be circulated in New York, Paris, Melbourne, Brussels, and Montreal,[59] aiming for a million signatures by the end of 1986.

---

[56] Denza, "Diplomatic agents," in R. Bernhardt, ed., *Encyclopedia of Public International Law*, Instalment 9 (1986), p. 95.

[57] *Washington Post*, 14 Mar. 1987.

[58] *Washington Post*, 28 May, 1988.

[59] *Times* (London), 15 Aug. 1986.

News of the petition was carried with photos in most of the London papers, under such supportive headlines as "Diplomats who get away with murder – Mother's plea on immunity" (*Daily Mail*) and "Getting way with murder" (*The People*). A *Daily Express* editorial headed "Diplomatic Impunity" said Mrs. Fletcher's campaign "deserves widespread support and official attention." *The People* editorial was more hard-hitting: "Diplomatic immunity . . . should be scrapped except for offences directly connected with diplomatic work." The *Daily Telegraph* editorial on August 18 acknowledged that most people would support the campaign to restrict diplomatic abuses, but also cautioned that "all moves must be taken with due respect to possible retaliation" against the country's own people abroad.

How are we to deal with such abusive practices, how penalize and prevent them? These are some of the gravest questions to be faced in considering, as we will in chapter 7, the outlook for diplomatic immunity in the coming decades.

Espionage. Embassies and consulates, each with their respective immunities, are sometimes involved in the business of spying, yet another characteristic of diplomatic practice in our time. It is not an easy topic to discuss for publication. The most influential handbook of diplomatic practice, *Satow's Guide*, does not refer to the subject (either in Sir Nevile Bland's 1956 edition or in Lord Gore-Booth's in 1979). In contrast, Eric Clark's popularly-styled *Corps diplomatique* in 1973 has a whole candid, irreverent twenty-page chapter called "Embassies and Espionage," and almost every year some former C.I.A. or other national intelligence service retiree writes a book about experiences in and out of embassy positions. It is a subject rather like sex in the Victorian period, in which a young man's request for advice on practice could be met either with the silence of propriety or, in other situations, with such worldly candor as "Don't have sex with your wife in the morning, because something better might come along during the day."

B. Sen's *A Diplomat's Handbook of International Law and Practice*, 1965 edition, touches on the subject only indirectly, noting that "spy incidents" have generally not precipitated breaks in relations (p. 195), and that consuls may encounter resistance and delays when they seek to contact their fellow nationals detained on the charge of spying (p. 323). Sen cites cases in Hungary and Czechoslovakia, though the status of the accused is not mentioned.

Spying by a diplomatic agent is one of the criminal offenses covered by diplomatic immunity. When apprehended, the diplomat may be transferred by the sending state, or if not, he is likely to be declared *persona non grata* by the receiving state.

In practice, it cannot be ignored that spying from diplomatic missions and consulates does occur and that national intelligence agencies have made use of the privileges and immunities of diplomats to assist their work. Diplomatic missions and consulates, as mentioned in chapter 3, do have the recognized function of "ascertaining by all lawful means conditions and developments in the receiving State, and reporting thereon to the Government of the sending State."[60] What is not acceptable in normal diplomatic practice is the clandestine collection of information, including payments to agents within a country, or even the overly intensive use of local citizens as sources of many kinds of sensitive information.

The subject of embassies and espionage is also complicated by the fact that in some countries even the overt collection of information is regarded as espionage. In such countries, the mere possession of a camera, a radio receiver, or even a typewriter is viewed with the suspicion that such equipment might be used for spying. Authoritarian or weak and nervous regimes may overreact toward diplomats who have good local contacts. Probably more intelligence agents have been declared *persona non grata* because of a suspicion that they were involved in internal plotting than because they were gathering information.

Soviet diplomatic missions have frequently been suspected of including a disproportionate number of intelligence personnel, many of them under other labels. Prof. T.J. Uldricks describes the situation in *The Times Survey of Foreign Ministries of the World*, 1982 (p. 535):

The embassies of the USSR frequently have the largest foreign mission staff in the country to which they are accredited. This has given rise to speculation that the Soviet missions house large numbers of KGB officials, some of whom enjoy immunity as diplomats. Estimates of the percentage of intelligence agents in the Soviet missions range from 40 to 45 percent in certain Western countries and up to 75 percent in some Third World countries. One of the functions of these KGB officials is to monitor the performance and loyalty of the embassy staff. Another . . . is to gather intelligence. . . . For example, members of the Soviet embassy in Mexico City were implicated in an attempt to procure sensitive technical data from a defence contractor, the TRW Corporation, in southern California. Sometimes these KGB diplomats are active in the political life of the country to which they are assigned. This was apparently the case when S.M. Kudriatsev (who had previously operated an atomic spy ring in Ottawa) was appointed

---

[60] Article 3 of the diplomatic convention and article 5 of the consular convention. (Perhaps a cynic or a lawyer might argue that even secret gathering of information was covered by the *alia* or *inter alia* that precedes the list of functions in the diplomatic convention.)

ambassador to Cuba in 1960, the year of Castro's consolidation of power. Normally, however, the KGB and military intelligence (GRU) officials occupy less conspicuous posts as third secretaries or attachés.

Partly with such situations in mind, the 1961 Vienna Convention specifies (article 7): "In the case of military, naval, and air attachés, the receiving State may require their names to be submitted beforehand, for its approval." For it is thought that those categories of positions are particularly sensitive from the security, and sometimes political, standpoint. The 1961 Convention also gives the receiving state the right (article 11) to "require that the size of a mission be kept within limits considered by it to be reasonable and normal" and to "refuse to accept officials of a particular category." In practice, receiving governments have sometimes required diplomatic missions to reduce their numbers, and whether so stated or not, this has been motivated by a conviction that spying was the real function of too many of the members of the mission. When the Soviet government has had to act on such requests, it has objected but complied, often retaliating by requesting reciprocal reductions in the embassy staff of the government concerned.

Between March and the end of October 1986, there was a major series of mutual expulsions of U.S. and Soviet diplomats on charges of spying and intelligence activities. The United States had informed the Soviets that spring that the size of their UN missions would need to be reduced. In August, the FBI arrested on charges of spying a Soviet scientific attaché at the United Nations, Gennadi Zakharov, who lacked diplomatic immunity. In apparent retaliation, the Soviets arrested an American correspondent, Nicholas S. Daniloff of *U.S. News and World Report*, on spying charges in Moscow. Both Zakharov and Daniloff were eventually allowed to return to their own countries in what was widely perceived, though officially denied, as an exchange deal. In the course of that half-year, reciprocal expulsions on charges of intelligence activities extended to many diplomats with immunity. The Russians expelled a total of eleven U.S. diplomats, and the Americans required the departure of twenty-five Soviet UN diplomats and fifty-five from the Soviet embassy and consulates in the United States, thereby achieving numerical parity between U.S. diplomats and consuls in the Soviet Union and Soviet counterparts in the United States.[61]

This episode was one of the larger and more recent examples of a host government's eventual impatience with the use for espionage of diplomats covered by immunity. It is an indication that spying is not

---

[61] *New York Times*, 1 Nov. 1986, *Washington Post*, 18 Dec. 1987, and numerous contemporary accounts.

tolerated in practice if it is on too large a scale. The incident also illustrates the willingness of the U.S. government to include UN secretariat employees in New York, with their international immunities, among the targets of its actions to curb spying. For the sake of harmonious international relations and smoothly working diplomatic contacts, as well as a better future for the institution of diplomatic immunity, it would clearly be preferable to have less spying from embassies and consulates.

7
FUTURE PROSPECTS

What seems to be the outlook for the institution of diplomatic privileges and immunities in the short term, say five to ten years, and the longer term, say ten to fifty years? It may seem a risky game to predict anything in the field of international relations amid the accelerating changes in technology, communications, and even such fundamentals as population during coming decades.

Diplomatic immunity, however, has a long history. Positive and negative changes currently under way seem fairly well balanced to ensure its survival. On the negative side are the instances of flagrant abuse and the trend toward a more dangerous international climate in which states have more to fear from diplomats' misbehavior than ever before. Balancing these is the positive function of diplomatic immunity in helping to keep open much-needed channels of communication between states of widely different ideologies, political systems, and levels of economic development. Another positive factor is that diplomatic immunity since the 1960s has become structured and legally stabilized by the Vienna Conventions. As an institution and an idea, it is more firmly established and better defined than ever before in history. Like the rules of grammar and spelling, it is more basic than technological innovations and can be used effectively by those who want to change, those who want to resist change, and the majority who just want to be neutral and survive.

Challenges to the Vienna Conventions

When dramatic, alarming, outrageous diplomatic abuses occur, one of the understandable reactions is to call for amending the Vienna Conventions. This is particularly likely to be proposed by editorialists, commentators, and legislators.

The Tehran embassy hostage crisis and the death of Policewoman Yvonne Fletcher raised the question again in the public mind. On the occasion of the second anniversary of Ms. Fletcher's murder, a London editorial called for scrapping diplomatic immunity "except for offences directly connected with diplomatic work."[1] The Ashman and Trescott book, *Outrage*, published in 1986, retold dozens of cases of diplomatic wrongdoing, from rape to parking

---

[1] *The People* (London), 17 Aug. 1986.

offenses, and concluded (p. 239), "The abuse of diplomatic immunity is a danger to us all." The authors did not specifically call for changes in the Vienna conventions, but Labour Party Member of Parliament and Shadow Home Secretary Gerald Kaufman, in a laudatory introduction to their book, said,

Plainly changes need to be made. . . . Renegotiation of the Vienna Convention governing diplomatic immunity seems the most logical step. This book will have made an important contribution if it plays its part in creating a climate that leads to such a re-negotiation.[2]

A subcommittee of the Senate Judiciary Committee in 1984 held hearings on a bill to make it a federal crime for foreign diplomats in the United States entitled to immunity under the Vienna conventions to use a firearm to commit a felony. Senator Jeremiah Denton acknowledged that the implementation of the bill would depend on amending the 1961 Vienna Convention, as proposed in a companion measure that had been referred to the Foreign Relations Committee.[3]

However, the State Department position on possible revisions of the Vienna conventions seems decidedly unenthusiastic. In July 1984, the department's principal deputy legal advisor, Daniel W. McGovern, sounding "a note of caution," explained to a Senate subcommittee:

The Vienna Convention . . . was developed by the International Law Commission . . . [which] is presently developing draft articles dealing with the diplomatic pouch and the diplomatic courier that are intended to supplement the provisions on those subjects in the Vienna Convention. The thrust of the Commission's draft is to expand privileges and immunities and to make it more difficult to control abuse of the diplomatic pouch. We are trying to discourage this mischievous exercise, which is sponsored by Bulgaria and encouraged by the entire Eastern bloc.

Looking to the circumstances of the near future Mr. McGovern warned:

Any initiatives that we might take to amend the Vienna Convention to cut back on privileges and immunities would be likely to be referred to the International Law Commission and linked with that body's work on the diplomatic pouch and the diplomatic courier. If this were to happen, prospects are that an unsatisfactory draft would be sent to a diplomatic confer-

---

[2] Kaufman became shadow foreign secretary following the June 1987 general election.

[3] U.S. Congress, Senate, Committee on the Judiciary, Subcommittee on Security and Terrorism, *Firearm Felonies by Foreign Diplomats, Hearings*, 24 July and 21 Sept. 1984, 98th cong., 2nd sess., p. 68.

ence. The product of such a conference could well be a convention with which we could not live, and disintegration of the rules of the Vienna Convention that benefit the United States.[4]

Thus far Congress seems to have been willing to accept the State Department's view, or at least not to insist on a U.S.initiative to revise the Vienna Conventions.

In June 1987, however, Senator Jesse Helms, the ranking Republican on the Foreign Relations Committee, introduced a bill, S. 1437, which would have had the effect of changing the U.S. adherence to some key provisions on diplomatic and consular immunity under the two Vienna conventions. The bill would have made members of diplomatic missions who were not diplomatic agents or consular officers subject to "the criminal jurisdiction of the United States (or of any State) for any crime of violence, . . . for drug trafficking, or for reckless driving or driving while intoxicated or under the influence of alcohol or drugs."

The State Department's refusal to support this proposed legislation was given before the Senate Committee on Foreign Relations in a reasoned statement by Selwa Roosevelt, the chief of protocol, on 5 August 1987. She pointed out that the proposed act would be "undermining long-standing international convention" and "would place the United States in violation of the Vienna convention." It would also violate the bilateral consular treaties of the United States "extending broader immunities for consular personnel," treaties which the United States in furtherance of its own interest had concluded on a reciprocal basis with the Soviet Union, the People's Republic of China, Bulgaria, the German Democratic Republic, Hungary, Poland, Romania, and the Philippines. She noted that the British Foreign Office had "concluded that it would be wrong to amend the Vienna convention as the solution to the abuse of diplomatic immunity but, instead, implemented a firmer policy in the application of the convention."[5]

In the same first session of the 100th Congress, Congressman Steven Solarz introduced a bill, H.R. 3036, "To provide redress for crimes committed by diplomats in the United States, and for other purposes," that called in great detail for revision of a number of diplomatic privileges and immunities. The bill included provisions that would (1) compensate victims of crimes committed by diplomats on the same basis as other victims of crimes; (2) require the

---

[4] Ibid., p. 79.
[5] Selwa Roosevelt, "Diplomatic Immunity and U.S. Interests," U.S. Department of State, Bureau of Public Affairs, *Current Policy* No.993. (Reproduced in appendix F of this book.)

State Department's Office of Foreign Missions to report annually on crimes committed in the United State by diplomats, giving the identity of the individual, the nature of the offense, whether it involved reckless or drunken driving, and the number and nature of other criminal offenses committed in the United States by that individual; (3) require the OFM to educate local police on the extent of diplomatic immunity under the Vienna Convention and encourage them to investigate, charge, and prosecute, to the extent possible under the convention, diplomats and their family members who commit serious criminal offences; (4) prevent the State Department from interfering with any investigation, charge, or prosecution of an alien who is a member of a foreign mission, a family member of such an alien, or any other alien not covered by diplomatic immunity, unless the secretary of state reports to the Congress within thirty days that a waiver is required by extraordinary foreign policy considerations or the national security; (5) require the director of the OFM to notify members of each foreign mission of the above-listed policies on criminal offences by diplomats; and (6) require the OFM to implement registration and departure procedures to identify those individuals with diplomatic immunity.

Further provisions called upon the secretary of state to request a waiver of immunity in cases of serious crimes or to require the offender's departure. The Immigration Act (8 United States Code 1182) would be amended to bar reentry by such persons, except for criminal proceedings or where their admission was determined to be in the national interest.

The Solarz bill also called for State Department review of any current policies according diplomats more favorable treatment than required under the Vienna Convention and for recommendations on ways to bring such treatment into line with treaty obligations and promote the observance of U.S. law by diplomats. In addition, the bill called for a review of procedures to conform the issuance of nonimmigrant visas to foreign diplomats with the treatment accorded American diplomats; for minimum coverage of one million dollars per incident to be required for liability insurance carried by diplomatic missions; and for presidential review of the treatment of diplomatic pouches under the Vienna Convention so as to preclude their being used for transporting unauthorized materials, particularly those incidental to terrorism, and to foster the adoption of measures against the use of pouches for illicit narcotics, explosives, and weapons.

The Helms and Solarz bills, though not enacted by the Congress in its 1987 session, are evidence of the way opinion in Congress is moving at the time of writing with respect to the future of diplomatic privileges and immunities. They also reflect a broad tendency in American public opinion of the late 1980s. This writer has repeatedly encountered a similar mood in conversations with persons in Washington and elsewhere in private business, the academic world, and other circles, including many seriously interested in foreign relations. This mood was reflected in the decision of the 68,000-member American Federation of Police to endorse the Solarz bill at its April 1988 meeting in New York. The president of the federation, Deputy Sheriff Dennis Ray Martin of Saginaw, Michigan, declared that the bill "will send a clear message to those lawbreakers who know our hands have been tied by the present laws."[6]

The results of the hearings and votes on the 1987 Helms and Solarz bills were incorporated in conference into section 137 of the State Department authorization bill[7] and signed into law by President Reagan on 24 December 1987. What had emerged was a requirement for a rather broad "study and report concerning the status of individuals with diplomatic immunity in the United States." The report was to focus on "the problem arising from diplomatic immunity from criminal prosecution and from civil suit."

The resulting findings and recommendations covering twelve areas were prepared by the Department of State and transmitted to the Senate Committee on Foreign Relations, the House Committee on Foreign Affairs, and the judiciary committees of both houses on 18 March 1988.[8] The report was notably detailed and responsive to congressional concerns. It thus provides a picture of the status of many problems and a guide to the direction of future U.S. practice.

Particularly instructive are a series of statistical tables. A list of "Special Cases – Unpaid Debts" of embassies and diplomats in Washington and New York as of the end of February 1988 (exhibits A-1 and A-2) catalogued amounts ranging from as little as $20 to a few in excess of $100,000. A number of fairly substantial debts were owed to hospitals.

---

[6] *Washington Post*, 14 April 1988.

[7] Foreign Relations Authorization Act, Fiscal Years 1988 and 1989, P.L. 100–204, Section 137, published in *Congressional Record – House*, 14 Dec. 1987, pp. 11301–2.

[8] *Study and Report Concerning the Status of Individuals with Diplomatic Immunity in the United States*, op. cit. (see p. 78, note 63 above).

Catalogues of "Alleged Criminal Cases" covered the period 1 August 1982 to 29 February 1988, grouped by nineteen types of incident, including "assault," "burglary," "drug-related," "sex" (with several subtypes), and "weapons." The disposition of each case was briefly indicated in phrases such as "Barred reentry into U.S.," "Sent home," "Pending," or "Embassy granted waiver of immunity, but U.S. Attorney's Office declined to pursue." The grand total for Washington was 147 cases, of which 30 involved

Table 1. ALLEGED CRIMINAL CASES (*Totals by Incident*)

Missions in Washington, D.C.
1 August 1982 – 29 February 1988

	Diplomat	Diplomat Dependent	Admin. & Tech.	A&T Dependent	Totals
Assault	4	11	5	4	24
Battery	–	1	–	–	1
Breaking into cars	–	1	–	–	1
Burglary	–	3	–	–	3
Child Abuse	1	–	1	–	2
Copyright Infringement & Violation of US Customs	1	–	–	–	1
Counterfeiting Money	–	–	–	1	1
Disorderly Conduct	–	2	1	–	3
Drug-Related:					
(a) Trafficking	–	2	1	–	3
(b) Possession	2	4	–	1	7
Embezzlement	–	1	1	–	2
Forgery	1	–	2	–	3
Harassment	2	–	–	–	2
Resisting Arrest	–	–	–	1	1
Robbery/Pocketbook Snatching	–	1	–	–	1
Sex:					
(a) Attempted Sexual Battery	–	–	1	–	1
(b) Indecent Exposure	2	–	4	2	8
(c) Indecent Liberties	–	1	–	1	2
(d) Rape	–	1	1	–	2
(e) Attempt to commit Rape	–	–	1	–	1
(f) Sexual Assault	–	1	1	–	2
(g) Soliciting	2	–	1	1	4
Shoplifting	10	23	11	9	53
Theft	–	6	2	1	9
Vandalism	–	–	–	1	1
Weapons	5	2	2	–	9
Totals	30	60	35	22	147

diplomats, 60 their dependents, 35 administrative and technical staff, and 22 their dependents. Table 1 [exhibit B-1(b) in the report] shows the subtotals by type of incident and category of accused. The comparable data for New York show a total of 44 alleged criminal cases, evenly divided between diplomats and their dependents. Administrative and technical personnel were not included because they do not have full criminal immunity. Table 2 [exhibit B-2(b)] shows the subtotals for New York.

Table 2. ALLEGED CRIMINAL CASES (*Totals by Incident*)

Missions to the United Nations,
1 August 1982 – 29 February 1988

	Diplomat	Diplomat Dependent	Totals
Assault	9	4	13
Drug Related:			
(a) Trafficking	–	3	3
Obtaining a Loan under			
False Pretenses	–	1	1
Reckless Endangerment	–	1	1
Sex:			
(a) Attempted Assault	–	1	1
(b) Soliciting	2	–	2
Shoplifting	4	6	10
Theft	3	4	7
Weapons: Possession	3	2	5
Weapons: Illegal Purchase and Export	1	–	1
Totals	22	22	44

(*Note.* Administrative and Technical and A&T Dependents do not have full criminal immunity.)

When one considers that these cases occurred over $5\frac{1}{2}$ years, the totals do not appear to loom large in the problem of controlling criminal activity in the two major urban areaas of New York and Washington. Indeed, in the year ending 31 May 1987, out of the 78,855 crimes reported in Washington, D.C., "no more than five which could be considered serious were committed by persons entitled to criminal immunity."[9]

A separate listing of "diplomatic motor vehicle operation violations" by missions in Washington during the period March 1986 to February 1988 (exhibit B-3) recorded a total of 24 cases. Again, this seemed relatively moderate. As the report notes (p. 5): "The combined population of persons entitled to full diplomatic privi-

[9] Richard Gookin, "Attacks on Immunity," *Foreign Service Journal*, Jan. 1988, p. 18.

leges and immunities in Washington and New York exceeds ten thousand.''

The State Department study responded to congressional questions as to whether the minimum liability insurance for missions and diplomats should be increased from $300,000 to $1 million. This question was carefully studied by the OFM, which consulted the insurance industry in detail. The department concluded that $300,000 was adequate because, among other reasons, 99 percent of cases fall within that figure and many U.S. states require even less. Furthermore, an increase to $1 million would substantially increase premiums so that some foreign missions could not afford automobile insurance at all. This could have harmful reciprocity implications, since governments whose missions are prevented from driving in the United States would likely impose similar restrictions on U.S. embassy and consulate personnel, thus paralyzing the overseas operations of the many U.S. agencies.[10]

Among the most basic and interesting matters dealt with in the study was the question raised in the Solarz bill of responsibility for compensating innocent victims of the abuses of diplomatic immunity. The Solarz bill had proposed that such victims could be added to the list of persons eligible to receive compensation through the Victims of Crime Act of 1984. In support, the State Department enunciated a clear principle: "The beneficiary of diplomatic immunity is fundamentally the United States Government because United States diplomatic personnel abroad could not function without diplomatic immunity. It therefore appears reasonable to spread the costs . . . among U.S. taxpayers . . . rather than to let it fall on the injured individuals. The funding required . . . should be viewed as a necessary cost of [the] conduct of foreign relations" (p. 57). The department noted that the practice of other countries could be a guide to setting up a fund. In Britain, such victims "have access to a Criminal Injuries Compensation Board," and similar practices exist in Canada (pp. 57, 59, 60).

The State Department's negative views on X-ray and other scanning of diplomatic pouches were reaffirmed in the study (pp. 54–55), in response to a congressional query about possible measures to prevent illicit use of such pouches for narcotics, explosives, or weapons. As the largest sender of such pouches, the U.S. government resists changes that would reduce the inviolability of pouches and argues specifically that "any provision which would allow scanning of the bag risks compromising the confidentiality of sensitive communications equipment" (p. 55).

---

[10] Testimony of John Condayan, acting director of OFM, to the U.S. House of Representatives Subcommittee on International Operations, 30 Mar. 1988.

The March 1988 report touches on other outstanding issues of practice respecting diplomatic immunity, including a survey of how countries interpret the Vienna Convention's definition of "family forming part of the household." In many respects, this report provides invaluable source material for students of the subject.

The British House of Commons Foreign Affairs Committee and Her Majesty's Government undertook a similar review of the Vienna Convention in 1984, in the aftermath of the fatal incident at the Libyan embassy in London and the secret attempt by the Nigerian high commission to remove a member of the Nigerian opposition from London. The December 1984 Commons Committee report, *The Abuse of Diplomatic Immunities and Privileges*, when dealing with the subject of possible changes in the Vienna Convention, certainly did not push the government to act. It said:

> Given the difficulties in the way of achieving any restrictive amendment to the Convention, and the doubtful net benefit to the UK of so doing, it would be wrong to regard amendment of the Vienna Convention as the solution to the problem of abuse of diplomatic immunities. Accordingly, the Government are right not to concentrate on amendment of the Convention as a major element in new policies to restrict abuse of immunities.[11]

In April 1985, the Government in turn published its report, *Diplomatic Immunities and Privileges* (Command Paper 9497), which responded to the Committee's questions and summarized the review. In the Command Paper, the Foreign Office dealt with possible changes in the Vienna Convention, both on one specific issue and as a general policy. They noted that Article 41 makes it a duty of diplomats to respect the laws of the receiving state. Therefore, "any change that strengthened this provision and enabled receiving states to enforce their own laws in respect of foreign diplomats could be valuable in dealing both with state-sponsored terrorism and more petty abuses. It could also however mean a corresponding reduction in the protection given to the personnel and facilities of sending states." The effect would "bear hardly on states that generally abide by the existing rules and lead in some cases to unjustified harassment. It could also restrict the ability of Governments, acting on behalf of their country and its citizens, to carry out legitimate business overseas."[12]

The Foreign and Commonwealth Office expressed general satisfaction and support toward the Vienna Convention as it stands, without revision, characterizing it as

---

[11] Quoted in *Diplomatic Immunities and Privileges*, Cmnd 9497, p. 7.
[12] Ibid., p. 6.

a codification of international law and practice going back many hundred years which was re-examined carefully by the international community before it was agreed in 1961 . . . [and] is almost universally respected. 145 states have become parties. The 1964 Diplomatic Privileges Act gave effect to it in the UK. Those very few states which are not parties give general effect to its terms. In practice it has become the modern customary law so that termination of [British] acceptance of the Convention (even if legally possible) would leave us in substantially the same position. It has provided a framework which is explicit and clear in many respects but nevertheless leaves room for common sense in its detailed interpretation and application.[13]

The FCO took a dim view of the practicability of amendments and found its skepticism shared by many other states following "extensive international soundings on the feasibility of amending . . . through renegotiation." The FCO found

widespread consensus that attempts to do so would not succeed. They could in fact create more problems than they would solve by opening up issues on which disagreements could surface and thrive. Given the ambiguities and grey areas, the process would be complex and time-consuming and would lead to a very confused position until the great majority of states accepted any amendments by ratification.[14]

In the light of the carefully considered attitudes of the United States and British governments that the Vienna Conventions in their present form are adequate and that any amendment process would be likely either to fail or to have results adverse to the interests of such relatively law-abiding states as themselves, it seems that for at least the next five or ten years, and probably well beyond that period, the international rules governing diplomatic immunity are not likely to change.

The view from the diplomatic trenches. What are the attitudes of the national organizations representing the interests of career diplomats toward the future of diplomatic privileges and immunities? Specifically, do they support the provisions of the Vienna Conventions on the status and immunities of diplomats as they stand, or do they want some amendments? Their members are the most directly affected by these questions, and their national organizations (there is no international federation of diplomatic organizations) are increasingly active in defending the interests of serving diplomats.

The American Foreign Service Association (AFSA) is the professional association and labor union of the U.S. Foreign Service. Its

13 Ibid., pp. 6–7.
14 Ibid., p. 7.

basic view is one of strong support for the principle of diplomatic immunity, and its representatives welcomed the efforts of OFM to secure better terms for U.S. embassies by applying the principle of reciprocity.[15]

At the time of the August 1987 hearings on the Helms bill (S. 1437) to restrict the immunity of diplomats' families and staff, AFSA President Perry Shankle expressed the association's concern "that recent calls for the United States to alter its obligations under the Vienna Convention on Diplomatic Relations could seriously jeopardize the freedom and even lives of those who represent the United States at foreign posts. . . . Diplomatic immunity serves as the very foundation on which communication between different nations is possible." In an authoritative statement in the Association's monthly magazine, Shankle affirmed that diplomatic immunity "allows a vital public service to be performed in areas of great risk. Without it the United States would be foolish to send representatives to the places where it most needs them." Senator Helms's approach, he said "will surely limit our ability to do our jobs and put us at risk."[16]

Concerned that the Helms bill would have the effect of "eliminating diplomatic immunity for families and staff members if other countries apply reciprocity," an AFSA committee took the positive step of proposing alternative language. Specific passages covered registration/departure procedures, waivers of immunity, declarations of *persona non grata* status, criminal prosecutions, and liability insurance requirements.[17]

The detailed views of organizations of British diplomats were elicited by the House of Commons Foreign Affairs Committee, when preparing its 1984 report, *The Abuse of Diplomatic Immunities and Privileges.*[18] Both the Trade Union Side of the Diplomatic Service and the Diplomatic Service Wives Association submitted memoranda, which were published as appendices 3 and 4 respectively of the report.[19] These memoranda are noteworthy as carefully considered public statements on some very practical matters. They come from a nation that was almost a superpower before that term was invented and which more recently has prudently

---

[15] "The Office of Foreign Missions: Reciprocity Leading to Equality," *Foreign Service Journal*, April 1986, pp. 42–44.

[16] Questions about Immunity," *Foreign Service Journal*, Oct. 1987, p. 3. See appendix E for full text of the AFSA statement.

[17] *Foreign Service Journal*, Dec. 1987, p. 54.

[18] House of Commons Report, Dec. 1984 [see note 7, chapter 1].

[19] Ibid., pp. 60–63. The views of the two groups reported here are culled from these appendixes, which are reproduced in appendixes H and I of this book.

adjusted to making a valued contribution to international relations through example and influence. The British have had long and extensive diplomatic experience in all regions of the world. Their strong endorsement of the Vienna Convention is indicative of the stake all nations' diplomats have in the continuation of the current international rules of diplomatic privileges and immunities.

The Trade Union Side of the Diplomatic Service (T.U.S.) made two general points. First, they "fully agree" with the Vienna Convention's preamble, which recalls that the purpose of diplomatic privileges and immunities is "not to benefit individuals but to ensure the efficient performance of the functions of diplomatic missions." Secondly, they oppose "relaxation of the strict provisions of the Convention." While such relaxation "might make it easier to prevent existing abuses by a small minority of diplomatic agents . . . it would penalize the majority by exposing them to arbitrary harassment, detention or other abuse by a host government, either in retaliation for acts by a sending State or because the existing rules of conduct were no longer taken so seriously."

The T.U.S. realistically recognized and deplored recent abuses of diplomatic immunity. In the immediate aftermath of the incidents involving the Libyan and Nigerian missions in London, the T.U.S. memorandum nevertheless warned that any resulting changes of policy by Britain should "not undermine the ability of our own Diplomatic Service personnel to operate effectively, or put them personally at risk as hostages for the acts and policies of the British Government." They noted instead that existing provisions of the Vienna Convention were a source for remedies. "Article 9 already allows a receiving State to declare a diplomat *persona non grata*, even before he has arrived. Article 11 allows a receiving State to limit the size of a mission. Personal baggage, but not the diplomatic bag itself, may be inspected in the presence of its owner under the provisions of Article 36." They believe "these measures could be effective if required as a last resort. They too are likely to cause retaliation. But they should not risk the kind of serious action against our representatives which Articles 29 to 31 (i.e., freedom from arrest and criminal jurisdiction) are designed to prevent."

Recent events had shown, the T.U.S. concluded, that there could be threats to the efficient operations of British posts abroad and even to "the safety of diplomatic service staff and their families, arising solely out of their position as agents of government: we do not think we can afford to relax the safeguards."

The British Diplomatic Service Wives Association (DSWA) had been asked by the Foreign Affairs Select Committee for views on "the practical advantages (or disadvantages) of the immunities granted under the 1961 Vienna Convention, variations in the practice of receiving countries . . . and any difficulties which Diplomatic Service families might expect if certain of the Convention's provisions were to be varied either by unilateral or bilateral agreement.''

The Wives Association, representing the spouses and other dependents of UK Diplomatic Service personnel, were strongly favorable to the *status quo* established under the Vienna Convention and pointed to its advantages. The most important was that families are protected even in tense or hostile situations. "Without such protection it is not difficult to imagine situations where governments and diplomats might be vulnerable through wives and children perhaps being attacked or held hostage.''

The DSWA also welcomed other advantages of the *status quo*, such as the ability to avoid intolerable living conditions due to difficult physical, economic, and political circumstances, as well as the Vienna Convention's clear support for opportunities for diplomatic dependents to take employment overseas. "Before the Vienna Convention the uncertainty over their immunity on professional matters (such as fraud or medical negligence) was often used as a reason for refusing permission.''

Noting the fundamental principle of reciprocity, the association warned against "any qualification affecting the immunities and protection of foreign diplomats in London," stating:

We are a stable country ruled by due process of law. Such will not be the case in all the countries where our diplomats serve, accompanied by their wives and families. The risks involved in departing from a strict interpretation of the Vienna Convention seem to us likely to fall disproportionately on our diplomats and their families and we would prefer them not to be run.

Improved compliance. An alternative option for the future of the Vienna Convention is to find means to encourage better compliance. The British Foreign and Commonwealth Office, commenting to the House of Commons committee on the views of friendly governments toward the possible amendment of the Convention, noted their emphasis on "the dangers to Western European interests as a whole which they believe would arise from re-opening the provisions of the Convention." They were concerned lest "the almost universally accepted framework on which diplomatic relations are based should . . . be put at risk because of abuse by a tiny minority of States," and some advocated "isolating any State which abuses the basic rules of the system."[20]

[20] House of Commons Report, Dec. 1984, pp. 11–12.

Pressed by the committee to describe more fully the idea of "isolation of States which abuse the Convention," the FCO provided an instructive reply:

In principle, we support the view that the international community should concentrate on isolating any State which abuses the basic rules of diplomatic relations. In practice, few Governments are willing to break off diplomatic relations with another country simply as a measure of support for an ally which has already done so – primarily because no government wishes to jeopardize its overseas trade unless there appears no alternative. Apart from a breach of diplomatic relations, the possibilities of isolation offered within the framework of the Convention include withdrawal of a mission, withdrawal of a head of mission as a mark of disapproval, downgrading the level of head of mission (e.g., from Ambassador to Chargé d'Affaires), and exemplary declarations of *persona non grata*. Such measures can be still more effective if they are carried out by a number of countries in concert. Moving away from the question of diplomatic representation, another possibility is to refuse to allow any official visits to or from the offending State. Trade sanctions have been shown over the years to be ineffective. It may sometimes be better to maintain a dialogue with States which abuse the norms of diplomatic behaviour than to sever all contacts. The number of States who have abused the Convention is small and each case would always have to be carefully assessed by Governments directly affected or contemplating sympathetic action.[21]

Prospects for Normal Practice by Revolutionary Regimes

There seems good reason to anticipate that even in the coming decade the present radical revolutionary regimes in the world will gradually adopt more normal attitudes toward diplomatic relations, including the accepted practice with respect to diplomatic immunity. No one government can expect to practice a markedly different style and substance in this field for long.

Postrevolutionary regimes often make the attempt. We have previously mentioned how the newly independent United States tried to symbolize its democratic character by appointing no ambassadors, only ministers. The United States also broke tradition by its "Benjamin Franklin" image of sending a representative to a royal court in plain dress, even on formal occasions. Benjamin Franklin, a quintessential American type and already famous as a world-class ideal social commoner, made the innovation a success in his own case. In time, however, America came to be represented by ambassadors, as well as ministers, and might even have followed through

21 Ibid., p. 87.

on its tentative experiment with diplomatic uniforms[22] had not most of the diplomatic corps moved into mufti.

Albania is an example of a post–World War II revolutionary government that evolved in the 1980s from a low standard toward more normal international behavior. Under Enver Hoxha, its Marxist-Stalinist leader from 1945 to his death in 1985, Albania showed little interest in formal diplomatic relations. Even in 1987, its government still had an idiosyncratic policy of refusing diplomatic ties with the Soviet Union and the United States, and referred to the two superpowers rather impartially as "the wolf and the jackal." However, under Hoxha's successor, Ramiz Alia, Albania in 1987 established relations with Bolivia, Canada, Jordan, the Philippines, and West Germany. There were 17 embassies in Tirana, and Albania had diplomatic relations with 110 countries. *Sunday Times* correspondent John Witherow, in a review of Albania's behavior, described it as "scouring the globe in search of friends" and seeking to "rejoin the world community."[23]

The postrevolutionary Russian regime also expressed itself through changes in diplomatic practice. They renamed their foreign ministry the People's Commissariat for Foreign Affairs (the acronym was Narkomindel). In the early years, according to T.J. Uldricks,

Soviet representatives often attempted to assist revolutionary movements in countries to which they were accredited. . . . Soviet diplomatic pouches occasionally carried instructions and funds for foreign radicals. . . . By 1921, however, the Kremlin had begun to learn that revolutions could not be provoked by the intrigues of diplomats and that such attempts undermined the relationship between the Soviet representative and the government to which he was accredited. Thereafter the Narkomindel began to dissociate itself from such activities.

During this period, the Soviets also began increasingly to make use of "diplomatic notes, formal negotiations, even secret treaties," in place of "diplomacy by proclamation and denunciation. The

---

[22] An example of a formal uniform for a U.S. ambassador is on display at Anderson House, the national headquarters of the Society of the Cincinnati, 2118 Massachusetts Avenue, N.W., in Washington, D.C. The uniform includes a gold-trimmed tailcoat and trousers and a "fore-and-aft" hat. It belonged to a career diplomat, Larz Anderson, who served early in the twentieth century as minister to Belgium and ambassador to Japan. E.J. Applewhite, *Washington Itself: An Informal Guide to the Capital of the United States* (New York: Alfred A. Knopf, 1981), pp. 60–61.

[23] "Lost Kingdom Strives for Self-discovery," *Sunday Times* (London), 20 Sept. 1987.

necessities of protecting the USSR imposed the usages of bourgeois diplomacy on the Kremlin's representatives."[24]

The continuing trend toward normalization of Soviet diplomatic practice is illustrated by a series of articles on diplomacy in the Soviet magazine *International Affairs*, published in Moscow in Russian, English, and French by the All-Union Znaniye Society. The Moscow *International Affairs* (not to be confused with the British Royal Institute of International Affairs quarterly of the same name) had few articles on diplomacy in 1984 and 1985, and those were historical and propagandistic in nature, e.g., "Soviet Diplomacy during the Great Patriotic War" in November 1984. In 1985, the journal began to publish articles which threw some light on Soviet attitudes toward diplomatic practice. One by V. Morozov, "Diplomatic Academy of the USSR Ministry of Foreign Affairs Marks Its 50th Anniversary," stated (p.151): "Half of all Soviet diplomats are graduates of the Academy. Among them are 179 ambassadors. . . ."

In 1986, there were at least seven articles on diplomatic practice: "Recognition and Establishment of Diplomatic Relations," "Diplomatic Missions," "Diplomatic Privileges and Immunities," "The Diplomatic Corps," "Diplomatic Correspondence," "The Development of Diplomatic Services and Today's World," and "Consular Activities." In 1987 the series continued with "Diplomatic Protocol," "The Establishment and Development of Soviet-Spanish Diplomatic Relations," and "The Early Days of Soviet Diplomatic Service."

The articles tended to be elementary. In fact, several of them were presented as "The ABC of Diplomacy." They had no revolutionary or even reformist line. A few were even occasionally interesting. For example, O. Pavlov in his article on the diplomatic corps and its dean mentioned that the tradition of seniority at the post is not always observed in Africa. "Certain African countries, former French colonies, appoint the ambassador of France the doyen, while in Togo the decision taken in 1984 makes ambassadors of the FRG and France the doyen and vice-doyen of the diplomatic corps regardless of the period of their stay in the country. In Burkina Faso the doyen is always an ambassador from an African country."[25]

In the same issue, O. Pavlov's article on diplomatic correspondence, after a review of the characteristic forms of notes, aide-mémoires, etc., solemnly continues with the customary prac-

---

[24] Teddy J. Uldricks, "The Tsarist and Soviet Ministry of Foreign Affairs," in Steiner, *Times Survey of Foreign Ministries,* pp. 527–28.

[25] *International Affairs* (Moscow), August 1986, p. 138.

tices of exchanging diplomatic calling cards. This seems a far cry from the days of the Narkomindel. The reader may be reminded of the (probably apocryphal) remark of Leon Trotsky upon hearing that the wives of the Politburo members were meeting weekly in the afternoon to drink tea and play cards, "Comrades, the revolution is over!"

In recent years the charge of abusing diplomatic immunity as a cover for state-sponsored terrorism has been leveled at Libya, Iran, Syria, and, to a lesser extent, Iraq. Cuba and South Yemen are others. Bulgaria has been suspected of doing this kind of dirty work for the Soviet Union. In January 1988, the United States added North Korea to its list of states practising international terrorism. The U.S. move came after a woman who said she was the daughter of a North Korean diplomat confessed to planting the bomb that blew up a South Korean civilian aircraft in flight under the direct orders of the son of North Korean leader Kim Il Sung.[26]

The Iraqi military coup of July 1958 caused the burning of the British embassy, but the new dictator, General Qasim, soon expressed regret and willingness to pay compensation. The Khomeini regime in Iran and the Chinese during their cultural revolution were guilty of allowing the violation of embassy premises and the persons of diplomats, including heads of mission. In Tehran, the offenses occurred against the U.S. embassy in 1979–80. In Beijing, it was the British embassy that suffered in 1967. The Iranian government is still apparently completely unrepentant. The Chinese government, in contrast, undertook in 1971 to pay the cost of rebuilding the chancery premises.[27]

These events are probably too recent to permit a clear conclusion for the future, but the history of the past two centuries indicates that regimes no less extreme than the ones we know today eventually settled down and behaved normally in their diplomatic practices.

It seems likely that during the next thirty years some old regimes will be swept away and new and, in some cases, revolutionary successors will appear. One dare not venture any specific predictions! Wherever this happens, however, embassies and diplomats may be threatened with violence. Security measures and communications facilities will be severely tested. The lives and careers of some currently young diplomats who will then be ambassadors will be in danger.

For them, it may be of small comfort to reflect that in time the behavior of volatile regimes tends to subside into predictability and

---

[26] *Washington Post*, 21 Jan. 1988.
[27] *Satow's Guide*, 5th ed., p. 197.

that there is more calm than storm in the world's political weather. For our purpose of envisioning the outlook for diplomatic immunity, however, there is some consolation in realizing that it is likely to go on being widely respected.

The Functional Approach to Immunity

There seems little doubt that the trend toward functional emphasis in matters of diplomatic privileges and immunities will continue. Where is this likely to lead in the long term?

There will probably be a persistent attempt to hold down the number of persons who are entitled to full immunity. Both Vienna Conventions had this effect, as we have seen, and the experience of the post-Vienna period has confirmed the wisdom of the drafters.

Foreign ministries will increasingly regulate the foreign missions in their countries, as permitted by the conventions. One powerful regulatory tool will be control of the number of diplomatic agents, trying to keep their numbers constant or even reduced. The tighter control on numbers along with firmer regulation will make the problems of diplomatic immunity more manageable.

The total number of persons involved in diplomatic and other intergovernmental relations, however, seems likely to increase inexorably. This will be due to the growing volume of official international business and its increasingly specialized character. Governments will continue to expand the areas in which they collaborate, as they are already doing in such relatively new fields as pollution control, airport security, illegal drug traffic, disaster aid, development aid, and weather observation, among others. Such activities require official agreements, funding, periodic inspections and progress assessments, official travel, conferences, files, and reports. Some of the work can he contracted out; substantial amounts will be entrusted to international organizations, mainly UN subsidiaries. But despite such tactics and despite the labor-saving advantages of computers, word processors, and jet aircraft, more officials will be required.

Those who are diplomatic agents, including all existing and many new categories of specialized attachés, will need full diplomatic immunity. Some of their assistants will need at least partial immunity. The functional criterion will be applied. Do they and their offices need privileges and immunities in order to work effectively? A restrictive policy may be attempted, but it will be working against heavy pressures from the agencies and individuals. It is hard to see the outcome.

A crisis may develop at some point, perhaps in the aftermath of an ugly incident. A series of problems in developing countries may point to a need to provide privileges and immunities for foreign officials and technicians. The sending governments may firmly insist on them to guarantee their nationals' safety. The receiving states may resist, even refuse. The sending states may then find that recruitment for such service is not possible, thereby jeopardizing some costly, valuable programs. This could become another facet of the North-South problem, along with "Northern" complaints of excessive levels of indebtedness and "Southern" complaints of economic exploitation. Perhaps a creative solution will have to come from a source in the South who is sympathetic to the problems of the North.

National Security Considerations

The interests of national security seem able to override considerations of diplomatic immunity, even in the 1980s. That will almost certainly be more and more the case as the century closes. This is a shadowy area where one can only speculate on how the question would arise.

In the sixteenth century and later, some ambassadors were discovered to have plotted to incite changes of monarchs in England and France.[28] When it happened in the reign of Queen Elizabeth I, eminent lawyers held that "an ambassador who incited insurrection against the ruler to whom he was accredited forfeited his privileges and could be tried." The queen chose to imprison the ambassador briefly, then expelled him.[29] Similar *persona non grata* reactions were taken in other cases.

However, there is now a general conviction that although the world may have become more civilized and sophisticated, it has also become far more dangerous. This has unquestionably been the situation since the invention of nuclear weapons and the further potential dangers of toxic and biological weapons. The whole subject becomes more nightmarish the more one looks into it.

A diplomat caught plotting a nuclear attack might still have a good chance of being expelled rather than imprisoned or executed. However, the inviolability of embassy premises or of its sealed pouch might well not be respected, depending entirely on the strength of the receiving government's evidence for suspicion.

Even short of such doomsday scenarios, the climate of opinion is shifting. Parliaments and courts, both national and international,

---

[28] *Satow's Guide*, 5th ed., p. 124.
[29] Ibid.

will probably be increasingly prone to uphold the right of a government when it acts to override diplomatic immunity on grounds of state security. In a 1947 opinion involving Soviet spies in Canada, Canadian Justice Bissonnette ruled that "the diplomatic agent must do or attempt nothing against the safety of the State that has consented to receive him."[30] The intervening years have only underscored the validity of his view, and the coming years will surely further confirm it.

On balance, it seems safe to predict that as long as there are independent sovereign states, there will be a strong functional need for diplomatic privileges and immunities. The institution of immunity for the accredited, resident representatives of such states has been a constructive factor. It has ensured an essential minimum of independence and freedom for those representatives. Immunity has enabled diplomats to work abroad with the peace of mind required for success in performing difficult tasks in a sometimes hostile environment. At some distant time when the nation-states – with their different languages, cultures, histories, legal systems, and levels of stability – learn to get along with each other as well as the culturally diverse cantons of Switzerland do, then diplomatic immunity may become an anachronism.

The world may take a zigzag but ultimately successful course in that direction. A long time from now, such a dream could be realized. After all, the harmonious body politic of Switzerland emerged from the history of only a few centuries. One can hope that the world's peoples will be as fortunate as the Swiss.

In the meantime, however, all diplomats and their families and, indirectly, the citizens of each country should be thankful for the well-established institution of diplomatic immunity and for the Vienna Conventions of 1961 and 1963, in particular, which do so much to promote the generally orderly climate of international relations.

[30] C.E. Wilson, *Diplomatic Privileges and Immunities,* p. 83.

APPENDIXES

APPENDIXES

A

Vienna Convention on Diplomatic Relations

Done at Vienna on 18 April 1961

Entered into force on 24 April 1964, in accordance with article 51

The States Parties to the present Convention,

Recalling that peoples of all nations from ancient times have recognized the status of diplomatic agents,

Having in mind the purposes and principles of the Charter of the United Nations concerning the sovereign equality of States, the maintenance of international peace and security, and the promotion of friendly relations among nations,

Believing that an international convention on diplomatic intercourse, privileges and immunities would contribute to the development of friendly relations among nations, irrespective of their differing constitutional and social systems,

Realizing that the purpose of such privileges and immunities is not to benefit individuals but to ensure the efficient performance of the functions of diplomatic missions as representing States,

Affirming that the rules of customary international law should continue to govern questions not expressly regulated by the provisions of the present Convention,

Have agreed as follows:

Article 1

For the purpose of the present Convention, the following expressions shall have the meanings hereunder assigned to them:

(a) the "head of the mission" is the person charged by the sending State with the duty of acting in that capacity;

(b) the "members of the mission" are the head of the mission and the members of the staff of the mission;

(c) the "members of the staff of the mission" are the members of the diplomatic staff, of the administrative and technical staff and of the service staff of the mission;

(d) the "members of the diplomatic staff" are the members of the staff of the mission having diplomatic rank;

(e) a "diplomatic agent" is the head of the mission or a member of the diplomatic staff of the mission;

(f) the "members of the administrative and technical staff" are the

Sources: United Nations, *Treaty Series*, vol. 500 pp. 95ff. U.S. Department of State, *United States Treaties and Other International Agreements*, TIAS 7502. Ratifications, accessions, and successions from *Multilateral Treaties Deposited with the Secretary-General*, Status as at 31 December 1985 (New York: United Nations, 1986), pp. 52–53.

members of the staff of the mission employed in the administrative and technical service of the mission;
(g) the "members of the service staff" are the members of the staff of the mission in the domestic service of the mission;
(h) a "private servant" is a person who is in the domestic service of a member of the mission and who is not an employee of the sending State;
(i) the "premises of the mission" are the buildings or parts of buildings and the land ancillary thereto, irrespective of ownership, used for the purposes of the mission including the residence of the head of the mission.

Article 2

The establishment of diplomatic relations between States, and of permanent diplomatic missions, takes place by mutual consent.

Article 3

1. The functions of a diplomatic mission consist *inter alia* in:
(a) representing the sending State in the receiving State;
(b) protecting in the receiving State the interests of the sending State and of its nationals, within the limits permitted by international law;
(c) negotiating with the Government of the receiving State;
(d) ascertaining by all lawful means conditions and developments in the receiving State, and reporting thereon to the Government of the sending State;
(e) promoting friendly relations between the sending State and the receiving State, and developing their economic cultural and scientific relations.
2. Nothing in the present Convention shall be construed as preventing the performance of consular functions by a diplomatic mission.

Article 4

1. The sending State must make certain that the *agrément* of the receiving State has been given for the person it proposes to accredit as head of the mission to that State.
2. The receiving State is not obliged to give reasons to the sending State for a refusal of *agrément*.

Article 5

1. The sending State may, after it has given due notification to the receiving States concerned, accredit a head of mission or assign any member of the diplomatic staff, as the case may be, to more than one State, unless there is express objection by any of the receiving States.
2. If the sending State accredits a head of mission to one or more other States it may establish a diplomatic mission headed by a *chargé d'affaires ad interim* in each State where the head of mission has not his permanent seat.
3. A head of mission or any member of the diplomatic staff of the mission may act as representative of the sending State to any international organization.

Article 6

Two or more States may accredit the same person as head of mission to another State, unless objection is offered by the receiving State.

Article 7

Subject to the provisions of Articles 5, 8, 9 and 11, the sending State may freely appoint the members of the staff of the mission. In the case of military, naval or air attachés, the receiving State may require their names to be submitted beforehand, for its approval.

Article 8

1. Members of the diplomatic staff of the mission should in principle be of the nationality of the sending State.
2. Members of the diplomatic staff of the mission may not be appointed from among persons having the nationality of the receiving State, except with the consent of that State which may be withdrawn at any time.
3. The receiving State may reserve the same right with regard to nationals of a third State who are not also nationals of the sending State.

Article 9

1. The receiving State may at any time and without having to explain its decision, notify the sending State that the head of the mission or any member of the diplomatic staff of the mission is *persona non grata* or that any other member of the staff of the mission is not acceptable. In any such case, the sending State shall, as appropriate, either recall the person concerned or terminate his functions with the mission. A person may be declared *non grata* or not acceptable before arriving in the territory of the receiving State.
2. If the sending State refuses or fails within a reasonable period to carry out its obligations under paragraph 1 of this Article, the receiving State may refuse to recognize the person concerned as a member of the mission.

Article 10

1. The Ministry for Foreign Affairs of the receiving State, or such other ministry as may be agreed, shall be notified of:
   (*a*) the appointment of members of the mission, their arrival and their final departure or the termination of their functions with the mission;
   (*b*) the arrival and final departure of a person belonging to the family of a member of the mission and, where appropriate, the fact that a person becomes or ceases to be a member of the family of a member of the mission;
   (*c*) the arrival and final departure of private servants in the employ of persons referred to in sub-paragraph (*a*) of this paragraph and, where appropriate, the fact that they are leaving the employ of such persons;
   (*d*) the engagement and discharge of persons resident in the receiving State as members of the mission or private servants entitled to privileges and immunities.
2. Where possible, prior notification of arrival and final departure shall also be given.

Article 11

1. In the absence of specific agreement as to the size of the mission, the receiving State may require that the size of a mission be kept within limits considered by it to be reasonable and normal, having regard to circumstances and conditions in the receiving State and to the needs of the particular mission.
2. The receiving State may equally, within similar bounds and on a non-discriminatory basis, refuse to accept officials of a particular category.

Article 12

The sending State may not, without the prior express consent of the receiving State, establish offices forming part of the mission in localities other than those in which the mission itself is established.

Article 13

1. The head of the mission is considered as having taken up his functions in the receiving State either when he has presented his credentials or when he has notified his arrival and a true copy of his credentials has been presented to the Ministry for Foreign Affairs of the receiving State, or such ministry as may be agreed, in accordance with the practice prevailing in the receiving State which shall be applied in a uniform manner.
2. The order of presentation of credentials or of a true copy thereof will be determined by the date and time of the arrival of the head of the mission.

Article 14

1. Heads of mission are divided into three classes, namely:
(*a*) that of ambassadors or nuncios accredited to Heads of State, and other heads of mission of equivalent rank;
(*b*) that of envoys, ministers and internuncios accredited to Heads of State;
(*c*) that of *chargés d'affaires* accredited to Ministers for Foreign Affairs.
2. Except as concerns precedence and etiquette, there shall be no differentiation between heads of mission by reason of their class.

Article 15

The class to which the heads of their missions are to be assigned shall be agreed between States.

Article 16

1. Heads of mission shall take precedence in their respective classes in the order of the date and time of taking up their functions in accordance with Article 13.
2. Alterations in the credentials of a head of mission not involving any change of class shall not affect his precedence.
3. This article is without prejudice to any practice accepted by the receiving State regarding the precedence of the representative of the Holy See.

Article 17

The precedence of the members of the diplomatic staff of the mission shall be notified by the head of the mission to the Ministry for Foreign Affairs or such other ministry as may be agreed.

Article 18

The procedure to be observed in each State for the reception of heads of mission shall be uniform in respect of each class.

Article 19

1. If the post of head of the mission is vacant, or if the head of the mission is unable to perform his functions, a *chargé d'affaires ad interim* shall act provisionally as head of the mission. The name of the *chargé d'affaires ad interim* shall be notified, either by the head of the mission or, in case he is unable to do so, by the Ministry for Foreign Affairs of the sending State to the Ministry for Foreign Affairs of the receiving State or such other ministry as may be agreed.

2. In cases where no member of the diplomatic staff of the mission is present in the receiving State, a member of the administrative and technical staff may, with the consent of the receiving State, be designated by the sending State to be in charge of the current administrative affairs of the mission.

Article 20

The mission and its head shall have the right to use the flag and emblem of the sending State on the premises of the mission, including the residence of the head of the mission, and on his means of transport.

Article 21

1. The receiving State shall either facilitate the acquisition on its territory, in accordance with its laws, by the sending State of premises necessary for its mission or assist the latter in obtaining accommodation in some other way.

2. It shall also, where necessary, assist missions in obtaining suitable accommodation for their members.

Article 22

1. The premises of the mission shall be inviolable. The agents of the receiving State may not enter them, except with the consent of the head of the mission.

2. The receiving State is under a special duty to take all appropriate steps to protect the premises of the mission against any intrusion or damage and to prevent any disturbance of the peace of the mission or impairment of its dignity.

3. The premises of the mission, their furnishings and other property thereon and the means of transport of the mission shall be immune from search, requisition, attachment or execution.

Article 23

1. The sending State and the head of the mission shall be exempt from all national, regional or municipal dues and taxes in respect of the premises of the mission, whether owned or leased, other than such as represent payment for specific services rendered.

2. The exemption from taxation referred to in this Article shall not apply to such dues and taxes payable under the law of the receiving State by persons contracting with the sending State or the head of the mission.

Article 24

The archives and documents of the mission shall be inviolable at any time and wherever they may be.

Article 25

The receiving State shall accord full facilities for the performance of the functions of the mission.

Article 26

Subject to its laws and regulations concerning zones entry into which is prohibited or regulated for reasons of national security, the receiving State shall ensure to all members of the mission freedom of movement and travel in its territory.

Article 27

1. The receiving State shall permit and protect free communication on the part of the mission for all official purposes. In communicating with the Government and the other missions and consulates of the sending State, wherever situated, the mission may employ all appropriate means, including diplomatic couriers and messages in code or cipher. However, the mission may install and use a wireless transmitter only with the consent of the receiving State.

2. The official correspondence of the mission shall be inviolable. Official correspondence means all correspondence relating to the mission and its functions.

3. The diplomatic bag shall not be opened or detained.

4. The packages constituting the diplomatic bag must bear visible external marks of their character and may contain only diplomatic documents or articles intended for official use.

5. The diplomatic courier, who shall be provided with an official document indicating his status and the number of packages constituting the diplomatic bag, shall be protected by the receiving State in the performance of his functions. He shall enjoy personal inviolability and shall not be liable to any form of arrest or detention.

6. The sending State or the mission may designate diplomatic couriers *ad hoc*. In such cases the provisions of paragraph 5 of this Article shall also apply, except that the immunities therein mentioned shall cease to apply when such a courier has delivered to the consignee the diplomatic bag in his charge.

7. A diplomatic bag may be entrusted to the captain of a commercial aircraft scheduled to land at an authorized port of entry. He shall be provided with an official document indicating the number of packages constituting the bag but he shall not be considered to be a diplomatic courier. The mission may send one of its members to take possession of the diplomatic bag directly and freely from the captain of the aircraft.

Article 28

The fees and charges levied by the mission in the course of its official duties shall be exempt from all dues and taxes.

Article 29

The person of a diplomatic agent shall be inviolable. He shall not be liable to any form of arrest or detention. The receiving State shall treat him with due respect and shall take all appropriate steps to prevent any attack on his person, freedom or dignity.

Article 30

1. The private residence of a diplomatic agent shall enjoy the same inviolability and protection as the premises of the mission.
2. His papers, correspondence and, except as provided in paragraph 3 of Article 31, his property, shall likewise enjoy inviolability.

Article 31

1. A diplomatic agent shall enjoy immunity from the criminal jurisdiction of the receiving State. He shall also enjoy immunity from its civil and administrative jurisdiction, except in the case of:
(a) a real action relating to private immovable property situated in the territory of the receiving State, unless he holds it on behalf of the sending State for the purposes of the mission;
(b) an action relating to succession in which the diplomatic agent is involved as executor, administrator, heir or legatee as a private person and not on behalf of the sending State;
(c) an action relating to any professional or commercial activity exercised by the diplomatic agent in the receiving State outside his official functions.
2. A diplomatic agent is not obliged to give evidence as a witness.
3. No measures of execution may be taken in respect of a diplomatic agent except in the cases coming under sub-paragraphs (a), (b), and (c) of paragraph 1 of this Article, and provided that the measures concerned can be taken without infringing the inviolability of his person or of his residence.
4. The immunity of a diplomatic agent from the jurisdiction of the receiving State does not exempt him from the jurisdiction of the sending State.

Article 32

1. The immunity from jurisdiction of diplomatic agents and of persons enjoying immunity under Article 37 may be waived by the sending State.
2. Waiver must always be express.

3. The initiation of proceedings by a diplomatic agent or by a person enjoying immunity from jurisdiction under Article 37 shall preclude him from invoking immunity from jurisdiction in respect of any counter-claim directly connected with the principal claim.

4. Waiver of immunity from jurisdiction in respect of civil or administrative proceedings shall not be held to imply waiver of immunity in respect of the execution of the judgment, for which a separate waiver shall be necessary.

Article 33

1. Subject to the provisions of paragraph 3 of this Article, a diplomatic agent shall with respect to services rendered for the sending State be exempt from social security provisions which may be in force in the receiving State.

2. The exemption provided for in paragraph 1 of this Article shall also apply to private servants who are in the sole employ of a diplomatic agent, on condition:

(a) that they are not nationals of or permanently resident in the receiving State; and

(b) that they are covered by the social security provisions which may be in force in the sending State or a third State.

3. A diplomatic agent who employs persons to whom the exemption provided for in paragraph 2 of this Article does not apply shall observe the obligations which the social security provisions of the receiving State impose upon employers.

4. The exemption provided for in paragraphs 1 and 2 of this Article shall not preclude voluntary participation in the social security system of the receiving State provided that such participation is permitted by that State.

5. The provisions of this Article shall not affect bilateral or multilateral agreements concerning social security concluded previously and shall not prevent the conclusion of such agreements in the future.

Article 34

A diplomatic agent shall be exempt from all dues and taxes, personal or real, national, regional or municipal, except:

(a) indirect taxes of a kind which are normally incorporated in the price of goods or services;

(b) dues and taxes on private immovable property situated in the territory of the receiving State, unless he holds it on behalf of the sending State for the purposes of the mission;

(c) estate, succession or inheritance duties levied by the receiving State, subject to the provisions of paragraph 4 of Article 39;

(d) dues and taxes on private income having its source in the receiving State and capital taxes on investments made in commercial undertakings in the receiving State;

(e) charges levied for specific services rendered;

(f) registration, court or record fees, mortgage dues and stamp duty, with respect to immovable property, subject to the provisions of Article 23.

Article 35

The receiving State shall exempt diplomatic agents from all personal services, from all public service of any kind whatsoever, and from military obligations such as those connected with requisitioning, military contributions and billeting.

Article 36

1. The receiving State shall, in accordance with such laws and regulations as it may adopt, permit entry of and grant exemption from all customs duties, taxes, and related charges other than charges for storage, cartage and similar services, on:
   (a) articles for the official use of the mission;
   (b) articles for the personal use of a diplomatic agent or members of his family forming part of his household, including articles intended for his establishment.
2. The personal baggage of a diplomatic agent shall be exempt from inspection, unless there are serious grounds for presuming that it contains articles not covered by the exemptions mentioned in paragraph 1 of this Article, or articles the import or export of which is prohibited by the law or controlled by the quarantine regulations of the receiving State. Such inspection shall be conducted only in the presence of the diplomatic agent or of his authorized representative.

Article 37

1. The members of the family of a diplomatic agent forming part of his household shall, if they are not nationals of the receiving State, enjoy the privileges and immunities specified in Articles 29 to 36.
2. Members of the administrative and technical staff of the mission, together with members of their families forming part of their respective households, shall, if they are not nationals of or permanently resident in the receiving State, enjoy the privileges and immunities specified in Articles 29 to 35, except that the immunity from civil and administrative jurisdiction of the receiving State specified in paragraph 1 of Article 31 shall not extend to acts performed outside the course of their duties. They shall also enjoy the privileges specified in Article 36, paragraph 1, in respect of articles imported at the time of first installation.
3. Members of the service staff of the mission who are not nationals of or permanently resident in the receiving State shall enjoy immunity in respect of acts performed in the course of their duties, exemption from dues and taxes on the emoluments they receive by reason of their employment and the exemption contained in Article 33.
4. Private servants of members of the mission shall, if they are not nationals of or permanently resident in the receiving State, be exempt from dues and taxes on the emoluments they receive by reason of their employment. In other respects, they may enjoy privileges and immunities only to the extent admitted by the receiving State. However, the receiving State must exercise its jurisdiction over those persons in such a manner as not to interfere unduly with the performance of the functions of the mission.

Article 38

1. Except insofar as additional privileges and immunities may be granted by the receiving State, a diplomatic agent who is a national of or permanently resident in that State shall enjoy only immunity from jurisdiction, and inviolability, in respect of officials acts performed in the exercise of his functions.

2. Other members of the staff of the mission and private servants who are nationals of or permanently resident in the receiving State shall enjoy privileges and immunities only to the extent admitted by the receiving State. However, the receiving State must exercise its jurisdiction over those persons in such a manner as not to interfere unduly with the performance of the functions of the mission.

Article 39

1. Every person entitled to privileges and immunities shall enjoy them from the moment he enters the territory of the receiving State on proceeding to take up his post or, if already in its territory, from the moment when his appointment is notified to the Ministry for Foreign Affairs or such other ministry as may be agreed.

2. When the functions of a person enjoying privileges and immunities have come to an end, such privileges and immunities shall normally cease at the moment when he leaves the country, or on expiry of a reasonable period in which to do so, but shall subsist until that time, even in case of armed conflict. However, with respect to acts performed by such a person in the exercise of his functions as a member of the mission, immunity shall continue to subsist.

3. In case of the death of a member of the mission, the members of his family shall continue to enjoy the privileges and immunities to which they are entitled until the expiry of a reasonable period in which to leave the country.

4. In the event of the death of a member of the mission not a national of or permanently resident in the receiving State or a member of his family forming part of his household, the receiving State shall permit the withdrawal of the movable property of the deceased, with the exception of any property acquired in the country the export of which was prohibited at the time of his death. Estate, succession and inheritance duties shall not be levied on movable property the presence of which in the receiving State was due solely to the presence there of the deceased as a member of the mission or as a member of the family of a member of the mission.

Article 40

1. If a diplomatic agent passes through or is in the territory of a third State, which has granted him a passport visa if such visa was necessary, while proceeding to take up or to return to his post, or when returning to his own country, the third State shall accord him inviolability and such other immunities as may be required to ensure his transit or return. The same shall apply in the case of any members of his family enjoying privileges or

immunities who are accompanying the diplomatic agent, or travelling separately to join him or to return to their country.

2. In circumstances similar to those specified in paragraph 1 of this Article, third States shall not hinder the passage of members of the administrative and technical or service staff of a mission, and of members of their families, through their territories.

3. Third States shall accord to official correspondence and other official communications in transit, including messages in code or cipher, the same freedom and protection as is accorded by the receiving State. They shall accord to diplomatic couriers, who have been granted a passport visa if such visa was necessary, and diplomatic bags in transit the same inviolability and protection as the receiving State is bound to accord.

4. The obligations of third States under paragraph 1, 2 and 3 of this Article shall also apply to the persons mentioned respectively in those paragraphs, and to official communications and diplomatic bags, whose presence in the territory of the third State is due to *force majeure.*

Article 41

1. Without prejudice to their privileges and immunities, it is the duty of all persons enjoying such privileges and immunities to respect the laws and regulations of the receiving State. They also have a duty not to interfere in the internal affairs of that State.

2. All official business with the receiving State entrusted to the mission by the sending State shall be conducted with or through the Ministry for Foreign Affairs of the receiving State or such other ministry as may be agreed.

3. The premises of the mission must not be used in any manner incompatible with the functions of the mission as laid down in the present Convention or by other rules of general international law or by any special agreements in force between the sending and the receiving State.

Article 42

A diplomatic agent shall not in the receiving State practise for personal profit any professional or commercial activity.

Article 43

The function of a diplomatic agent comes to an end, *inter alia*:
(a) on notification by the sending State to the receiving State that the function of the diplomatic agent has come to an end;
(b) on notification by the receiving State to the sending State that, in accordance with paragraph 2 of Article 9, it refuses to recognize the diplomatic agent as a member of the mission.

Article 44

The receiving State must, even in case of armed conflict, grant facilities in order to enable persons enjoying privileges and immunities, other than nationals of the receiving State, and members of the families of such persons irrespective of their nationality, to leave at the earliest possible moment. It must, in particular, in case of need, place at their disposal the necessary means of transport for themselves and their property.

Article 45

If diplomatic relations are broken off between two States, or if a mission is permanently or temporarily recalled:

(a) the receiving State must, even in case of armed conflict, respect and protect the premises of the mission, together with its property and archives;

(b) the sending State may entrust the custody of the premises of the mission, together with its property and archives, to a third State acceptable to the receiving State;

(c) the sending State may entrust the protection of its interests and those of its nationals to a third State acceptable to the receiving State.

Article 46

A sending State may with the prior consent of a receiving State, and at the request of a third State not represented in the receiving State, undertake the temporary protection of the interests of the third State and of its nationals.

Article 47

1. In the application of the provisions of the present Convention, the receiving State shall not discriminate as between States.

2. However, discrimination shall not be regarded as taking place:

(a) where the receiving State applies any of the provisions of the present Convention restrictively because of a restrictive application of that provision to its mission in the sending State;

(b) where by custom or agreement States extend to each other more favourable treatment than is required by the provisions of the present Convention.

Article 48

The present Convention shall be open for signature by all States Members of the United Nations or of any of the specialized agencies or Parties to the Statute of the International Court of Justice, and by any other State invited by the General Assembly of the United Nations to become a Party to the Convention, as follows: until 31 October 1961 at the Federal Ministry for Foreign Affairs of Austria and subsequently, until 31 March 1962, at the United Nations Headquarters in New York.

Article 49

The present Convention is subject to ratification. The instruments of ratification shall be deposited with the Secretary-General of the United Nations.

Article 50

The present Convention shall remain open for accession by any State belonging to any of the four categories mentioned in Article 48. The instruments of accession shall be deposited with the Secretary-General of the United Nations.

Article 51

1. The present Convention shall enter into force on the thirtieth day following the date of deposit of the twenty-second instrument of ratification or accession with the Secretary-General of the United Nations.
2. For each State ratifying or acceding to the Convention after the deposit of the twenty-second instrument of ratification or accession, the Convention shall enter into force on the thirtieth day after deposit by such State of its instrument of ratification or accession.

Article 52

The Secretary-General of the United Nations shall inform all states belonging to any of the four categories mentioned in Article 48:

(a) of signatures to the present Convention and of the deposit of instruments of ratification or accession, in accordance with Articles 48, 49 and 50;
(b) of the date on which the present Convention will enter into force, in accordance with Article 51.

Article 53

The original of the present Convention, of which the Chinese, English, French, Russian and Spanish texts are equally authentic, shall be deposited with the Secretary-General of the United Nations, who shall send certified copies thereof to all States belonging to any of the four categories mentioned in Article 48.

IN WITNESS WHEREOF the undersigned Plenipoteniaries, being duly authorized thereto by their respective Governments, have signed the present Convention.

DONE AT VIENNA, this eighteenth day of April one thousand nine hundred and sixty-one.

STATES RATIFYING, ACCEDING TO, AND SUCCEEDING TO THE VIENNA CONVENTION ON DIPLOMATIC RELATIONS

	Signature	Ratification, accession (a), succession (d)
Afghanistan		6 Oct 1965 a
Albania	18 Apr 1961	
Algeria		14 Apr 1964 a
Argentina	18 Apr 1961	10 Oct 1963
Australia	30 Mar 1962	26 Jan 1968
Austria	18 Apr 1961	28 Apr 1966
Bahamas		17 Mar 1977 d
Bahrain		2 Nov 1971 a
Bangladesh		13 Jan 1978 d
Barbados		6 May 1968 d
Belgium	23 Oct 1961	2 May 1968
Benin		27 Mar 1967 a
Bhutan		7 Dec 1972 a
Bolivia		28 Dec 1977 a
Botswana		11 Apr 1969 a
Brazil	18 Apr 1961	25 Mar 1965
Bulgaria	18 Apr 1961	17 Jan 1968
Burma		7 Mar 1980 a
Burundi		1 May 1968 a
Byelorussian SSR	18 Apr 1961	14 May 1964
Cameroon		4 Mar 1977 a
Canada	5 Feb 1962	26 May 1966
Cape Verde		30 Jul 1979 a
Central African Rep.	28 Mar 1962	19 Mar 1973
Chad		3 Nov 1977 a

	Signature	Ratification, accession (a), succession (d)
Chile	18 Apr 1961	9 Jan 1968
China*		25 Nov 1975 a
Colombia	18 Apr 1961	5 Apr 1973
Congo		11 Mar 1963 a
Costa Rica	14 Feb 1962	9 Nov 1964
Cuba	16 Jan 1962	26 Sep 1963
Cyprus		10 Sep 1968 a
Czechoslovakia	18 Apr 1961	24 May 1963
Denmark	18 Apr 1961	2 Oct 1968
Djibouti		2 Nov 1978 a
Dominican Rep.	30 Mar 1962	14 Jan 1964
Ecuador	18 Apr 1961	21 Sep 1964
Egypt		9 Jun 1964 a
El Salvador		9 Dec 1965 a
Equatorial Guinea		30 Aug 1976 a
Ethiopia		22 Mar 1979 a
Fiji		21 Jun 1971 d
Finland	20 Oct 1961	9 Dec 1969
France	30 Mar 1962	31 Dec 1970
Gabon		2 Apr 1964 a
German Dem. Rep.		2 Feb 1973 a
Germany, Fed. Rep. of*	18 Apr 1961	11 Nov 1964
Ghana	18 Apr 1961	28 Jun 1962
Greece	29 Mar 1962	16 Jul 1970
Guatemala	18 Apr 1961	1 Oct 1963

Country	Signature		Ratification/Accession	
Guinea			10 Jan	1968 a
Guyana			28 Dec	1972 a
Haiti			2 Feb	1978 a
Holy See	18 Apr	1961	17 Apr	1964
Honduras			13 Feb	1968 a
Hungary	18 Apr	1961	24 Sep	1965
Iceland			18 May	1971 a
India			15 Oct	1965 a
Indonesia			4 Jun	1982 a
Iran	27 May	1961	3 Feb	1965
Iraq	20 Feb	1962	15 Oct	1963
Ireland	18 Apr	1961	10 May	1967
Israel	18 Apr	1961	11 Aug	1970
Italy	13 Mar	1962	25 Jun	1969
Ivory Coast			1 Oct	1962 a
Jamaica			5 Jun	1963 a
Japan	26 Mar	1962	8 Jun	1964
Jordan			29 Jul	1971 a
Kampuchea, Dem.			31 Aug	1965 a
Kenya			1 Jul	1965 a
Kiribati			2 Apr	1982 d
Korea, Dem. People's Rep. of			29 Oct	1980 a
Korea, Rep. of*	28 Mar	1962	28 Dec	1970
Kuwait			23 Jul	1969 a
Laos			3 Dec	1962 a
Lebanon	18 Apr	1961	16 Mar	1971
Lesotho			26 Nov	1969 a
Liberia	18 Apr	1961	15 May	1962
Libya			7 Jun	1977 a
Liechtenstein	18 Apr	1961	8 May	1964
Luxembourg	2 Feb	1962	17 Aug	1966
Madagascar			31 Jul	1963 a
Malawi			19 May	1965 a
Malaysia			9 Nov	1965 a
Mali			28 Mar	1968 a
Malta*			7 Mar	1967 d
Mauritania			16 Jul	1962 a
Mauritius			18 Jul	1969 d
Mexico	18 Apr	1961	16 Jun	1965
Mongolia			5 Jan	1967 a
Morocco			19 Jun	1968 a
Mozambique			18 Nov	1981 a
Nauru			5 May	1978 d
Nepal			28 Sep	1965 a
Netherlands			7 Sep	1984 a
New Zealand	28 Mar	1962	23 Sep	1970
Nicaragua			31 Oct	1975 a
Niger			5 Dec	1962 a
Nigeria	31 Mar	1962	19 Jun	1967
Norway	18 Apr	1961	24 Oct	1967
Oman			31 May	1974 a
Pakistan	29 Mar	1962	29 Mar	1962
Panama	18 Apr	1961	4 Dec	1963
Papua New Guinea			4 Dec	1975 d
Paraguay			23 Dec	1969 a
Peru			18 Dec	1968 a
Philippines	20 Oct	1961	15 Nov	1965
Poland	18 Apr	1961	19 Apr	1965
Portugal			11 Sep	1968 a
Romania	18 Apr	1961	15 Nov	1968
Rwanda			15 Apr	1964 a
San Marino	25 Oct	1961	8 Sep	1965
Sao Tome & Principe			3 May	1983 a

STATES RATIFYING, ACCEDING TO, AND SUCCEEDING TO THE VIENNA CONVENTION ON DIPLOMATIC RELATIONS (*continued*)

	Signature	Ratification, accession (a), succession (d)
Saudi Arabia		10 Feb 1981 a
Senegal	18 Apr 1961	12 Oct 1972
Seychelles		29 May 1979 a
Sierra Leone		13 Aug 1962 a
Somalia		29 Mar 1968 a
South Africa	28 Mar 1962	21 Nov 1967 a
Spain		2 Jun 1978
Sri Lanka	18 Apr 1961	13 Apr 1981 a
Sudan		25 Apr 1969 a
Swaziland		
Sweden	18 Apr 1961	21 Mar 1967
Switzerland	18 Apr 1961	30 Oct 1963
Syria		4 Aug 1978 a
Tanzania	27 Feb 1962	5 Nov 1962
Thailand	30 Oct 1961	23 Jan 1985
Togo		27 Nov 1970 a
Tonga		31 Jan 1973 d

	Signature	Ratification, accession (a), succession (d)
Trinidad & Tobago		19 Oct 1965 a
Tunisia		24 Jan 1968 a
Turkey		6 Mar 1985 a
Tuvalu*		15 Sep 1982 d
Uganda		15 Apr 1965 a
Ukrainian SSR	18 Apr 1961	12 Jun 1964
USSR	18 Apr 1961	25 Mar 1964
United Arab Emirates		24 Feb 1977 a
UK	11 Dec 1961	1 Sep 1964
USA	29 Jun 1961	13 Nov 1972
Uruguay	18 Apr 1961	10 Mar 1970
Venezuela	18 Apr 1961	16 Mar 1965
Vietnam*		26 Aug 1980 a
Yemen, Dem.		24 Nov 1976 a
Yugoslavia	18 Apr 1961	1 Apr 1963
Zaire	18 Apr 1961	19 Jul 1965
Zambia*		16 Jun 1975 d

*States that made declarations or reservations upon ratification, accession or succession. These, followed by objections thereto, can be found in United Nations, *Multilateral Treaties*, 1986, op. cit., pp. 53–66.

B

Vienna Convention on Consular Relations

Done at Vienna on 24 April 1963

Entered into force on 19 March 1967, in accordance with article 77

The States Parties to the present Convention,

Recalling that consular relations have been established between peoples since ancient times,

Having in mind the Purposes and Principles of the Charter of the United Nations concerning the sovereign equality of States, the maintenance of international peace and security, and the promotion of friendly relations among nations,

Considering that the United Nations Conference on Diplomatic Intercourse and Immunities adopted the Vienna Convention on Diplomatic Relations which was opened for signature on 18 April 1961,

Believing that an international convention on consular relations, privileges and immunities would also contribute to the development of friendly relations among nations, irrespective of their differing constitutional and social systems,

Realizing that the purpose of such privileges and immunities is not to benefit individuals but to ensure the efficient performance of functions by consular posts on behalf of their respective States,

Affirming that the rules of customary international law continue to govern matters not expressly regulated by the provisions of the present Convention,

Have agreed as follows:

Article 1
Definitions

1. For the purposes of the present Convention, the following expressions shall have the meanings hereunder assigned to them:

(*a*) "consular post" means any consulate-general, consulate, vice consulate or consular agency;

(*b*) "consular district" means the area assigned to a consular post for the exercise of consular functions;

(*c*) "head of consular post" means the person charged with the duty of acting in that capacity;

(*d*) "consular officer" means any person, including the head of a consular post, entrusted in that capacity with the exercise of consular functions;

(*e*) "consular employee" means any person employed in the administrative or technical service of a consular post;

(*f*) "member of the service staff" means any person employed in the domestic service of a consular post;

Sources: United Nations, *Treaty Series*, vol. 596, pp. 261ff. Ratifications, accessions, and successions from *Mutilateral Treaties*, op. cit., pp. 70–71.

(g) "members of the consular post" means consular officers, consular employees and members of the service staff;

(h) "members of the consular staff" means consular officers, other than the head of a consular post, consular employees and members of the service staff;

(i) "member of the private staff" means a person who is employed exclusively in the private service of a member of the consular post;

(j) "consular premises" means the buildings or parts of buildings and the land ancillary thereto, irrespective of ownership, used exclusively for the purposes of the consular post;

(k) "consular archives" includes all the papers, documents, correspondence, book, films, tapes and registers of the consular post, together with the ciphers and codes, the card-indexes and any article of furniture intended for their protection or safe keeping.

2. Consular officers are of two categories, namely career consular officers and honorary consular officers. The provisions of Chapter II of the present Convention apply to consular posts headed by career consular officers, the provisions of Chapter III govern consular posts headed by honorary consular officers.

3. The particular status of members of the consular posts who are nationals or permanent residents of the receiving State is governed by Article 71 of the present Convention.

CHAPTER I. CONSULAR RELATIONS IN GENERAL

SECTION I. ESTABLISHMENT AND CONDUCT OF CONSULAR RELATIONS

Article 2
Establishment of consular relations

1. The establishment of consular relations between States takes place by mutual consent.

2. The consent given to the establishment of diplomatic relations between two States implies, unless otherwise stated, consent to the establishment of consular relations.

3. The severance of diplomatic relations shall not *ipso facto* involve the severance of consular relations.

Article 3
Exercise of consular functions

Consular functions are exercised by consular posts. They are also exercised by diplomatic missions in accordance with the provisions of the present Convention.

Article 4
Establishment of a consular post

1. A consular post may be established in the territory of the receiving State only with the State's consent.

2. The seat of the consular post, its classification and the consular district

shall be established by the sending State and shall be subject to the approval of the receiving State.

3. Subsequent changes in the seat of the consular post, its classification or the consular district may be made by the sending State only with the consent of the receiving State.

4. The consent of the receiving State shall also be required if a consulate-general or a consulate desires to open a vice-consulate or a consular agency in a locality other than that in which it is itself established.

5. The prior express consent of the receiving State shall also be required for the opening of an office forming part of an existing consular post elsewhere than at the seat thereof.

Article 5
Consular functions

Consular functions consist in:

(a) protecting in the receiving State the interests of the sending State and of its nationals, both individuals and bodies corporate, within the limits permitted by international law;

(b) furthering the development of commercial, economic, cultural and scientific relations between the sending State and the receiving State and otherwise promoting friendly relations between them in accordance with the provisions of the present Convention;

(c) ascertaining by all lawful means conditions and developments in the commercial, economic, cultural and scientific life of the receiving State, reporting thereon to the Government of the sending State and giving information to persons interested;

(d) issuing passports and travel documents to nationals of the sending State, and visas or appropriate documents to persons wishing to travel to the sending State;

(e) helping and assisting nationals, both individuals and bodies corporate, of the sending State;

(f) acting as notary and civil registrar and in capacities of a similar kind, and performing certain functions of an administrative nature, provided that there is nothing contrary thereto in the laws and regulations of the receiving State;

(g) safeguarding the interests of nationals, both individuals and bodies corporate, of the sending States in cases of succession *mortis causa* in the territory of the receiving State, in accordance with the laws and regulations of the receiving State;

(h) safeguarding, within the limits imposed by the laws and regulations of the receiving State, the interests of minors and other persons lacking full capacity who are nationals of the sending State, particularly where any guardianship or trusteeship is required with respect to such persons;

(i) subject to the practices and procedures obtaining in the receiving State, representing or arranging appropriate representation for nationals of the sending State before the tribunals and other authorities of the receiving State, for the purpose of obtaining, in accordance with the laws and regulations of the receiving State, provisional measures for the preservation of the rights and interests of these nationals, where, because of absence or any other reason, such nationals are unable at the proper time to assume the defence of their rights and interest;

(*j*) transmitting judicial and extra-judicial documents or executing letters rogatory or commissions to take evidence for the courts of the sending State in accordance with international agreements in force or, in the absence of such international agreements, in any other manner compatible with the laws and regulations of the receiving State;

(*k*) exercising rights of supervision and inspection provided for in the laws and regulations of the sending State in respect of vessels having the nationality of the sending State, and of aircraft registered in that State, and in respect of their crews;

(*l*) extending assistance to vessels and aircraft mentioned in sub-paragraph,

(*m*) of this Article, and to their crews, taking statements regarding the voyage of a vessel, examining and stamping the ship's papers, and, without prejudice to the powers of the authorities of the receiving State, conducting investigations into any incidents which occurred during the voyage, and settling disputes of any kind between the master, the officers and the seamen in so far as this may be authorized by the laws and regulations of the sending State;

(*n*) performing any other functions entrusted to a consular post by the sending State which are not prohibited by the laws and regulations of the receiving State or to which no objection is taken by the receiving State or which are referred to in the international agreements in force between the sending State and the receiving State.

Article 6
Exercise of consular functions outside the consular district
A consular officer may, in special circumstances, with the consent of the receiving State, exercise his functions outside his consular district.

Article 7
Exercise of consular functions in a third State
The sending State may, after notifying the States concerned, entrust a consular post established in a particular State with the exercise of consular functions in another State, unless there is express objection by one of the States concerned.

Article 8
Exercise of consular functions on behalf of a third State
Upon appropriate notification to the receiving State, a consular post of the sending State may, unless the receiving State objects, exercise consular functions in the receiving State on behalf of a third State.

Article 9
Classes of heads of consular posts

1. Heads of consular posts are divided into four classes, namely
(a) consuls-general;
(b) consuls;
(c) vice-consuls;
(d) consular agents.
2. Paragraph 1 of this Article in no way restricts the right of any of the Contracting Parties to fix the designation of consular officers other than the heads of consular posts.

Article 10
Appointment and admission of heads of consular posts

1. Heads of consular posts are appointed by the sending State and are admitted to the exercise of their functions by the receiving State.
2. Subject to the provisions of the present Convention, the formalities for the appointment and for the admission of the head of a consular post are determined by the laws, regulations, and usages of the sending State and of the receiving State respectively.

Article 11
The consular commission or notification of appointment

1. The head of a consular post shall be provided by the sending State with a document, in the form of a commission or similar intrument, made out for each appointment, certifying his capacity and showing, as a general rule, his full name, his category and class, the consular district and the seat of the consular post.
2. The sending State shall transmit the commission or similar instrument through the diplomatic or other appropriate channel to the Government of the State in whose territory the head of a consular post is to exercise his functions.
3. If the receiving State agrees, the sending State may, instead of a commission or similar instrument, send to the receiving State a notification containing the particulars required by paragraph 1 of this Article.

Article 12
The exequatur

1. The head of a consular post is admitted to the exercise of his functions by an authorization from the receiving State termed an *exequatur*, whatever the form of this authorization.
2. A State which refused to grant an *exequatur* is not obliged to give to the sending State reasons for such refusal.
3. Subject to the provisions of Articles 13 and 15, the head of a consular post shall not enter upon his duties until he has received an *exequatur*.

Article 13
Provisional admission of heads of consular posts

Pending delivery of the *exequatur*, the head of a consular post may be admitted on a provisional basis to the exercise of his functions. In that case, the provisions of the present Convention shall apply.

Article 14
Notification to the authorities of the consular district

As soon as the head of a consular post is admitted even provisionally to the exercise of his functions, the receiving State shall immediately notify the competent authorities of the consular district. It shall also ensure that the necessary measures are taken to enable the head of a consular post to carry out the duties of his office and to have the benefit of the provisions of the present Convention.

Article 15
Temporary exercise of the functions of the head of a consular post

1. If the head of a consular post is unable to carry out his functions or the position of head of consular post is vacant, an acting head of post may act provisionally as head of the consular post.
2. The full name of the acting head of post shall be notified either by the diplomatic mission of the sending State or, if that State has no such mission in the receiving State, by the head of the consular post, or, if he is unable to do so, by any competent authority of the sending State, to the Ministry for Foreign Affairs of the receiving State or to the authority designated by that Ministry. As a general rule, this notification shall be given in advance. The receiving State may make the admission as acting head of post of a person who is neither a diplomatic agent nor a consular officer of the sending State in the receiving State conditional on its consent.
3. The competent authorities of the receiving State shall afford assistance and protection to the acting head of post. While he is in charge of the post, the provisions of the present Convention shall apply to him on the same basis as to the head of the consular post concerned. The receiving State shall not, however, be obliged to grant to an acting head of post any facility, privilege or immunity which the head of the consular post enjoys only subject to conditions not fulfilled by the acting head of post.
4. When, in the circumstances referred to in paragraph 1 of this Article, a member of the diplomatic staff of the diplomatic mission of the sending State in the receiving State is designated by the sending State as an acting head of post, he shall, if the receiving State does not object thereto, continue to enjoy diplomatic privileges and immunities.

Article 16
Precedence as between heads of consular posts

1. Heads of consular posts shall rank in each class according to the date of the grant of the *exequatur*.

2. If, however, the head of a consular post before obtaining the *exequatur* is admitted to the exercise of his functions provisionally, his precedence shall be determined according to the date of the provisional admission; this precedence shall be maintained after the granting of the *exequatur*.

3. The order of precedence as between two or more heads of consular posts who obtained the *exequatur* or provisional admission on the same date shall be determined according to the dates on which their commissions or similar instruments or the notifications referred to in paragraph 3 of Article 11 were presented to the receiving State.

4. Acting heads of posts shall rank after all heads of consular posts and, as between themselves, they shall rank according to the dates on which they assumed their functions as acting heads of posts as indicated in the notifications given under paragraph 2 of Article 15.

5. Honorary consular officers who are heads of consular posts shall rank in each class after career heads of consular posts, in the order and according to the rules laid down in the foregoing paragraphs.

6. Heads of consular posts shall have precedence over consular officers not having that status.

Article 17
Performance of diplomatic acts by consular officers

1. In a State where the sending State has no diplomatic mission and is not represented by a diplomatic mission of a third State, a consular officer may, with the consent of the receiving State, and without affecting his consular status, be authorized to perform diplomatic acts. The performance of such acts by a consular officer shall not confer upon him any right to claim diplomatic privileges and immunities.

2. A consular officer may, after notification addressed to the receiving State, act as representative of the sending State to any inter-governmental organization. When so acting, he shall be entitled to enjoy any privileges and immunities accorded to such a representative by customary international law or by international agreements; however, in respect of the performance by him of any consular function, he shall not be entitled to any greater immunity from jurisdiction than that to which a consular officer is entitled under the present Convention.

Article 18
Appointment of the same person by two or more States as a consular officer

Two or more States may, with the consent of the receiving State, appoint the same person as a consular officer in that State.

Article 19
Appointment of members of consular staff

1. Subject to the provisions of Articles 20, 22 and 23, the sending State may freely appoint the members of the consular staff.

2. The full name, category and class of all consular officers, other than the head of a consular post, shall be notified by the sending State to the receiving State in sufficient time for the receiving State, if it so wishes, to exercise its rights under paragraph 3 of Article 23.

3. The sending State may, if required by its laws and regulations, request the receiving State to grant an *exequatur* to a consular officer other than the head of a consular post.

4. The receiving State may, if required by its laws and regulations, grant an *exequatur* to a consular officer other than the head of a consular post.

Article 20
Size of the consular staff

In the absence of an express agreement as to the size of the consular staff, the receiving State may require that the size of the staff be kept within limits considered by it to be reasonable and normal, having regard to circumstances and conditions in the consular district and to the needs of the particular consular post.

Article 21
Precedence as between consular officers of a consular post

The order of precedence as between the consular officers of a consular post and any change thereof shall be notified by the diplomatic mission of the sending State or, if that State has no such mission in the receiving State, by the head of the consular post, to the Ministry for Foreign Affairs of the receiving State or to the authority designated by the Ministry.

Article 22
Nationality of consular officers

1. Consular officers should, in principle, have the nationality of the sending State.

2. Consular officers may not be appointed from among persons having the nationality of the receiving State except with the express consent of that State which may be withdrawn at any time.

3. The receiving State may reserve the same right with regard to nationals of a third State who are not also nationals of the sending State.

Article 23
Persons declared non grata

1. The receiving State may at any time notify the sending State that a consular officer is *persona non grata* or that any other member of the consular staff is not acceptable. In that event, the sending State shall, as the case may be, either recall the person concerned or terminate his functions with the consular post.

2. If the sending State refuses or fails within a reasonable time to carry out its obligations under paragraph 1 of this Article, the receiving State may, as the case may be, either withdraw the *exequatur* from the person concerned or cease to consider him as a member of the consular staff.

3. A person appointed as a member of consular post may be declared

unacceptable before arriving in the territory of the receiving State or, if already in the receiving State, before entering on his duties with the consular post. In any such case, the sending State shall withdraw his appointment.

4. In the cases mentioned in paragraphs 1 and 3 of this Article, the receiving State is not obliged to give to the sending State reasons for its decision.

Article 24
Notification to the receiving State of appointments, arrivals and departures

1. The Ministry for Foreign Affairs of the receiving State or the authority designated by that Ministry shall be notified of:

(a) the appointment of members of a consular post, their arrival after appointment to the consular post, their final departure or the termination of their functions and any other changes affecting their status that may occur in the course of their service with the consular post;

(b) the arrival and final departure of a person belonging to the family of a member of a consular post forming part of his household and, where appropriate, the fact that a person becomes or ceases to be such a member of the family;

(c) the arrival and final departure of members of the private staff and, where appropriate, the termination of their service as such;

(d) the engagement and discharge of persons resident in the receiving State as members of a consular post or as members of the private staff entitled to privileges and immunities.

2. When possible, prior notification of arrival and final departure shall also be given.

SECTION II. END OF CONSULAR FUNCTIONS

Article 25
Termination of the functions of a member of a consular post

The functions of a member of a consular post shall come to an end *inter alia*:

(a) on notification by the sending State to the receiving State that his functions have come to an end;

(b) on withdrawal of the *exequatur*;

(c) on notification by the receiving State to the sending State that the receiving State has ceased to consider him as a member of the consular staff.

Article 26
Departure from the territory of the receiving State

The receiving State shall, even in case of armed conflict, grant to members of the consular post and members of the private staff, other than nationals of the receiving State, and to members of their families forming part of their households irrespective of nationality, the necessary time and facilities to enable them to prepare their departure and to leave at the earliest possible moment after the termination of the functions of the members concerned.

In particular, it shall, in case of need, place at their disposal the necessary means of transport for themselves and their property other than property acquired in the receiving State the export of which is prohibited at the time of departure.

Article 27
Protection of consular premises and archives and of the interests of the sending State in exceptional circumstances

1. In the event of the severance of consular relations between two States:
   (a) the receiving State shall, even in case of armed conflict, respect and protect the consular premises, together with the property of the consular post and the consular archives;
   (b) the sending State may entrust the custody of the consular premises, together with the property contained therein and the consular archives, to a third State acceptable to the receiving State;
   (c) the sending State may entrust the protection of its interests and those of its nationals to a third State acceptable to the receiving State.
2. In the event of the temporary or permanent closure of a consular post, the provisions of sub-paragraph (a) of paragraph 1 of this Article shall apply. In addition,
   (a) if the sending State, although not represented in the receiving State by a diplomatic mission, has another consular post in the territory of that State, that consular post may be entrusted with the custody of the premises of the consular post which has been closed, together with the property contained therein and the consular archives, and, with the consent of the receiving State, with the exercise of consular functions in the district of that consular post; or
   (b) if the sending State has no diplomatic mission and no other consular post in the receiving State, the provisions of sub-paragraphs (b) and (c) of paragraph 1 of this Article shall apply.

CHAPTER II. FACILITIES, PRIVILEGES AND IMMUNITIES RELATING TO CONSULAR POSTS, CAREER CONSULAR OFFICERS AND OTHER MEMBERS OF A CONSULAR POST

SECTION I. FACILITIES, PRIVILEGES AND IMMUNITIES RELATING TO A CONSULAR POST

Article 28
Facilities for the work of the consular post

The receiving State shall accord full facilities for the performance of the functions of the consular post.

Article 29
Use of national flag and coat-of-arms

1. The sending State shall have the right to the use of its national flag and coat-of-arms in the receiving State in accordance with the provisions of this Article.

2. The national flag of the sending State may be flown and its coat-of-arms displayed on the building occupied by the consular post and at the entrance door thereof, in the residence of the head of the consular post and on his means of transport when used on official business.
3. In the exercise of the right accorded by this Article regard shall be had to the laws, regulations and usages of the receiving State.

Article 30
Accommodation

1. The receiving State shall either facilitate the acquisition on its territory, in accordance with its laws and regulations, by the sending State of premises necessary for its consular post or assist the latter in obtaining accommodation in some other way.
2. It shall also, where necessary, assist the consular post in obtaining suitable accommodation for its members.

Article 31
Inviolability of the consular premises

1. Consular premises shall be inviolable to the extent provided in this Article.
2. The authorities of the receiving State shall not enter that part of the consular premises which is used exclusively of the purpose of the work of the consular post except with the consent of the head of the consular post or of this designee or the head of the diplomatic mission of the sending State. The consent of the head of the consular post may, however, be assumed in case of fire or other disaster requiring prompt protective action.
3. Subject to the provisions of paragraph 2 of this Article, the receiving State is under a special duty to take all appropriate steps to protect the consular premises against any intrusion or damage and to prevent any disturbance of the peace of the consular post or impairment of its dignity.
4. The consular premises, their furnishings, the property of the consular post and its means of transport shall be immune from any form of requisition for purposes of national defence or public untility. If expropriation is necessary for such purposes, all possible steps shall be taken to avoid impeding the performance of consular functions, and prompt, adequate and effective compensation shall be paid to the sending State.

Article 32
Exemption from taxation of consular premises

1. Consular premises and the residence of the career head of consular post of which the sending State or any person acting on its behalf is the owner or lessee shall be exempt from all national, regional or municipal dues and taxes whatsoever, other than such as represent payment for specific services rendered.
2. The exemption from taxation referred to in paragraph 1 of this Article shall not apply to such dues and taxes if under the law of the receiving State, they are payable by the person who contracted with the sending State or with the person acting on its behalf.

Article 33
Inviolability of the consular archives and documents

The consular archives and documents shall be inviolable at all times and wherever they may be.

Article 34
Freedom of movement

Subject to its laws and regulations concerning zones entry into which is prohibited or regulated for reasons of national security, the receiving State shall ensure freedom of movement and travel in its territory to all members of the consular post.

Article 35
Freedom of communication

1. The receiving State shall permit and protect freedom of communication on the part of the consular post for all official purposes. In communicating with the Government, the diplomatic missions and other consular posts, wherever situated, of the sending State, the consular post may employ all appropriate means, including diplomatic or consular couriers, diplomatic or consular bags and messages in code or cipher. However, the consular post may install and use a wireless transmitter only with the consent of the receiving State.

2. The official correspondence of the consular post shall be inviolable. Official correspondence means all correspondence relating to the consular post and its functions.

3. The consular bag shall be neither opened nor detained. Nevertheless, if the competent authorities of the receiving State have serious reason to believe that the bag contains something other than the correspondence, documents or articles referred to in paragraph 4 of this Article, they may request that the bag be opened in their presence by an authorized representative of the sending State. If this request is refused by the authorities of the sending State, the bag shall be returned to its place of origin.

4. The packages constituting the consular bag shall bear visible external marks of their character and may contain only official correspondence and documents or articles intended exclusively for official use.

5. The consular courier shall be provided with an official document indicating his status and the number of packages constituting the consular bag. Except with the consent of the receiving State he shall be neither a national of the receiving State, nor, unless he is a national of the sending State, a permanent resident of the receiving State. In the performance of his functions he shall be protected by the receiving State. He shall enjoy personal inviolability and shall not be liable to any form of arrest or detention.

6. The sending State, its diplomatic missions and its consular posts may designate consular couriers *ad hoc*. In such cases the provisions of paragraph 5 of this Article shall also apply except that the immunities therein mentioned shall cease to apply when such a courier has delivered to the consignee the consular bag in his charge.

7. A consular bag may be entrusted to the captain of a ship or of a commercial aircraft scheduled to land at an authorized port of entry. He shall be provided with an official document indicating the number of packages constituting the bag, but he shall not be considered to be a consular courier. By arrangement with the appropriate local authorities, the consular post may send one of its members to take possession of the bag directly and freely from the captain of the ship or of the aircraft.

Article 36
Communication and contact with nationals of the sending State

1. With a view to facilitating the exercise of consular functions relating to nationals of the sending State:
   (*a*) consular officers shall be free to communicate with nationals of the sending State and to have access to them. Nationals of the sending State shall have the same freedom with respect to communication with and access to consular officers of the sending State;
   (*b*) if he so requests, the competent authorities of the receiving State shall, without delay, inform the consular post of the sending State if, within its consular district, a national of that State is arrested or committed to prison or to custody pending trial or is detained in any other manner. Any communication addressed to the consular post by the person arrested, in prison, custody or detention shall be forwarded by the said authorities without delay. The said authorities shall inform the person concerned without delay of his rights under this sub-paragraph;
   (*c*) consular officers shall have the right to visit a national of the sending State who is in prison, custody or detention, to converse and correspond with him and to arrange for his legal representation. They shall also have the right to visit any national of the sending State who is in prison, custody or detention in their district in pursuance of a judgement. Nevertheless, consular officers shall refrain from taking action on behalf of a national who is in prison, custody or detention if he expressly opposes such action.
2. The rights referred to in paragraph 1 of this Article shall be exercised in conformity with the laws and regulations of the receiving State, subject to the proviso, however, that the said laws and regulations must enable full effect to be given to the purposes for which the rights accorded under this Article are intended.

Article 37
Information in cases of deaths, guardianship or trusteeship, wrecks and air accidents

If the relevant information is available to the competent authorities of the receiving State, such authorities shall have the duty:
   (*a*) in the case of the death of a national of the sending State, to inform without delay the consular post in whose district the death occurred;
   (*b*) to inform the competent consular post without delay of any case where the appointment of a guardian or trustee appears to be in the interests of a minor or other person lacking full capacity who is a national of the

sending state. The giving of this information shall, however, be without prejudice to the operation of the laws and regulations of the receiving State concerning such appointments;
(c) if a vessel, having the nationality of the sending State, is wrecked or runs aground in the territorial sea or internal waters of the receiving State, or if an aircraft registered in the sending State suffers an accident on the territory of the receiving State, to inform without delay the consular post nearest to the scene of the occurrence.

Article 38
Communication with the authorities of the receiving State

In the exercise of their functions, consular officers may address:
(a) the competent local authorities of their consular district;
(b) the competent central authorities of the receiving State if and to the extent that this is allowed by the laws, regulations and usages of the receiving State or by the relevant international agreements.

Article 39
Consular fees and charges

1. The consular post may levy in the territory of the receiving State the fees and charges provided by the laws and regulations of the sending State for consular acts.
2. The sums collected in the form of the fees and charges referred to in paragraph 1 of this Article, and the receipts for such fees and charges, shall be exempt from all dues and taxes in the receiving State.

SECTION II. FACILITIES, PRIVILEGES AND IMMUNITIES RELATING TO CAREER
CONSULAR OFFICERS AND OTHER MEMBERS OF A CONSULAR POST

Article 40
Protection of consular officers

The receiving State shall treat consular officers with due respect and shall take all appropriate steps to prevent any attack on their persons, freedom or dignity.

Article 41
Personal inviolability of consular officers

1. Consular officers shall not be liable to arrest or detention pending trial, except in the case of a grave crime and pursuant to a decision by the competent judicial authority.
2. Except in the case specified in paragraph 1 of this Article, consular officers shall not be committed to prison or be liable to any other form of restriction on their personal freedom save in execution of a judicial decision of final effect.
3. If criminal proceedings are instituted against a consular officer, he must appear before the competent authorties. Nevertheless, the proceedings shall be conducted with the respect due to him by reason of his official position

and, except in the case specified in paragraph 1 of this Article, in a manner which will hamper the exercise of consular functions as little as possible. When, in the circumstances mentioned in paragraph 1 of this Article, it has become necessary to detain a consular officer, the proceedings against him shall be instituted with the minimum of delay.

Article 42
Notification of arrest, detention or prosecution

In the event of the arrest or detention, pending trial, of a member of the consular staff, or of criminal proceedings being instituted against him, the receiving State shall promptly notify the head of the consular post. Should the latter be himself the object of any such measure, the receiving State shall notify the sending State through the diplomatic channel.

Article 43
Immunity from jurisdiction

1. Consular officers and consular employees shall not be amenable to the jurisdiction of the judicial or administrative authorities of the receiving State in respect of acts performed in the exercise of consular functions.

2. The provisions of paragraph 1 of this Article shall not, however, apply in respect of a civil action either:

(*a*) arising out of a contract concluded by a consular officer or a consular employee in which he did not contract expressly or impliedly as an agent of the sending State; or

(*b*) by a third party for damage arising from an accident in the receiving State caused by a vehicle, vessel or aircraft.

Article 44
Liability to give evidence

1. Members of a consular post may be called upon to attend as witnesses in the course of judicial or administrative proceedings. A consular employee or a member of the service staff shall not, except in the cases mentioned in paragraph 3 of this Article, decline to give evidence. If a consular officer should decline to do so, no coercive measure or penalty may be applied to him.

2. The authority requiring the evidence of a consular officer shall avoid interference with the performance of his functions. It may, when possible, take such evidence at his residence or at the consular post or accept a statement from him in writing.

3. Members of a consular post are under no obligation to give evidence concerning matters connected with the exercise of their functions or to produce official correspondence and documents relating thereto. They are also entitled to decline to give evidence as expert witnesses with regard to the law of the sending State.

Article 45
Waiver of privileges and immunities

1. The sending State may waive, with regard to a member of the consular post, any of the privileges and immunities provided for in Articles 41, 43 and 44.
2. The waiver shall in all cases be express, except as provided in paragraph 3 of this Article, and shall be communicated to the receiving State in writing.
3. The initiation of proceedings by a consular officer or a consular employee in a matter where he might enjoy immunity from jurisdiction under Article 43 shall preclude him from invoking immunity from jurisdiction in respect of any counter-claim directly connected with the principal claim.
4. The waiver of immunity from jurisdiction for the purposes of civil or administrative proceedings shall not be deemed to imply the waiver of immunity from the measures of execution resulting from the judicial decision; in respect of such measures, a separate waiver shall be necessary.

Article 46
Exemption from registration of aliens and residence permits

1. Consular officers and consular employees and members of their families forming part of their households shall be exempt from all obligations under the laws and regulations of the receiving State in regard to the registration of aliens and residence permits.
2. The provisions of paragraph 1 of this Article shall not, however, apply to any consular employee who is not a permanent employee of the sending State or who carries on any private gainful occupation in he receiving State or to any member of the family of any such employee.

Article 47
Exemption from work permits

1. Members of the consular post shall, with respect to services rendered for the sending State, be exempt from any obligations in regard to work permits imposed by the laws and regulations of the receiving State concerning the employment of foreign labour.
2. Members of the private staff of consular officers and of consular employees shall, if they do not carry on any other gainful occupation in the receiving State, be exempt from the obligations referred to in paragraph 1 of this Article.

Article 48
Social security exemption

1. Subject to the provisions of paragraph 3 of this Article, members of the consular post with respect to services rendered by them for the sending State, and members of their families forming part of their households, shall be exempt from social security provisions which may be in force in the receiving State.
2. The exemption provided for in paragraph 1 of this Article shall apply

also to members of the private staff who are in the sole employ of members of the consular post, on condition:

(*a*)   that they are not nationals of or permanently resident in the receiving State; and

(*b*)   that they are covered by the social security provisions which are in force in the sending State or a third State.

3. Members of the consular post who employ persons to whom the exemption provided for in paragraph 2 of this Article does not apply shall observe the obligations which the social security provisions of the receiving State impose upon employers.

4. The exemption provided for in paragraphs 1 and 2 of this Article shall not preclude voluntary participation in the social security system of the receiving State, provided that such participation is permitted by that State.

Article 49
Exemption from taxation

1. Consular officers and consular employees and members of their families forming part of their households shall be exempt from all dues and taxes, personal or real, national, regional or municipal, except:

(*a*)   indirect taxes of a kind which are normally incorporated in the price of goods or services;

(*b*)   dues or taxes on private immovable property situated in the territory of the receiving State, subject to the provisions of Article 32;

(*c*)   estate, succession or inheritance duties, and duties on transfers, levied by the receiving State, subject to the provisions of paragraph (*b*) of Article 51;

(*d*)   dues and taxes on private income, including capital gains, having its source in the receiving State and capital taxes relating to investments made in commercial or financial undertakings in the receiving State;

(*e*)   charges levied for specific services rendered;

(*f*)   registration, court or record fees, mortgage dues and stamp duties, subject to the provisions of Article 32.

2. Members of the service staff shall be exempt from dues and taxes on the wages which they receive for their services.

3. Members of the consular post who employ persons whose wages or salaries are not exempt from income tax in the receiving State shall observe the obligations which the laws and regulations of that State impose upon employers concerning the levying of income tax.

Article 50
Exemption from customs duties and inspection

1. The receiving State shall, in accordance with such laws and regulations as it may adopt, permit entry of and grant exemption from all customs duties, taxes, and related charges other than charges for storage, cartage and similar services, on:

(*a*)   articles for the official use of the consular post;

(*b*)   articles for the personal use of a consular officer or members of his family forming part of his household, including articles intended for his establishment. The articles intended for consumption shall not exceed the quantities necessary for direct utilization by the persons concerned.

2. Consular employees shall enjoy the privileges and exemptions specified in paragraph 1 of this Article in respect of articles imported at the time of first installation.

3. Personal baggage accompanying consular officers and members of their families forming part of their households shall be exempt from inspection. It may be inspected only if there is serious reason to believe that it contains articles other than those referred to in sub-paragraph (*b*) of paragraph 1 of this Article, or articles the import or export of which is prohibited by the laws and regulations of the receiving State or which are subject to its quarantine laws and regulations. Such inspection shall be carried out in the presence of the consular officer or member of his family concerned.

Article 51
Estate of a member of the consular post or of a member of his family

In the event of the death of a member of the consular post or of a member of his family forming part of his household, the receiving State:

(*a*) shall permit the export of the movable property of the deceased, with the exception of any such property acquired in the receiving State the export of which was prohibited at the time of his death;

(*b*) shall not levy national, regional or municipal estate, succession or inheritance duties, and duties on transfers, on movable property the presence of which in the receiving State was due solely to the presence in that State of the deceased as a member of the consular post or as a member of the family of a member of the consular post.

Article 52
Exemption from personal services and contributions

The receiving State shall exempt members of the consular post and members of their families forming part of their households from all personal services, from all public service of any kind whatsoever, and from military obligations such as those connected with requisitioning, military contributions and billeting.

Article 53
Beginning and end of consular privileges and immunities

1. Every member of the consular post shall enjoy the privileges and immunities provided in the present Convention from the moment he enters the territory of the receiving State on proceeding to take up his post or, if already in its territory, from the moment when he enters on his duties with the consular post.

2. Members of the family of a member of the consular post forming part of his household and members of his private staff shall receive the privileges and immunities provided in the present Convention from the date from

which he enjoys privileges and immunities in accordance with paragraph 1 of this Article or from the date of their entry into the territory of the receiving State or from the date of their becoming a member of such family or private staff, whichever is the latest.

3. When the functions of a member of the consular post have come to an end, his privileges and immunities and those of a member of his family forming part of his household or a member of his private staff shall normally cease at the moment when the person concerned leaves the receiving State or on the expiry of a reasonable period in which to do so, whichever is the sooner, but shall subsist until that time, even in case of armed conflict. In the case of the persons referred to in paragraph 2 of this Article, their privileges and immunities shall come to an end when they cease to belong to the household or to be in the service of a member of the consular post provided, however, that if such persons intend leaving the receiving State within a reasonable period thereafter, their privileges and immunities shall subsist until the time of their departure.

4. However, with respect to acts performed by a consular officer or a consular employee in the exercise of his functions, immunity from jurisdiction shall continue to subsist without limitation of time.

5. In the event of the death of a member of the consular post, the members of his family forming part of this household shall continue to enjoy the privileges and immunities accorded to them until they leave the receiving State or until the expiry of a reasonable period enabling them to do so, whichever is the sooner.

Article 54
Obligations of third States

1. If a consular officer passes through or is in the territory of a third State, which has granted him a visa if a visa was necessary, while proceeding to take up or return to his post or when returning to the sending State, the third State shall accord to him all immunities provided for by the other Articles of the present Convention as may be required to ensure his transit or return. The same shall apply in the case of any member of his family forming part of his household enjoying such privileges and immunities who are accompanying the consular officer or travelling separately to join him or to return to the sending State.

2. In circumstances similar to those specified in paragraph 1 of this Article, third States shall not hinder the transit through their territory of other members of the consular post or of members of their families forming part of their households.

3. Third States shall accord to official correspondence and to other official communications in transit, including messages in code or cipher, the same freedom and protection as the receiving State is bound to accord under the present Convention. They shall accord to consular couriers who have been granted a visa, if a visa was necessary, and to consular bags in transit, the same inviolability and protection as the receiving State is bound to accord under the present Convention.

4. The obligations of third States under paragraphs 1, 2 and 3 of this Article

shall also apply to the persons mentioned respectively in those paragraphs, and to official communications and to consular bags, whose presence in the territory of the third State is due to *force majeure.*

Article 55
Respect for the laws and regulations of the receiving State

1. Without prejudice to their privileges and immunities, it is the duty of all persons enjoying such privileges and immunities to respect the laws and regulations of the receiving State. They also have a duty not to interfere in the internal affairs of the State.
2. The consular premise shall not be used in any manner incompatible with the exercise of consular functions.
3. The provisions of paragraph 2 of this Article shall not exclude the possibility of offices of other institutions or agencies being installed in part of the building in which the consular premises are situated, provided that the premises assigned to them are separate from those used by the consular post. In that event, the said offices shall not, for the purposes of the present Convention, be considered to form part of the consular premises.

Article 56
Insurance against third party risks

Members of the consular post shall comply with any requirements imposed by the laws and regulations of the receiving State in respect of insurance against third party risks arising from the use of any vehicle, vessel or aircraft.

Article 57
Special privisions concerning private gainful occupation

1. Career consular officers shall not carry on for personal profit any professional or commercial activity in the receiving State.
2. Privileges and immunities provided in this Chapter shall not be accorded:
   (a) to consular employees or to members of the service staff who carry on any private gainful occupation in the receiving State;
   (b) to members of the family of a person referred to in sub-paragraph (a) of this paragraph or to members of his private staff;
   (c) to members of the family of a member of a consular post who themselves carry on any private gainful occupation in the receiving State.

CHAPTER III. REGIME RELATING TO HONORARY CONSULAR OFFICERS AND CONSULAR POSTS HEADED BY SUCH OFFICERS

Article 58
General provisions relating to facilities, privileges and immunities

1. Articles 28, 29, 30, 34, 35, 36, 37, 38 and 39, paragraphs 3 of Article 54 and paragraphs 2 and 3 of Article 55 shall apply to consular posts headed by an honorary consular officer. In addition, the facilities, privileges and

immunities of such consular posts shall be governed by Articles 59, 60, 61, and 62.

2. Articles 42 and 43, paragraph 3 of Article 44, Articles 45 and 53 and paragraph 1 of Article 55 shall apply to honorary consular officers. In addition, the facilities, privileges and immunities of such consular officers shall be governed by Articles 63, 64, 65, 66 and 67.

3. Privileges and immunities provided in the present Convention shall not be accorded to members of the family of an honorary consular officer or of a consular employee employed at a consular post headed by an honorary consular officer.

4. The exchange of consular bags between two consular posts headed by honorary consular officers in different States shall not be allowed without the consent of the two receiving States concerned.

Article 59
Protection of the consular premises

The receiving State shall take such steps as may be necessary to protect the consular premises of a consular post headed by an honorary consular officer against any intrusion or damage and to prevent any disturbance of the peace of the consular post or impairment of its dignity.

Article 60
Exemption from taxation of consular premises

1. Consular premises of a consular post headed by an honorary consular officer of which the sending State is the owner or lessee shall be exempt from all national, regional or municipal dues and taxes whatsoever, other than such as represent payment for specific services rendered.

2. The exemption from taxation referred to in paragraph 1 of this Article shall not apply to such dues and taxes if, under the laws and regulations of the receiving State, they are payable by the person who contracted with the sending State.

Article 61
Inviolability of consular archives and documents

The consular archives and documents of a consular post headed by an honorary consular officer shall be inviolable at all times and wherever they may be, provided that they are kept separate from other papers and documents and, in particular, from the private correspondence of the head of a consular post and of any person working with him, and from the materials, books or documents relating to their profession or trade.

Article 62
Exemption from customs duties

The receiving State shall, in accordance with such laws and regulations as it may adopt, permit entry of, and grant exemption from all customs duties, taxes, and related charges other than charges for storage, cartage and similar services on the following articles, provided that they are for the official use of a consular post headed by an honorary consular officer: coats-of-arms, flags, signboards, seals and stamps, books, official printed matter, office furniture, office equipment and similar articles supplied by or at the instance of the sending State to the consular post.

Article 63
Criminal proceedings

If criminal proceedings are instituted against an honorary consular officer, he must appear before the competent authorities. Nevertheless, the proceedings shall be conducted with the respect due to him by reason of his official position and except when he is under arrest or detention, in a manner which will hamper the exercise of consular functions as little as possible. When it has become necessary to detain an honorary consular officer, the proceedings against him shall be instituted with the minimum of delay.

Article 64
Protection of honorary consular officers

The receiving State is under a duty to accord to an honorary consular officer such protection as may be required by reason of his official position.

Article 65
Exemption from registration of aliens and residence permits

Honorary consular officers, with the exception of those who carry on for personal profit any professional or commercial activity in the receiving State, shall be exempt from all obligations under the laws and regulations of the receiving State in regard to the registration of aliens and residence permits.

Article 66
Exemption from taxation

An honorary consular officer shall be exempt from all dues and taxes on the remuneration and emoluments which he receives from the sending State in respect of the exercise of consular functions.

Article 67
Exemption from personal services and contributions

The receiving State shall exempt honorary consular officers from all personal services and from all public services of any kind whatsoever and from military obligations such as those connected with requisitioning, military contributions and billeting.

Article 68
Optional character of the institution of honorary consular officers

Each State is free to decide whether it will appoint or receive honorary consular officers.

CHAPTER IV. GENERAL PROVISIONS

Article 69
Consular agents who are not heads of consular posts

1. Each State is free to decide whether it will establish or admit consular agencies conducted by consular agents not designated as heads of consular posts by the sending State.
2. The conditions under which the consular agencies referred to in paragraph 1 of this Article may carry on their activities and the privileges and immunities which may be enjoyed by the consular agents in charge of them shall be determined by agreement between the sending State and the receiving State.

Article 70
Exercise of consular functions by diplomatic missions

1. The provisions of the present Convention apply also, so far as the context permits, to the exercise of consular functions by a diplomatic mission.
2. The names of members of a diplomatic mission assigned to the consular section or otherwise charged with the exercise of the consular functions of the mission shall be notified to the Ministry for Foreign Affairs of the receiving State or to the authority designated by that Ministry.
3. In the exercise of consular functions a diplomatic mission may address:
(a) the local authorities of the consular district;
(b) the central authorities of the receiving State if this is allowed by the laws, regulations and usages of the receiving State or by relevant international agreements.
4. The privileges and immunities of the members of a diplomatic mission referred to in paragraph 2 of this Article shall continue to be governed by the rules of international law concerning diplomatic relations.

Article 71
Nationals or permanent residents of the receiving State

1. Except in so far as additional facilities, privileges and immunities may be granted by the receiving State, consular officers who are nationals of or permanently resident in the receiving State shall enjoy only immunity from jurisdiction and personal inviolability in respect of official acts performed in the exercise of their functions, and the privileges provided in paragraph 3 of Article 44. So far as these consular officers are concerned, the receiving State shall likewise be bound by the obligation laid down in Article 42. If criminal proceedings are instituted against such a consular officer, the proceedings shall, except when he is under arrest or detention, be conducted in a manner which will hamper the exercise of consular functions as little as possible.
2. Other members of the consular post who are nationals of or permanently resident in the receiving State and members of their families, as well as members of the families of consular officers referred to in paragraph 1 of this Article, shall enjoy facilities, privileges and immunities only in so far as

these are granted to them by the receiving State. Those members of the families of members of the consular post and those members of the private staff who are themselves nationals of or permanently resident in the receiving State shall likewise enjoy facilities, privileges and immunities only in so far as these are granted to them by the receiving State. The receiving State shall, however, exercise its jurisdiction over those persons in such a way as not to hinder unduly the performance of the functions of the consular post.

Article 72
Non-discrimination

1. In the application of the provisions of the present Convention the receiving State shall not discriminate as between States.
2. However, discrimination shall not be regarded as taking place:
   (a) where the receiving State applies any of the provisions of the present Convention restrictively because of a restrictive application of that provision to its consular posts in the sending State;
   (b) where by custom or agreement States extend to each other more favourable treatment than is required by the provisions of the present Convention.

Article 73
Relationship between the present Convention and other international agreements

1. The provisions of the present Convention shall not affect other international agreements in force as between States parties to them.
2. Nothing in the present Convention shall preclude States from concluding international agreements confirming or supplementing or extending or amplifying the provisions thereof.

CHAPTER V. FINAL PROVISIONS

Article 74
Signature

The present Convention shall be open for signature by all States Members of the United Nations or of any of the specialized agencies or Parties to the Statute of the International Court of Justice, and by any other State invited by the General Assembly of the United Nations to become a Party to the Convention, as follows: until 31 October 1963 at the Federal Ministry for Foreign Affairs of the Republic of Austria and subsequently, until 31 March 1964, at the United Nations Headquarters in New York.

Article 75
Ratification

The present Convention is subject to ratification. The instruments of ratification shall be deposited with the Secretary-General of the United Nations.

Article 76
Accession

The present Convention shall remain open for accession by any State belonging to any of the four categories mentioned in Article 74. The instruments of accession shall be deposited with the Secretary-General of the United Nations.

Article 77
Entry into force

1. The present Convention shall enter into force on the thirtieth day following the date of deposit of the twenty-second instrument of ratification or accession with the Secretary-General of the United Nations.

2. For each State ratifying or acceding to the Convention after the deposit of the twenty-second instrument of ratification or accession, the Convention shall enter into force on the thirtieth day after deposit by such State of its instrument of ratification or accession.

Article 78
Notifications by the Secretary-General

The Secretary-General of the United Nations shall inform all States belonging to any of the four categories mentioned in Article 74:

(a) of signatures to the present Convention and of the deposit of instruments of ratification or accession, in accordance with Articles 74, 75 and 76;

(b) of the date on which the present Convention will enter into force, in accordance with Article 77.

Article 79
Authentic texts

The original of the present Convention, of which the Chinese, English, French, Russian and Spanish texts are equally authentic, shall be deposited with the Secretary-General of the United Nations, who shall send certified copies thereof to all States belonging to any of the four categories mentioned in Article 74.

IN WITNESS WHEREOF the undersigned Plenipotentiaries, being duly authorized thereto by their respective Governments, have signed the present Convention.

DONE AT VIENNA, this twenty-fourth day of April, one thousand nine hundred and sixty-three.

STATES RATIFYING, ACCEDING TO, AND SUCCEEDING TO THE VIENNA CONVENTION ON CONSULAR RELATIONS

Country	Signature	Ratification, accession (a), succession (d)
Algeria		14 Apr 1964 a
Argentina	24 Apr 1963	7 Mar 1967
Australia	31 Mar 1964	12 Feb 1973
Austria	24 Apr 1963	12 Jun 1969
Bahamas		17 Mar 1977 d
Bangladesh		13 Jan 1978 d
Belgium	31 Mar 1964	9 Sep 1970
Benin	24 Apr 1963	27 Apr 1979
Bhutan		28 Jul 1981 a
Bolivia	6 Aug 1963	22 Sep 1970
Brazil	24 Apr 1963	11 May 1967
Burkina Faso	24 Apr 1963	11 Aug 1964
Cameroon	21 Aug 1963	22 May 1967
Canada		18 Jul 1974 a
Cape Verde		30 Jul 1979 a
Central African Rep.	24 Apr 1963	
Chile	24 Apr 1963	9 Jan 1968
China*		2 Jul 1979 a
Colombia	24 Apr 1963	6 Sep 1972
Congo	24 Apr 1963	
Costa Rica	6 Jun 1963	29 Dec 1966
Cuba	24 Apr 1963	15 Oct 1965
Cyprus		14 Apr 1976 a
Czechoslovakia	31 Mar 1964	13 Mar 1968
Denmark	24 Apr 1963	15 Nov 1972
Djibouti		2 Nov 1978 a
Dominican Republic	24 Apr 1963	4 Mar 1964
Ecuador	25 Mar 1964	11 Mar 1965
Egypt		21 Jun 1965 a
El Salvador		19 Jan 1973 a
Equatorial Guinea		30 Aug 1976 a
Fiji		28 Apr 1972 a
Finland	28 Oct 1963	2 Jul 1980
France	24 Apr 1963	31 Dec 1970
Gabon	24 Apr 1963	23 Feb 1965
Germany, Fed. Rep. of*	31 Oct 1963	7 Sep 1971
Ghana	24 Apr 1963	4 Oct 1963
Greece		14 Oct 1975 a
Guatemala		9 Feb 1973 a
Guyana		13 Sep 1973 a
Haiti		2 Feb 1978 a
Holy See	24 Apr 1963	8 Oct 1970
Honduras		13 Feb 1968 a
Iceland		1 Jun 1978 a
India		28 Nov 1977 a
Indonesia		4 Jun 1982 a
Iran	24 Apr 1963	5 Jun 1975
Iraq		14 Jan 1970 a
Ireland	24 Apr 1963	10 May 1967
Israel	25 Feb 1964	
Italy	22 Nov 1963	25 Jun 1969
Ivory Coast	24 Apr 1963	

Jamaica		9 Feb 1976 a
Japan		3 Oct 1983 a
Jordan		7 Mar 1973 a
Kenya		1 Jul 1965 a
Kiribati		2 Apr 1982 d
Korea, Dem. People's Rep.		8 Aug 1984 a
Korea, Rep. of		2 Mar 1977 a
Kuwait	10 Jan 1964	31 Jul 1975
Laos		9 Aug 1973 a
Lebanon	24 Apr 1963	20 Mar 1975
Lesotho		26 Jul 1972 a
Liberia		28 Aug 1984 a
Liechtenstein	24 Apr 1963	18 May 1966
Luxembourg	24 Apr 1963	8 Mar 1972
Madagascar	24 Mar 1964	17 Feb 1967
Malawi		29 Apr 1980 a
Mali		28 Mar 1968 a
Mauritius		13 May 1970 a
Mexico	7 Oct 1963	16 Jun 1965
Morocco		23 Feb 1977 a
Mozambique		18 Apr 1983 a
Nepal		28 Sep 1965 a
Netherlands		17 Dec 1985 a
New Zealand		10 Sep 1974 a
Nicaragua		31 Oct 1975 a
Niger	24 Apr 1963	26 Apr 1966
Nigeria		22 Jan 1968 a
Norway	24 Apr 1963	13 Feb 1980
Oman		31 May 1974 a
Pakistan		14 Apr 1969 a
Panama	4 Dec 1963	28 Aug 1967
Papua New Guinea		4 Dec 1975 d
Paraguay		23 Dec 1969 a
Peru	24 Apr 1963	17 Feb 1978
Philippines	24 Apr 1963	15 Nov 1965
Poland	20 Mar 1964	13 Oct 1981
Portugal		13 Sep 1972 a
Romania		24 Feb 1972 a
Rwanda		31 May 1974 a
Sao Tome & Principe		3 May 1983 a
Senegal		29 Apr 1966 a
Seychelles		29 May 1979 a
Somalia		29 Mar 1968 a
Spain		3 Feb 1970 a
Suriname		11 Sep 1980 a
Sweden	8 Oct 1963	19 Mar 1974
Switzerland	23 Oct 1963	3 May 1965
Syria		13 Oct 1978 a
Tanzania		18 Apr 1977 a
Togo		26 Sep 1983 a
Tonga		7 Jan 1972 a
Trinidad & Tobago		19 Oct 1965 a
Tunisia		8 Jul 1964 a
Turkey		19 Feb 1976 a
Tuvalu		15 Sep 1982 d
United Arab Emirates		24 Feb 1977 a
UK	27 Mar 1964	9 May 1972
USA	24 Apr 1963	24 Nov 1969
Uruguay	24 Apr 1963	10 Mar 1970
Venezuela*	24 Apr 1963	27 Oct 1965
[Republic of South Viet-Nam]*		10 May 1973 a
Yugoslavia	24 Apr 1963	8 Feb 1965
Zaire	24 Apr 1963	15 Jul 1976

*Declaration or reservation. These can be found, together with objections thereto, in *Multilateral Treaties*, 1986, op. cit., pp. 71–75.

C

Judgment of the International Court of Justice, 24 May 1980, in the "Case Concerning United States Diplomatic and Consular Staff in Tehran" (*United States of America* v. *Iran*)

Selected paragraphs

Present: President Sir Humphrey Waldock; Vice-President Elias; Judges Forster, Gros, Lachs, Morozov, Nagendra Singh, Ruda, Mosler, Tarazi, Oda, Ago, El-Erian, Sette-Camara, Baxter; Registrar Aquarone

86. The rules of diplomatic law, in short, constitute a self-contained regime which, on the one hand, lays down the receiving State's obligations regarding the facilities, privileges and immunities to be accorded to diplomatic missions and, on the other, foresees their possible abuse by members of the mission and specifies the means at the disposal of the receiving State to counter any such abuse. These means are, by their nature, entirely efficacious, for unless the sending State recalls the member of the mission objected to forthwith, the prospect of the almost immediate loss of his privileges and immunities, because of the withdrawal by the receiving State of his recognition as a member of the mission, will in practice compel that person, in his own interest, to depart at once. But the principle of the inviolability of the persons of diplomatic agents and the premises of diplomatic missions is one of the very foundations of this long-established regime, to the evolution of which the traditions of Islam made a substantial contribution. The fundamental character of the principle of inviolability is, moreover, strongly underlined by the provisions of Articles 44 and 45 of the Convention of 1961 (cf. also Articles 26 and 27 of the Convention of 1963). Even in the case of armed conflict or to the case of a breach in diplomatic relations those provisions require that both the inviolability of the members of a diplomatic mission and of the premises, property and archives of the mission must be respected by the receiving State. Naturally, the observance of this principle does not mean – and this the Applicant Government [the United States of America] expressly acknowledges – that a diplomatic agent caught in the act of committing an assault or other offence may not, on occasion, be briefly arrested by the police of the receiving State in order to prevent the commission of the particular crime. But such eventualities bear no relation at all to what occurred in the present case.

87. In the present case, the Iranian Government did not break off diplomatic relations with the United States; and in response to a question put to

---

Source: International Court of Justice, *Reports of Judgments, Advisory Opinions and Orders*, 1980.

him by a Member of the Court, the United States Agent informed the Court that at no time before the events of 4 November 1979 had the Iranian Government declared, or indicated any intention to declare, any member of the United States diplomatic or consular staff in Tehran *persona non grata*. The Iranian Government did not, therefore, employ the remedies placed at its disposal by diplomatic law specifically for dealing with activities of the kind of which it now complains. Instead, it allowed a group of militants to attack and occupy the United States Embassy by force, and to seize the diplomatic and consular staff as hostages; instead, it has endorsed that action of those militants and has deliberately maintained their occupation of the Embassy and detention of its staff as a means of coercing the sending State. It has, at the same time, refused altogether to discuss this situation with representatives of the United States. The Court, therefore, can only conclude that Iran did not have recourse to the normal and efficacious means at its disposal, but resorted to coercive action against the United States Embassy and its staff.

91. At the same time the Court finds itself obliged to stress the cumulative effect of Iran's breaches of its obligations when taken together. A marked escalation of these breaches can be seen to have occurred in the transition from the failure on the part of the Iranian authorities to oppose the armed attack by the militants on 4 November 1979 and their seizure of the Embassy premises and staff, to the almost immediate endorsement by those authorities of the situation thus created, and then to their maintaining deliberately for many months the occupation of the Embassy and detention of its staff by a group of armed militants acting on behalf of the State for the purpose of forcing the United States to bow to certain demands. Wrongfully to deprive human beings of their freedom and to subject them to physical constraint in conditions of hardship is in itself manifestly incompatible with the principles of the Charter of the United Nations, as well as with the fundamental principles enunciated in the Universal Declaration of Human Rights. But what has above all to be emphasized is the extent and seriousness of the conflict between the conduct of the Iranian State and its obligations under the whole corpus of the international rules of which diplomatic and consular law is comprised, rules the fundamental character of which the Court must here again strongly affirm. In its Order of 15 December 1979, the Court made a point of stressing that the obligations laid on States by the two Vienna Conventions are of cardinal importance for the maintenance of good relations between States in the interdependent world of today. "There is no more fundamental prerequisite for the conduct of relations between States", the Court there said, "than the inviolability of diplomatic envoys and embassies, so that throughout history nations of all creeds and cultures have observed reciprocal obligations for that purpose". The institution of diplomacy, the Court continued, has proved to be "an instrument essential for effective co-operation in the international community, and for enabling States, irrespective of their differing constitutional and social systems, to achieve mutual understanding and to resolve their differences by peaceful means" (*I.C.J. Reports 1979*, p. 19).

92. It is a matter of deep regret that the situation which occasioned those observations has not been rectified since they were made. Having regard to their importance the Court considers it essential to reiterate them in the present Judgment. The frequency with which at the present time the principles of international law governing diplomatic and consular relations are set at naught by individuals or groups of individuals is already deplorable. But this case is unique and of very particular gravity because here it is not only private individuals or groups of individuals that have disregarded and set at naught the inviolability of a foreign embassy, but the government of the receiving State itself. Therefore in recalling yet again the extreme importance of the principles of law which it is called upon to apply in the present case, the Court considers it to be its duty to draw the attention of the entire international community, of which Iran itself has been a member since time immemorial, to the irreparable harm that may be caused by events of the kind now before the Court. Such events cannot fail to undermine the edifice of law carefully constructed by mankind over a period of centuries, the maintenance of which is vital for the security and well-being of the complex international community of the present day, to which it is more essential than ever that the rules developed to ensure the ordered progress of relations between its members should be constantly and scrupulously respected.

95. For these reasons,

THE COURT,

1. By thirteen votes to two,
Decides that the Islamic Republic of Iran, by the conduct which the Court has set out in this Judgment, has violated in several respects, and is still violating, obligations owed by it to the United States of America under international conventions in force between the two countries, as well as under long-established rules of general international law;
In Favour: President Sir Humphrey Waldock; Vice-President Elias; Judges Forster, Gros, Lachs, Nagendra Singh, Ruda, Mosler, Oda, Ago, El-Erian, Sette-Camara and Baxter.
Against: Judges Morozov and Tarazi.

2. By thirteen votes to two,
Decides that the violations of these obligations engage the responsibility of the Islamic Republic of Iran towards the United States of America under international law;
In Favour: President Sir Humphrey Waldock; Vice-President Elias; Judges Forster, Gros, Lachs, Nagendra Singh, Ruda, Mosler, Oda, Ago, El-Erian, Sette-Camara and Baxter.
Against: Judges Morozov and Tarazi.

3. Unanimously,
Decides that the Government of the Islamic Republic of Iran must immediately take all steps to redress the situation resulting from the events of

4 November 1979 and what followed from these events, and to that end:

(*a*) must immediately terminate the unlawful detention of the United States Chargé d'affaires and other diplomatic and consular staff and other United States nationals now held hostage in Iran, and must immediately release each and every one and entrust them to the protecting Power (Article 45 of the 1961 Vienna Convention on Diplomatic Relations);

(*b*) must ensure that all the said persons have the necessary means of leaving Iranian territory, including means of transport;

(*c*) must immediately place in the hands of the protecting Power the premises, property, archives and documents of the United States Embassy in Tehran and of its Consulates in Iran;

4. Unanimously,

Decides that no member of the United States diplomatic or consular staff may be kept in Iran to be subjected to any form of judicial proceedings or to participate in them as a witness;

5. By twelve votes to three,

Decides that the Government of the Islamic Republic of Iran is under an obligation to make reparation to the Government of the United States of America for the injury caused to the latter by the events of 4 November 1979 and what followed from these events;

In Favour: President Sir Humphrey Waldock; Vice-President Elias; Judges Forster, Gros, Negendra Singh, Ruda, Mosler, Oda, Ago, El-Erian, Sette-Camara and Baxter.

Against: Judges Lachs, Morozov and Tarazi.

6. By fourteen votes to one,

Decides that the form and amount of such reparation, failing agreement between the Parties, shall be settled by the Court, and reserves for this purpose the subsequent procedure in the case.

In Favour: President Sir Humphrey Waldock; Vice-President Elias; Judges Forster, Gros, Lachs, Nagendra Singh, Ruda, Mosler, Tarazi, Oda, Ago, El-Erian, Sette-Camara and Baxter.

Against: Judge Morozov.

Done in English and in French, the English text being authoritative, at the Peace Palace, The Hague, this twenty-fourth day of May, one thousand nine hundred and eighty, in three copies, one of which will be placed in the archives of the Court, and the others transmitted to the Government of the United States of America and the Government of the Islamic Republic of Iran, respectively.

Judge Lachs appends a separate opinion to the Judgment of the Court.

Judge Morozov and Tarazi append dissenting opinions to the Judgment of the Court.

D

Excerpts from U.S. Department of State *Guidance for Law Enforcement Officers, February 1988*

This is a booklet designed for federal, state, and local law enforcement officers. It "explains how properly to identify (and verify the identity of)" personnel of foreign missions entitled to privileges and immunities and how to handle incidents involving such personnel.

INCIDENTS; GUIDANCE FOR POLICE

General

The vast majority of the persons entitled to privileges and immunities in the United States are judicious in their actions and keenly aware of the significance attached to their actions as representatives of their sending country. On rare occasions, however, a member of this class or of his or her family may be involved in a criminal law violation. The more common violations involve traffic offenses such as illegal parking, speeding, and, less frequently, driving while intoxicated.

Whatever the offense or circumstances of contact, police officers should keep in mind that such persons are official representatives of foreign governments who are to be accorded the maximum degree of respect possible in the circumstances. It is not an exaggeration to say that police handling of incidents in this country may have a direct effect on the treatment of U.S. diplomatic or consular personnel abroad.

When, in the course of responding to or investigating an apparent violation of criminal law, a police officer is confronted with a person claiming immunity, official Department of State identification should immediately be requested in order to verify the person's status and immunity. Should the individual be unable to produce satisfactory identification, and the situation would normally warrant arrest or detention, the officer should inform the individual that he or she will be detained until proper identity can be confirmed. As described previously, this can be accomplished by contacting the appropriate Department of State office.

When proper identification is available, the individual's immunity should be fully respected to the degree to which the particular individual is entitled. If it is established that the individual is entitled to the full inviolability and immunity of a *diplomatic agent*, he or she may not be arrested and should not, except in extraordinary circumstances (see *Personal Inviolability vs. Public Saftey* below), be handcuffed or detained in any way. However, in an incident involving any person entitled to

---

Source: U.S. Department of State, Office of Protocol and Office of Foreign Missions, *Guidance for Law Enforcement Officers: Personal Rights and Immunities of Foreign Diplomatic and Consular Personnel*, February 1988, pp. 15–19 and 21.

immunity, the officer should record all pertinent details from the identity card and fully record the details and circumstances of the incident in accordance with normal police procedures. As is further explained below, proper documentation of incidents is essential to permit the Department of State to take consequential steps, should they be considered appropriate.

Personal Inviolability vs. Public Safety

Personal inviolability is enjoyed to some degree by a majority of foreign diplomatic or consular personnel. In its most extreme form, this inviolability precludes arrest or detention in any form and forbids U.S. authorities from intruding into their residences, automobiles, or other property. All such personal inviolability is, however, qualified by the understanding, well established in international law, that the host country does not give up its right to protect the safety and welfare of its populace and retains the right, in extraordinary circumstances, to prevent the commission of a crime. Thus, in circumstances where public safety is in imminent danger or it is apparent that a serious crime may otherwise be committed, police authorities may intervene to the extent necessary to halt such activity. This naturally includes the power of the police to defend themselves from personal harm.

Traffic Enforcement

Stopping a diplomatic or consular officer and issuing a traffic citation does not constitute arrest or detention and is permissible, although signature of the citation by such individual may not be required. Accordingly, a police officer should never hesitate to follow normal procedures to intervene in a traffic violation which he or she has observed – even if immunity ultimately bars any further action at the scene, the officer should always stop persons committing moving violations, issue a citation if appropriate, and report the incident in accordance with usual procedures. Sobriety tests may be offered in accordance with local procedures but may not be required or compelled. If the police officer judges the individual to be intoxicated, the officer should not (even in the case of diplomatic agents) permit the individual to continue to drive. The officer's primary concern in this connection should be the safety of the community and of the intoxicated individual. Depending on the circumstances, the following options are available. The officer may, with the individual's permission, take the individual to the police station or other location where he or she may recover sufficiently to drive. The officer may summon, or allow the individual to summon, a friend or relative to drive; or the police officer may call a taxi for the individual. If appropriate, the police may choose to provide the individual with transportation.

In any event, the police officer involved with the incident should fully document the facts of the incident and the identity of the individual, and a written report of the incident should be promptly forwarded to the Department of State (in serious cases, report by telephone is also urged). It is Department of State policy to suspend the operator's license of foreign mission personnel not considered to be responsible drivers, and this policy may only be effectively enforced if all driving-related infractions (DWI, reckless driving, etc.) are fully reported to the Department of State.

The property of a person enjoying full immunity, including his or her vehicle, may not be searched or seized. Such vehicles may not be impounded or "booted" but may be towed the distance necessary to remove them from obstructing traffic or endangering public safety. If the vehicle is suspected of being stolen or used in the commission of a crime, occupants of the vehicle may be required to present vehicle documentation to permit police verification of the vehicle's status through standard access to "NLETS." Should the vehicle prove to have been stolen or to have been used by unauthorized persons in the commission of a crime, the inviolability to which the vehicle would normally be entitled must be considered temporarily suspended, and normal search of the vehicle and, if appropriate, its detention, are permissible.

Correct Understanding of Immunity

Frequently (and erroneously), immunity is understood to mean pardon, total exoneration, or total release from the responsibility to comply with the law. In actuality, immunity is simply a legal barrier which precludes U.S. courts from exercising jurisdiction over cases against persons who enjoy it and in no way releases such persons from the duty, embodied in international law, to respect the laws and regulations of the United States. Even those who properly understand the concept of immunity sometimes believe that it is senseless to waste valuable police time in the investigation and paperwork essential to building a legal case, when there is no possibility that a conviction will result. This too is an incorrect perception. It can never be ascertained with certainty at the investigation stage that the person involved will continue to enjoy immunity when his or her government is confronted with the alleged criminal actions of such person and, in any event, there are diplomatic remedies available to deal with such persons even when immunity bars prosecution and conviction. As is explained in greater detail below, there are a number of important reasons for police authorities to give careful attention to the documentation of incidents involving persons enjoying privileges and immunities. Such incidents should always be promptly reported to the Department of State.

Waiver of Immunity

Even though individuals ultimately enjoy the protections afforded by diplomatic or consular privileges and immunities, as indicated above, it is for the benefit of the sending country that these protections are actually devised. This concept is well established in international law and explains the fact that the individual concerned does not "own" the immunity; such immunity may always be waived, in whole or in part, by the country which employs such person. While waiver of immunity in the face of criminal charges is not common, it is routinely sought and occasionally granted. The Department's ability to secure such waiver may depend to a large degree on the strength (and documentation) of the case at issue. Similarly, it is of little avail for the Department to secure waiver of immunity in a particular case, if the case has not been developed with sufficient care and completeness to permit a successful subsequent prosecution. Proper documentation and reporting by law enforcement authorities plays a critical role in both of these respects.

The Persona Non Grata (PNG) Procedure

The criminal immunity which foreign diplomatic and consular personnel enjoy protects them, to the extent that it is not waived by their government, from the normal jurisdiction of the courts in respect of alleged criminal activity. One of the oldest concepts of international diplomatic law, however, is that host countries may strip persons who become unacceptable to them of their privileges and immunities allowing such persons only a reasonable time to remove themselves from the territory of the host country. This is known as the *persona non grata* (PNG) procedure, it may be employed by the host country at any time, and there is no requirement, under international law, for such countries to justify their action. For the United States, however, use of this procedure has inherent constraints. Even though their immunity may deprive such persons of due process in the formal sense, it is felt that in most cases this remedy should be employed only when there is reasonable certainty that a criminal act has actually been committed. The United States's reputation for being a society governed by the rule of law is not served if it may be pointed to as having acted in an arbitrary, capricious, or prejudiced manner in invoking the extreme diplomatic tool of declaring a foreign diplomat PNG. Similarly, any PNG action which the U.S. Government is not able to defend in appropriate detail may be understood by the other country involved as a political action and might thus result in the reciprocal PNG of an entirely innocent American diplomat abroad. *A high standard of police investigation, records, and reporting in diplomatic incident cases is therefore essential to permit the Department responsibly to exercise the diplomatic tools available to remove persons engaged in criminal activity from the United States.*

Official Acts Immunity

As explained above, official acts immunity is not a *prima facie* bar to the exercise of jurisdiction by U.S. courts. Rather, it is an affirmative defense to be raised before the U.S. court with subject matter jurisdiction over the alleged crime. If such court, in the full light of all the relevant facts, determines that the action complained of was an official act, only at that point does international law preclude the further exercise of jurisdiction by the U.S. court. *Because the judicial determination in a case of this type is very much dependent on the facts surrounding the incident, a full and complete police report may be critical in permitting the court to make a just decision.*

Termination of Immunity

Criminal immunity, to the extent that it is enjoyed by a particular individual and to the extent that it is not waived by the sending State concerned, precludes the exercise by courts of the United States of jurisdiction over alleged criminal activity by such persons, whether such activity occurred

Appendix D

DIPLOMATIC AND CONSULAR PRIVILEGES AND IMMUNITIES
SUMMARY OF LAW ENFORCEMENT ASPECTS

	Category	May Be Arrested or Detained	Residence May Be Entered Subject to Ordinary Procedures	May be Issued Traffic Citation
Diplomatic	Diplomatic Agent	No[2]	No	Yes
	Member of Admin. and Tech. Staff	No[2]	No	Yes
	Service Staff	Yes[1]	Yes	Yes
Consular	Career Consular Officers	Yes, if for a felony & pursuant to a warrant[1]	Yes[4]	Yes
	Honorary Consular Officers	Yes	Yes	Yes
	Consular Employees	Yes[1]	Yes	Yes
International Organizations	International Organization Staff[3]	Yes[3]	Yes[3]	Yes
	Diplomatic-Level Staff of Missions to Int'l Orgs.	No[2]	No	Yes
	Support Staff of Missions to International Organizations	Yes	Yes	Yes

[1]This table presents general rules. Particularly in the cases indicated, the employees of certain foreign countries may enjoy *higher* levels of privileges and immunities on the basis of special bilateral agreements.

[2]Reasonable constraints, however, may be applied in emergency circumstances involving self-defense, public safety, or the prevention of serious criminal acts.

[3]A small number of senior officers are entitled to be treated identically to "diplomatic agents."

[4]Note that consular residences are sometimes located within the official consular premises. In such cases, *only* the official office space is protected from police entry.

May be Subpoenaed as Witness	May be Prosecuted	Recognized Family Member
No	No	Same as sponsor (full immunity & inviolability).
No	No	Same as sponsor (full immunity & inviolability).
Yes	No — for official acts. Otherwise, Yes[1]	No immunity or inviolability.[1]
No — for official acts. Testimony may not be compelled in any case.	No — for official acts. Otherwise, Yes[1]	No immunity or inviolability.[1]
No — for official acts. Yes, in all other cases.	No — for official acts. Otherwise, Yes	No immunity or inviolability.
No — for official acts. Yes, in all other cases.	No — for official acts. Otherwise, Yes[1]	No immunity or inviolability.[1]
Yes[3]	No — for official acts. Otherwise, Yes[3]	No immunity or inviolability.
No	No	Same as sponsor (full immunity & inviolability).
Yes	No — for official acts. Otherwise, Yes	No immunity or inviolability.

during or prior to the period during which such person enjoys criminal immunity in the United States. This jurisdictional bar is, however, not a perpetual benefit for such person. With the exception of immunity for official acts (which subsists indefinitely), criminal immunity expires upon the termination of the diplomatic or consular tour of the individual enjoying such immunity, including a reasonable period of time for such person to depart the U.S. territory. Thereafter, if the law enforcement authorities of the United States can obtain personal jurisdiction over a person alleged to have committed criminal acts in the United States, normal prosecution may go forward. This assumes, of course, that the case against such individual has been adequately developed at the time of the alleged action and that any applicable statute of limitations has not run. Obviously, careful and complete police work is required at the time of the alleged crime in order to lay the basis for such delayed prosecution, and it is important that the charges against such person be pushed as far as possible in the U.S. judicial system in order to lay the basis for such prosecution. Obtaining an indictment, information, or arrest warrant, even though they would be without immediate legal effect, would lay the basis for a prosecution at a later date. Moreover, the existence of an outstanding arrest warrant may be entered into the records of the U.S. immigration authorities and thus serve to bar the subsequent issuance of a U.S. visa permitting such person to enter the United States.

It also should be kept in mind that persons who once resided in the United States in a status affording criminal immunity may later return for pleasure or otherwise under conditions affording them no criminal immunity. Additionally, in the case of serious crimes and with respect to foreign countries with which the United States enjoys an extradition relationship, it is not precluded under international law that international extradition may be effected.

E

Excerpt from Foreign and Commonwealth Office Memorandum, 6 June 1984

The following is excerpted from evidence presented to the Foreign Affairs Committee on 20 June 1984. It is in answer to the question: "What provisions of the Vienna Convention are regarded by Her Majesty's Government as ambiguous or as raising particular problems of interpretation or implementation?"

Answer

19. *Article 3(e)* refers to the development of cultural relations between the sending and the receiving state. We do not interpret this as meaning that we are obliged to accept cultural centres and institutes as premises of the mission. Some countries dispute this view. Acceptance of such buildings as premises would lead to considerable cost to the Exchequer, since buildings accepted as premises of a mission are entitled to diplomatic rating relief. (See comment of Article 34(b) below.)

20. *Article 22.2* refers to the special duty of the receiving state to take all appropriate steps to protect the premises of a mission. This provision sometimes gives rise to difficulties of application: for example where the Government could not have known in advance of a particular threat, or where a mission has failed to take adequate steps to protect the security of its own premises against intruders.

21. *Article 25* states that the receiving state shall accord full facilities for the performance of the functions of a mission. This vague obligation has been interpreted by some missions as obliging HMG to provide them with extensive parking facilities in Central London – an interpretation which we do not accept.

22. *Article 27.3* states that the diplomatic bag shall not be opened or detained. Some states argue that this Article excludes the electronic scanning of a bag as being a form of constructive opening. On the other hand it may be argued that the Convention stops short of according "inviolability" to the bag and that the negotiators who were fully conscious of the dangers of abuse did not intend to exclude external examination by equipment or by dogs as some kind of safeguard for the receiving state.

Source: House of Commons, Foreign Affairs Committee, *The Abuse of Diplomatic Immunities and Privileges*, Report with an Annex, together with the Proceedings of the Committee; Minutes of Evidence Taken on 20 June and 2 and 18 July in the last Session of Parliament; and Appendices, London, 12 Dec. 1984, pp. 4–5.

23. The interpretation of *Article 31(a)* dealing with immunity in relation to private immovable property, and *Article 34(b)*, dealing with exceptions to relief from taxes and rates [property taxes – *ed.*] has caused difficulties of interpretation as regards principal private residences. It is however for a court of law, and not for the FCO, to determine whether a diplomat is entitled to immunity in any particular case; and there have been several reported English cases on Article 31.1(a).

24. *Article 36.1* refers to exemption from customs duties "in accordance with such laws and regulations" as the receiving state may adopt. This reference is normally intrepreted as a justification for quantitative restrictions imposed on cars, spirits and tobacco products. We have recently tightened up our restrictions on cars. Some missions have found these restrictions hard to accept.

25. The terms "members of their families forming part of their respective households" in Article 37.1 has caused some problems of interpretation. The Vienna Conference failed to agree on a definition of the term and it is for each state to apply a reasonable interpretation of it. The practice applied in the UK has not been generally challenged but individual cases such as adult students in their twenties living away from home give rise to difficulty.

26. There is no satisfactory definition of "permanently resident" in *Article 38.1* (and elsewhere in the Convention). Some diplomats stay in London for many years, particularly those married to British nationals. The UK have over the years evolved a consistent practice, set out in a Note to Missions of 27 January 1969 (text at Annex B) which has not been generally challenged, but individual case still give rise to difficulty.

27. We know that some diplomats engage in business activities in direct contravention of *Article 42*. We have no powers to prevent this, except by the extreme sanction of declaring them *persona non grata*.

28. Some states interpret the wording of *Article 45(a)* as meaning that the premises of a mission continue to be inviolable even after a break in diplomatic relations. We do not share this view.

F

Statement by Selwa Roosevelt, Chief of Protocol, before the Senate Committee on Foreign Relations, 5 August 1987

I appear here today pursuant to Chairman [Claiborne] Pell's invitation to the Department of State to submit its views on S. 1437, introduced by Senator Helms. I am responsible for the accreditation of foreign government personnel in the United States. By virtue of their status as members of diplomatic missions, consular posts, and international organizations, they are entitled to certain privileges and immunities.

Diplomatic Immunity: Background and Purposes

I will begin by discussing immunity and briefly explaining its purpose. Diplomatic immunity is a fundamental principle of international law under which certain foreign officials are not subject to the jurisdiction of local courts or other authorities for official or personal activities. The reason for immunity is simple and basic: it is to assure that diplomatic representatives are able to carry out the official business of their governments without undue influence or interference from the host country. It enables them to work in an environment of freedom, independence, and security. It was not designed to benefit individuals but rather to ensure the efficient performance of the functions of the mission.

Diplomatic immunity has its roots in antiquity. In our country, statutes extending immunity to diplomats were first enacted by the Congress in 1790. The customary international law of diplomatic immunity was later codified in 1961 when the Vienna Convention on Diplomatic Relations was drafted. This treaty entered into force for the United States in 1972. In 1978, the Diplomatic Relations Act repealed the 1790 status and established the Vienna convention as the definitive U.S. law on the subject. The corresponding law governing consular immunity is the Vienna Convention on Consular Relations of 1963. I have attached to my statement a chart which shows the degree of immunity accorded to personnel of diplomatic missions and consular posts [see p. 248].

Having given this background, I want to make very clear that the Department of State abhors any wrong-doing on the part of persons entitled to immunity. I am not here to defend the indefensible, that is, the unlawful acts of persons having immunity. The serious abuses of those immunities – although rare – which have brought this matter to your attention concern me deeply, and I have worked hard during my 5 years as Chief of Protocol to institute a more effective response to instances of diplomatic crime. I

Source: "Diplomatic Immunity and U.S. Interests," Current Policy No. 993, U.S. Department of State, Bureau of Public Affairs. Washington, D.C., August 1987.

have established a reputation in the diplomatic community for toughness. I cannot overemphasize how strongly I feel and have always felt about this issue. At the same time, we have to bring rational thinking to this subject. We must weigh extreme remedial measures against the grave injury that those measures could cause to U.S. interests.

Concern for U.S. Interests Abroad

With all due respect, we cannot support this proposal for a most elemental reason: it would be detrimental to U.S. interests abroad. Regardless how grievous these matters may be, our own national interest must take precedence over any other consideration.

In a world where discord and disagreement are prevalent in relations among states, the principle of immunity is something the community of nations has agreed upon. We are an honorable nation; we are not an Iran. We have set our signature on a treaty. Enactment of this bill would place the United States in violation of its international obligations. We do not believe that our government, to which so many others look for guidance, should abrogate its responsibility under international law.

If the U.S. Government unilaterally alters its treaty obligation, we surely will invite more harmful reciprocal action. Let's consider what might happen if similar legislation were passed in other countries. The bill would eliminate immunity for crimes of violence, defined as "the use, attempted use or threatened use of physical force against the person or property of another." This is a large category of crimes. Other countries might respond by eliminating immunity even more broadly.

Similarly, the terms "reckless driving", "drug trafficking," and "driving under the influence of alcohol or drugs" might be interpreted broadly by other countries. In addition, even if another country eliminated immunity for precisely the same crimes that the bill would cover, Americans still would face unequal treatment. Those serving in countries with similar legislation could be arrested, detained, and questioned until the matter was fully adjudicated. In the United States, persons might be free on bail pending trial, but in another country, they might be held for months.

Once the floodgates are open, other governments may not mirror this bill in the response they make. They could go beyond the measures proposed by the bill, for example, by limiting the immunities of diplomatic agents. Or they might choose to keep intact the immunity of administrative and technical staff for violent crimes but eliminate their immunity for other crimes, such as espionage.

The language of the proposed legislation covers only members of the administrative and technical staff and the service staff of diplomatic missions and consular employees. Persons not affected would be diplomatic agents, members of their families, and family members of the administrative and technical staffs of embassies.

Based on a review of our files for a recent 12-month period and a review of the Ashman-Trescott book, *Diplomatic Crime*, we find that only two incidents would have been addressed by this legislation. In light of the fact that only two people would have been "brought to justice" had this legislation been in force previously, we ask whether its passage, undermining longstanding international convention, would really serve our best interest, especially when you consider that so many Americans and their dependents are serving overseas?

The members of the administrative and technical staff of an embassy must have full criminal immunity in order to perform their jobs effectively. These personnel perform tasks fundamental to the operation of the embassy. Many of them, including communicators who transmit encoded messages and secretaries who type the missions' classified documents, engage in very sensitive work. They and their families could be subjected to the same pressures that diplomats face. We cannot take great comfort in the full immunity of the ambassador, of the FBI legal attache, of a military attache, or of the personnel of other agencies engaged throughout the world in such sensitive work as fighting terrorism and drugs, if we know that those who do their clerical work and transmit their classified material back to Washington could be interrogated and jailed by hostile receiving-state authorities.

The Need for Immunity

If the intent of the bill is also to reduce the immunity of family members of diplomats and family members of the administrative and technical staff – as we have been led to believe informally – we cannot support the proposal.

Under the Vienna Convention on Diplomatic Relations, members of the family of a diplomatic agent have full criminal immunity, as do members of the administrative and technical staff of a mission and their families. Lower level members of embassy staffs have criminal immunity for their official acts. In addition, under the Vienna Convention on Consular Relations, consular employees have criminal immunity for acts performed in the exercise of consular functions. These immunities, which serve important objectives, all would be curtailed if the bill were enacted.

We believe complete immunity from criminal jurisdiction assured to diplomats is fundamental to diplomatic relations. Diplomats could not perform their duties if they faced criminal liability under local law for normal performance of their jobs or if they could be harassed by the receiving state bringing false charges. Moreover, the diplomat's own immunity would be meaningless if his family residing with him did not have the same immunities. The threat of actions against family members could be used to intimidate the diplomat.

Can you imagine the specter of the American Ambassador's spouse involved in an automobile accident being taken away by the police in certain countries – to be held in jail according to local statute? Or worse, being held on trumped-up charges? Think of the implications. Of course, we couldn't respond in kind because our system does not operate that way.

The U.S. judicial system in premised on the rule of law, and many of the potential abuses that I have just described may seem far-fetched to an American. But U.S. personnel from a variety of agencies serve overseas in countries where the risks that I have just outlined are very real indeed. If the

United States were to reduce the immunities of diplomatic personnel here, I am certain that foreign states would reciprocate by restricting the immunities accorded to U.S. personnel. Our embassies in hostile foreign countries will not be able to do their jobs effectively if the children of diplomats could be imprisoned as a means to pressure them and if the members of the administrative and technical staff face the risk of imprisonment.

So far I have only addressed the effect of the bill on our personnel at embassies. But the bill would also affect some personnel at consulates. Although the proposed legislation would not affect consular officers, it would affect consular employees, who perform in consulates the same functions that administrative and technical staff perform in embassies. The immunity from jurisdiction accorded to consular officers and consular employees by the Vienna Convention on Consular Relations, as I noted before, is much more limited than the regime which applies to diplomats. Consular immunity applies only to acts performed in the exercise of consular functions, i.e., to "official acts". When a case is brought, the court determines whether the acts were performed in the exercise of consular functions. Family members have no official acts and have no immunity. Thus, consular officers are now subject to jurisdiction with respect to most "crimes of violence", as, indeed, are consular employees. While consular officers and employees may raise their functional immunity as a defense in connection with a speeding charge or accident, this itself is not a bar to judicial action. The courts would determine whether or not such a defense would apply.

Thus, even with respect to the more limited immunity accorded consular employees, the bill would place the United States in violation of the Vienna convention and would put U.S. personnel at risk of reciprocal measures. There may, moreover, be instances in which a consular officer is charged with a violent crime for an act performed in the exercise of consular functions. For example, a hostile country might charge a U.S. consular officer with assault if he took measures to defend himself against physical attack by a disgruntled visa applicant. The United States should be entitled to assert consular immunity to prevent the case from going forward. This measure, if enacted, could provoke reciprocal legislation which would bar such asserting of immunity.

At this point, I should point out that there are countries with which the United States has concluded treaties extending broader immunities for consular personnel. The United States has entered into such agreements with the Soviet Union, the People's Republic of China (P.R.C.), Bulgaria, the German Democratic Republic (G.D.R.), Hungary, Poland, and Romania. A similar agreement also exists with the Philippines. (Bulgaria, the G.D.R., and Romania have no consular posts in the United States.) Thus, our consular employees in such countries as the U.S.S.R. and the P.R.C. have full criminal immunity, and we are obligated to provide the same immunities to consular employees of those countries. The proposed legislation, therefore, would violate these bilateral agreements in addition to violating the Vienna conventions.

Recent Steps

While the Department of State cannot support the proposed legislation, which would call into question the entire framework of diplomatic immunity, we have taken a variety of steps to curtail abuses of diplomatic immunity that are wholly consistent with international law.

Incidentally, it may be of interest to the committee that the British Foreign Office instituted a full review of the Vienna convention in the aftermath of the fatal shooting of a policewoman by a gunman in the Libyan Embassy and the attempted abduction of a Nigerian exile. The British concluded that it would be wrong to amend the Vienna convention as the solution to the abuse of diplomatic immunity but, instead, implemented a firmer policy in the application of the convention.

I should like to take this opportunity to inform the committee of recent steps we have taken.

Barring Reentry. Some years ago, I initated a system to bar the reentry into the United States of serious offenders entitled to criminal immunity at the time of expulsion. The names of the offenders are entered into the Department's worldwide automated visa lookout system so that should an offender seek another visa, the application is held up until the Department's advice can be obtained. The names also are given to the central office of the Immigration Service to alert ports of entry that arrivals of such persons arc to be reported immediately to the Department.

We have found, however, that the system was not perfect and that, in at least three cases, the persons expelled reentered the United States. To prevent any other such occurrence, we will ensure that the diplomatic visa is canceled before an alleged offender leaves the country. Should the person leave before this is done, we will inform the mission concerned that the principal alien cannot be replaced until the visa has been canceled.

Police Guidance. In March [1987] the Department published updated and more comprehensive written guidance for law enforcement officers on the handling of incidents involving foreign diplomatic and consular personnel. It has been distributed nationwide. I am happy to make this booklet available to the committee. As you will see, we have pointed out the necessity for careful and complete police work at the time of the incident in order to lay the basis for possible future prosecution when immunity ceases to exist. In other words we urge that charges be pursued as far as possible in our judicial system. After the offender leaves the United States, the existence of an oustanding arrest warrant may be entered into the records of the immigration authorities. The existence of the warrant and the knowledge that the Federal Government will assist in serving the warrant would deter an offender from attempting to return to the United States.

In the recently publicized Afghan auto case, we learned that New York law enforcement authorities discontinued the investigation on the assumption that the driver was immune. You might be interested to know that neither the U.S. Mission to the United Nations nor the Office of Protocol was consulted in making this determination. However, as soon as the mission learned of this, it asked the police to reopen the investigation. We did this because we believe firmly that in all of these cases, the facts must be brought to light.

CRIMINAL IMMUNITY

DIPLOMATIC				CONSULAR	
Diplomats* (Ambassador, Ministers, Counselors, 1st, 2nd, and 3rd Secretaries, Attaches)	**Administrative and Technical Staff** (Clerks, Typists, Procurement Officers)	**Service Staff** (Drivers, Gardeners, Cooks, Security Guards)	**Personal Servants** (Maids, Butlers)	**Consular Officers** (Consuls General, Consuls, Vice Consuls)	**Consular Employees** (Clerks, Typists)
FULL CRIMINAL IMMUNITY	FULL CRIMINAL IMMUNITY	CRIMINAL IMMUNITY FOR OFFICIAL ACTS ONLY	NO IMMUNITY	CRIMINAL IMMUNITY FOR OFFICIAL ACTS ONLY	CRIMINAL IMMUNITY FOR OFFICIAL ACTS ONLY
Family Members FULL CRIMINAL IMMUNITY	**Family Members** FULL CRIMINAL IMMUNITY	**Family Members** NO IMMUNITY	**Family Members** NO IMMUNITY	**Family Members** NO IMMUNITY	**Family Members** NO IMMUNITY

*This category includes diplomats at the Organization of American States and members of missions to the United Nations and a small number of persons at the World Bank and International Monetary Fund.

By special agreement, on a reciprocal basis, all personnel at the Embassies of the People's Republic of China and the U.S.S.R and members of their families enjoy full criminal immunity.

By special agreement, on a reciprocal basis, personnel and members of their families at the consulates of the following countries enjoy full criminal immunity: Hungary, People's Republic of China, Poland, Philippines, and U.S.S.R.

Parental Responsibility. In particularly egregious cases involving juvenile offenders, I have had the entire family expelled from the United States. This policy ensures that parents will be fully accountable for the acts of their children.

Traffic Offenses. In September 1985 the Department's Office of Foreign Missions instituted a program to monitor traffic violations and increase the observance of traffic laws and regulations. Under the program, the Department assesses points for all traffic violations using the American Association of Motor Vehicle Administrator's standardized point system. The accumulation of eight points during a 2-year period may result in the loss of the privilege to drive in this country. Persons with unpaid parking violations incur one point for each ticket. Speeding violations are assessed at two or four points depending upon the rate of speed, and persons driving while intoxicated are assessed eight points. Up to this time, 15 drivers' licenses have been permanently suspended. We do not permit a member of the diplomatic community who has operated a motor vehicle under the influence of alcohol to operate a motor vehicle in the United States again. The program has had a salutary effect on the driving habits of privileged personnel.

Firearms. In May 1986, we reissued a circular on the subject of firearms, pointing out that failure to comply with local laws and regulations pertaining to firearms will subject the offender to expulsion.

Identification Documents. Recently, the Office of Protocol began issuing newly designed identification documents to all embassy personnel entitled to any degree of immunity. The cards identify the individual, state the type of immunity which he has, and provide phone numbers to call 24 hours a day if a law enforcement official has questions. In cases where immunity is limited, the cards state that the bearer is not immune from arrest. Similar cards will be issued to consular officers and employees next year.

Definition of "Members of the Family". The Vienna convention requires the parties to extend privileges and immunities to family members forming part of the household but does not define family members. In May 1986, we informed the missions that we would set age limits beyond which the Department on longer would extend privileges and immunities to dependent children. The cutoff age is 21, unless the child is a full-time student, in which case the age limitation is 23. This step has reduced the number of persons entitled to privileges and immunities.

We are continually reviewing means to reduce the numbers of persons entitled to immunity. For example, we are not obligated by the Vienna convention to extend full immunity to aliens "permanently resident in the

United States''. Accordingly, we propose to terminate privileges and immunities for locally hired members of embassy staffs who have resided in the United States for 10 years or more.

In closing, I wish to express my appreciation for this opportunity to present the Department's views on this sensitive matter. Also, I wish to assure you again that we stand ready to take action in any situation where a person with immunity acts contrary to the law.

G

Statement by the American Foreign Service Association, October 1987

Questions about Immunity

Diplomatic Immunity serves the same function for the Foreign Service employee as does the policeman's bullet-proof vest: it allows a vital public service to be performed in areas of great risk. Without it the United States would be foolish to send representatives to the places where it most needs them. Thus we are greatly troubled by recent proposals to radically change this valuable and proven system.

The most recent of these has been put forth by Senator Jesse Helms. Responding to criticism of the current immunity arrangements agreed to in the Vienna Convention of 1961, the senator would remove protection from family and staff members of foreign diplomats posted here who are charged with drug trafficking, violent crimes, or reckless driving. We do not argue that these people should be free to break our laws and get away with it by hiding behind immunity, but that another way should be found to deal with the problem that does not weaken the protection of immunity for our people abroad – as would surely occur as reciprocity is invoked around the world.

Senator Helms's proposal would not affect the immunity of consular and diplomatic officials themselves, but our communicators and secretaries, not to mention our spouses and children, would be subject to legal and political systems that are often sharply at variance with ours or are controlled by states that could use them to harass and intimidate us. Without immunity, what is to prevent an unfriendly country from arresting and imprisoning the spouse of an official who delivers a diplomatic rebuke? Must we return to the days when the messenger who brought unpleasant news had his head sent back home on a plate?

Under the convention, the United States may not take judicial action against a diplomat. But that does not mean that he or she must go unpunished or that justice must be denied the victim. The State Department can declare the perpetrator persona non grata, urge the embassy to waive his or her immunity, or ask the sending state to compensate the victim. In addition, U.S. law has been updated so that foreign missions are now required to insure their drivers for liability, and the State Department can revoke their licenses. A new bill would go even further by creating a system in which victims could be compensated through a special fund when other procedures fail.

We understand the anguish of those who have been unfortunate victims of criminal acts perpetrated by foreign representatives in our country.

Source: Foreign Service Journal (Washington, D.C.), October 1987, p. 3.

Diplomatic immunity certainly should not be used as a shield to permit criminal actions. But neither should the remedy be worse than the illness. AFSA is presenting its own proposals to address these concerns while opposing Senator Helms's approach, which will surely limit our ability to do our jobs and put us at risk.

Perry Shankle, President

H

Memorandum by the Trade Union Side of the Diplomatic Service

Diplomatic Immunities and Privileges (DIP 10)

Introduction

1. The Trade Union Side of the Diplomatic Service Whitley Council were pleased to receive an invitation from the Foreign Affairs Select Committee to submit evidence for their enquiry into diplomatic immunities and privileges. This is a subject of close concern to members of the Diplomatic Service in their working lives in British missions overseas.

General Considerations

2. The preamble to the 1961 Vienna convention on Diplomatic Relations recalls that peoples of all nations from ancient times have recognised the status of diplomatic agents. It subsequently points out that the purpose of the privileges and immunities conferred by the Convention is not to benefit individuals but to ensure the efficient performance of the functions of diplomatic missions as representing States. We fully agree with this. The provisions of the Vienna Convention do not exist so as to grant the staff of diplomatic services a particular personal status, but so as to ensure that they can carry out their duties without interference, including in our case, the protection of British subjects overseas. Relaxation of the strict provisions of the Convention might make it easier to prevent existing abuses by a small minority of diplomatic agents. But it would penalise the majority by exposing them to arbitrary harassment, detention or other abuse by a host government, either in retaliation for acts by a sending State or because the existing rules of conduct were no longer taken so seriously. We could then be faced with the kind of unacceptable action against innocent people which any change in the Convention would be designed to prevent.

3. Happily nearly all governments honour their obligations to diplomatic agents. But there are sufficient examples of severe abuse of the Vienna Convention to convince us that it is essential for the agreed international framework to remain in force. The ordeal suffered by American diplomats in Tehran in 1979–80 is well known, and our own people in Tehran came under threat at the same time. The most notorious recent case affecting British diplomatic agents was the sacking of the British mission in Peking in 1967 and the physical assaults on staff. In the Stalin era British and other

---

Source: Appendix 3 to the Minutes of Evidence, taken on 20 June and 2 and 18 July [1984], House of Commons, Foreign Affairs Committee, *The Abuse of Diplomatic Immunities and Privileges*, 12 December 1984, op. cit., pp. 60–61.

western diplomats were not infrequently named in show trials. It is not difficult to imagine what could have happened to them if they had not been protected by the diplomatic immunities subsequently codified in the Vienna Convention.

Specific Articles of the Vienna Convention

4. We should like to comment specifically on the implications of certain articles of the Vienna Convention for our staff overseas. The list is illustrative, not comprehensive: all the provisions of the Convention may be relevant from time to time.

Article 7

This article states that a sending State may freely appoint the members of staff of their mission, with the exception of the Head of Post. We would be concerned at any proposal to give the receiving State the right to require a *curriculum vitae* of new members of staff and to accept or reject them in advance, beyond the right already conferred in Article 9 (paragraph 5 below). This could lead to staff being rejected because they had served in a country of which the host government did not approve, and deprive an officer for this and other reasons of a posting for which his qualifications and personal circumstances well suited him.

Article 27

This prescribes the inviolability of the official correspondence of a diplomatic mission. If the correspondence of certain missions in London became subject to search, retaliation would be inevitable. It is important for the morale, efficiency and security of our staff overseas, particularly in difficult and dangerous posts like Beirut, to be confident of remaining in confidential written contact with home base. Disruption or confiscation of correspondence, apart from the damage to the work of the mission, would feel to staff like the cutting off of a lifeline. It would also endanger the security of individuals, since the collection of personal information is a well-established technique of hostile intelligence services.

Articles 29, 30 and 31

These articles, providing immunity from arrest and criminal jurisdiction (unless waived by the sending State) and the safeguarding of residences of diplomatic agents, are the most important for the protection of our staff overseas. We are conscious of the public criticism in Britain of the immunity enjoyed by diplomats here, arising not just from the recent Anglo/Libyan crisis but also from serious cases over a number of years, for example of driving while under the influence of drink and drugs. Immunity from prosecution for parking offences is another contentious problem. Our own staff overseas therefore take particular care, in accordance with Article 41 of the Vienna Convention, to respect the laws and regulations of receiving States, and the same applies to our allies. Exceptions are rare. But any relaxation of

Articles 29 to 31 would risk action against our representatives abroad, most likely in countries where we would have little faith in the conduct of the police and legal proceedings. Without the universally agreed provisions of the Vienna Convention, it would be difficult to give us the protection to do the job properly. Exceptions agreed between a limited number of States would not be an answer: political circumstances might change and cause dangers not envisaged at the time of the agreement.

Existing Constraints on Diplomatic Agents

5. We deplore abuses of diplomatic immunity and recognise that recent events have called into question whether existing procedures are adequate. But it is important that any resulting changes of policy do not undermine the ability of our own Diplomatic Service personnel to operate effectively, or put them personally at risk as hostages for the acts or policies of the British Government. We suggest that a remedy may lie in the existing provisions of the Vienna Convention. Article 9 already allows a receiving State to declare a diplomat *persona non grata*, even before he has arrived. Article 11 allows a receiving State to limit the size of a mission. Personal baggage, but not the diplomatic bag itself, may be inspected in the presence of its owner under the provisions of Article 36. These measures could be effective if required as a last resort. They too are likely to cause retaliation. But they should not risk the kind of serious action against our representatives which Articles 29 to 31 are designed to prevent.

Conclusion

6. The Vienna Convention on Diplomatic Relations, which defines the immunities and privileges to be accorded to diplomatic agents, is essential for the efficient performance of our tasks overseas and for the safety of diplomatic services staff and their families. Recent experience has shown that there is a real threat to our representatives, arising solely out of their position as agents of government: we do not think we can afford to relax the safeguards.

I

Memorandum by the Diplomatic Service Wives Association, 19 June 1984

Diplomatic Immunities and Privileges (DIP 14)

1. The Diplomatic Service Wives Association welcomes the opportunity to submit evidence to the Foreign Affairs Select Committee in its enquiry into diplomatic immunities and privileges. We were invited to give our view on "the practical advantages (or disadvantages) of the immunities and privileges granted under the 1961 Vienna Convention, variations in the practice of receiving countries in interpreting the Convention, and any difficulties which Diplomatic Service families might expect if certain of the Convention's provisions were to be varied either by unilateral or bilateral agreement".

2. The Diplomatic Service Wives Association represents spouses of permanent and seconded home-based UK Diplomatic Service personnel of all ranks at home and abroad. They are all likely to accompany Diplomatic Service officers who are liable to serve in posts abroad, which vary widely in size, scope and conditions from, for example, large posts such as Washington, Moscow and Lagos, medium size posts such as Dar-es-Salaam, Vienna and Kuala Lumpur, to small posts as different as Georgetown, Guyana, Ulan Bator and Brazzaville. Questions which concern the safety and well-being of the dependants and families of HM Diplomatic Service are the particular concern of the Association, which constitutes their only independent collective voice.

3. The 1961 Vienna Convention on Diplomatic Relations does not mention spouses specifically. Article 37 however extends the immunities and privileges specified in Articles 29 to 36 to "members of the family of a diplomatic agent forming part of his household if they are not nationals of the receiving State". Qualified privileges and immunities from civil and administrative jurisdiction are also extended under Article 37 to members of the administrative and technical staff of a mission and to "members of their families forming part of their respective households, if they are not nationals of or permanently resident in the receiving State".

4. Differing concepts of "family" around the world made it impossible at the time of the Convention to agree a definition of what exactly was meant by the phrase "members of the family. . .forming part of their household". States therefore retain some flexibility about which members of a family are entitled to immunities and privileges, and settle difficult or unusual cases by agreement with individual missions. In receiving diplo-

---

Source: Appendix 4, House of Commons, Foreign Affairs Committee, *The Abuse of Diplomatic Immunities and Privileges,* 12 December 1984, op. cit., pp. 61–63.

matic families the UK generally interprets the provisions to include the spouse and children under eighteen, together in exceptional circumstances with certain other persons such as the parent of a diplomat living with him, a family member who fulfils the social duties of a hostess, or adult student children residing with the diplomat on vacations. DSWA has no knowledge of any restrictive interpretation of the terms causing difficulty to wives or families of diplomats abroad, although husbands have sometimes found their privileges or immunities questioned.

5. The extension of immunities and privileges to spouses and families has long been established. It derives from the need to protect diplomats from harassment particularly by means of "framed" or politically motivated legal proceedings, so that they can do the job they are sent to do, whatever the situation in the receiving State. Families are regarded essentially as extensions of the persons of the diplomats themselves. The protection of diplomatic dependents has therefore been regarded as quite as necessary as that of the diplomats, to ensure the diplomats' independence and their ability to carry on their governments' business however unpopular their country, their mission or their instructions.

6. Under the Vienna Convention, therefore, spouses and affected children of accredited diplomats are not liable to arrest or detention, their homes, their property (including most strikingly their cars) and their papers are inviolable, they are immune from the criminal jurisdiction of the receiving State and from the civil and administrative jurisdiction, and they are immune from the taxes and customs duties of the receiving State. Diplomatic dependants do not however enjoy immunity from the civil and administrative jurisdiction of the receiving State in respect of any action relative to any professional or commercial activity.

7. The effect of these immunities in practice is to ensure that in States where difficult conditions or tense or hostile relations prevail, families are protected from being used as a means of indirect pressure or intimidation of either individual diplomats or the British government. Without such protection it is not difficult to imagine situations where governments and diplomats might be vulnerable through wives and children perhaps being attacked or held hostage.

8. An advantage of the immunities can be to help make life tolerable in countries where difficult physical, economic or political conditions prevail. They allow some latitude for the preservation of the way of life usual at home. The family is spared having to master the local laws on taxation or residence permits for example. Such advantages are, however, an incidental, if logical, consequence of the immunities.

9. Articles 29–36 are essentially safeguards enabling diplomatic relations between States to be carried on despite adverse conditions, though they are open to abuse. The British government requires high standards of behaviour from its diplomats and their families abroad. Article 41 of the Vienna Convention obliges those protected by immunities and privileges to respect the laws and regulations of the receiving State and our families abroad are

under instructions not to abuse their status by, for example, non-payment of parking fines. For any serious abuses the UK government can waive the immunity from prosecution of a diplomat or member of his family, or can send an offender home.

10. The only significant respect in which the DSWA is aware of major variations in the interpretation of the Convention as it affects their members is in how it affects their opportunities to take paid employment abroad. The family of a diplomatic agent is not covered by the terms of Article 42 which prohibits a diplomatic agent from practising any professional or commercial activity for personal profit. Interpretation and practice in this area varies. The UK takes a generous view and allows members of diplomatic families in the UK to work. Some countries, such as the US and Canada, insist on reciprocal arrangements before allowing dependants to take up employment. Others such as Switzerland, Belgium, Spain, Federal Republic of Germany, France and Zimbabwe require dependants of diplomats to have work permits or official permission to take up paid employment. But in general the clear understanding in the Convention that family members are not in principle excluded from professional or commercial activity or employment has been helpful. Before the Vienna Convention the uncertainty over their immunity on professional matters (such as fraud or medical negligence) was often used as a reason for refusing permission.

11. DSWA recognises that the recent appalling events in London have raised important questions about the way the provisions of the Vienna Convention are interpreted. It would be profoundly uneasy, however, about any moves which could have the effect of weakening the protection afforded by Articles 29 to 36 of the Convention to our diplomats and their families abroad. The principle of reciprocity which underlies all immunities has perhaps nowhere been more evident than in the procedures attending the evacuation of Diplomatic Service personnel and their families in safety from Libya. Once any qualification affecting the immunities and protection of foreign diplomats in London is made, then the immunity and protection afforded to our officers and families abroad will inevitably be similarly qualified. We are a stable country ruled by due process of law. Such will not be the case in all the countries where our diplomats serve, accompanied by their wives and families. The risks involved in departing from a strict interpretation of the Vienna Convention seem to us likely to fall disproportionately on our diplomats and their families and we would prefer them not to be run.

12. Variations of the Convention's provisions by bilateral agreements seem to us to involve the possibility, by abrogating its universality, of undermining the credibility of the Convention, and likely to lead to confusion in its application. Moreover the circumstances in which a bilaterally agreed derogation from the Convention seemed appropriate could change with a change of regime or other circumstances; yet withdrawal from the agreement could be seen as a political act in itself, and therefore impossible to undertake without risk. The likelihood of multilateral agreement to amend-

ment of the Convention within a reasonable period seems small. The rules are too generally accepted as the basic framework of international relations.

13. Whilst it may sometimes be abused by some governments or individuals from some countries, and whilst its provisions may only be essential in some States some of the time, the Vienna Convention on Diplomatic Relations would rapidly be undermined if it were not universal or came to be seen as discriminating between "good" and "bad" States. Although it may on occasions be subject to abuse it constitutes, in essence, vital protection for British Diplomatic Service officers carrying out their duties abroad and, by extension, their families. We would very much regret any alterations which might weaken the protection it affords.

19 June 1984

J

A Postscript from the Author:
Advice to Junior Foreign Service Officers Concerning Diplomatic and Consular Immunities

The goal of these personal suggestions is, first, to help you to support your country's policy and to enhance its image in matters of diplomatic privileges and immunities. Secondly, it is to help you do your job well as an individual career Foreign Service officer. Since my own experience has been in the U.S. Foreign Service, I write here with U.S. references. Readers from other countries can substitute their own appropriate references.

The tactical key to long-term success in this field, as in so many other aspects of diplomacy, is to strive to win without triumphing. And if the facts of a situation put you on the defensive, and you cannot win, be a reasonable, dignified loser, avoid drama, and make the other side's victory as inconspicuous as possible.

As part of your early professional training, take time to read carefully the two Vienna Conventions of 1961 and 1963. Then turn to *Satow's Guide to Diplomatic Practice* and read the relevant chapters – in the latest (5th) edition, chapters 14 through 19, with chapter 27 on consuls' immunities and chapter 40 on those of international organizations.

Before going to a new post, particularly if you are to be in charge or if you are to be deputy to the officer-in-charge or a political officer or a consul, you will have a schedule of Washington consultations and preparations. After you have called at the Office of the Assistant Secretary and after you've had a talk or a luncheon meeting with the officer in charge of your country's affairs, you will confer with other interested offices and agencies. Include in your rounds a call on the Legal Adviser's Office. Don't just touch base there, but mention what you've read and ask their suggestions on recent developments with respect to immunity. What is the general situation in your country of assignment? How are diplomats and consuls and their premises treated there? Have there been any interesting cases involving U.S. or other nations' diplomats, the A.I.D. mission or Peace Corps or USIA and its premises? Were there any relevant bilateral agreements or significant reservations when the country adhered to the Vienna Conventions? Are there any interesting issues of reciprocity in U.S. official relations? Is there anything distinctive in the country's attitude to foreign diplomats or the legal status of foreigners in general? Some of these questions might well be raised with the Protocol Office and the Office of Foreign Missions.

Take with you to your post a copy of the handy five-page leaflet on "privileges and immunities" issued by the Department of State's Overseas Briefing Center in February 1986 (*What Do I Do Now?* Department of State Publication 9296, Dept. and Foreign Service 325, Supplement, Revised February 1986). Have your spouse and your older children read it (it has a column on "family members"), and, if necessary, ask them a few questions about it to indicate your own interest. You might also take a copy of the Office of Protocol/Office of Foreign Missions booklet *Guidance for Law Enforcement Officers: Personal Rights and Immunities of Foreign Diplomatic and Consular Personnel*, published in February 1988. That can be a succinct indication of U.S. policy and practice, in case issues of reciprocity arise at your post.

When you arrive at your post, you'll meet all the staff and be briefed and oriented. Among the practical points to cover, especially if it's a large post, is to find out who handles the subject of immunity. It might be a function spread among the political section, the administrative office, and the consul general. When making calls and meeting local officials, take note of the officers in charge of protocol at the ministry of foreign affairs and perhaps spot some active subordinate in that office. Make his acquaintance, know his office and home telephone number, and build a bridge of friendly contact in case you ever need to use it.

From the day of your arrival, respect local laws. Do not, for example, commit traffic offenses or park illegally. Don't let your family or servants do so. Even if other officers at your mission or at other nations' missions are not being careful and punctilious, don't follow their example. Don't be brusque with police or hurry offhandedly past guards, especially when the atmosphere is tense. Turn a pleasant face to persons in authority, and show you know they have a job to do and you have an important job too.

If you're unlucky, you may find yourself threatened with a violation of your diplomatic immunity. For example, the police may try to arrest you or to search your car or to enter your house for an investigation or they may halt you at an unexpected checkpoint on your way to your office.

If that happens, be calm but firm and determined. Do not say or do anything which concedes your immunity. As you know, under State Department rules, neither the individual nor the mission can waive immunity without informing the department and securing its consent to the waiver. State clearly that you are a diplomat or consul, show identification as such, if possible. Know the words, even if you are unacquainted with much of the local language, for "diplomat," "embassy" or "consulate," "immunity," "freedom from arrest," and be able to use them even if the rest of your explanation has to be in English. Know these key words in French also if you are in many parts of Africa or the Middle East.

Without seeming to yield and without pressing direct questions, try to size up your situation. Does the action which is threatening to occur seem to be based on any reasonable grounds? For example, are they halting you for your own safety? In that case, you might ask to be escorted on your way to official business. Are your threateners inexperienced? Perhaps a request to see their supervisors may clear up your rights as a diplomat.

Be patient. Adopt a tone of understanding and of trying to help them avoid an incident or being overruled later by their superiors. If they are stubborn, be sure to invite them to make a phone call to their office and offer to call your office. "Let us clarify my rights. I'm confident you'll come to agree, etc."

If you're very unlucky, in spite of your best efforts, you may be hustled off or a sullen crowd may gather or other ominous signs may build up. Keep your position simple: "I am an American diplomat and must serve my ambassador (or consul general), (use his name). I have immunity to do my work for him. Your government will agree to that if you can ask a higher authority. I *insist* that you let me call my ambassador's office." As you are saying this, note the time and location and the identity, as exactly as possible, of the people who are threatening your dignity and inviolability. Good reporting uses such observations.

The probability – and you should appear to be confident of it – is that you will be released and assisted, willingly or grudgingly, to maintain your freedom and inviolability and to go your way unhampered. If your words and demeanor are not enough to keep you from being abused or even beaten, then be as brave as your inner resources permit.

If an incident involving diplomatic immunity occurs at your post (e.g., one of your fellow officers is detained or the embassy premises or a diplomatic pouch is violated), you may find yourself in a special meeting on the subject. The senior officers, such as the ambassador, the consul general, and the administrative officer, will probably be wise or at least wary. They will ask questions, and the replies may tend to be general or anecdotal. Do not compete with your seniors along those lines. When your turn comes [or you see a tactful opening], speak briefly, saying for example that this case clearly is (or is not) covered by a specific provision of the Vienna Conventions, which you cite. You recall from department briefings that the department likes to hear about such cases promptly and in detail, and you'd be willing to draft a cable or assist whoever else is assigned to draft one. You will need a couple of hours in which to check facts, find the latest on the status of the case, and a little more about the people involved.

If the senior officers like the sound of your offer and put the ball at your feet, focus your cable on what the department's regional bureau will want to know about the political importance of the case and on what the Legal Adviser's Office, the Protocol Office, and perhaps the Office of Foreign Missions will need. If you are of junior rank it is advisable to incorporate points made by senior officers. Draft the best conclusions possible at that early stage and give at least a couple of proposals for action, in order of preference (e.g., an oral démarche at the Foreign Ministry, more fact collecting, a temperate note, etc.). Clear it with all appropriate embassy divisions, always mentioning the urgency you feel.

If the cable goes out and time passes, return to your normal work but continue to assemble information and ideas on next steps. If the incident is closed locally and satisfactorily, report that good news promptly if you are the one to do so. But if the situation becomes ugly and far-reaching, don't be surprised to be displaced from your role by a senior, possibly the DCM. You may still be useful to him and perhaps be asked to accompany him or the ambassador on a call on the Foreign Minister.

Handling a delicate immunity case with good sense and political flair can also be helpful to your career. But don't be too legalistic, especially if you have legal training, for diplomatic work is traditionally and currently quite different from the law.

BIBLIOGRAPHY OF SUGGESTED READING
(alphabetically by authors within categories)

The Vienna Conventions of 1961 and 1963

Denza, Eileen. *Diplomatic Law: Commentary on the Vienna Convention on Diplomatic Relations.* London: British Institute of International and Comparative Law, 1976; Dobbs Ferry, N.Y.: Oceana Publications, 1976. E. Denza comments on the Vienna Convention of 1961, article by article, with unmatched expertise. She was a key member of the UK delegation to the Vienna Conference and for many years a specialist in the Foreign Office Protocol and International Conferences Department. She analyzes and summarizes the discussion at the conference and the practice of the United Kingdom and some other governments under the convention up to 1976. She manages to give answers in clear, nontechnical language even on subtle points.

Lee, L.T. *Vienna Convention on Consular Relations: With Texts and Commentaries on Vienna Convention on Diplomatic Relations, 1961, United States-Soviet Consular Convention, 1964, Draft European Convention on Consular Functions.* Durham, N.C.: Rule of Law Press, 1966. A detailed scholarly work by a specialist in consular law and practice. In addition to an account of the content and negotiating history of the convention, many interesting topics are briefly explored, such as the relationship of consuls to unrecognized governments (pp. 180–82), to the United Nations (pp. 182–88), and to the solemnization of marriages (pp. 65–67). Part four of the book, "Privileges and Immunities," gives a thorough discussion. The text of the US-Soviet Consular Convention of 1964 is conveniently made available in an appendix (pp. 299–309).

UN Legislative Series. *Laws and Regulations regarding Diplomatic and Consular Privileges and Immunities.* New York: United Nations, 1958. (ST/IEG/SER.B/7.) And *Supplement.* 1963.

Guides to diplomatic practice

Feltham, R.G. *Diplomatic Handbook.* 4th ed. London and New York: Longman, 1982. Chapter 5 (pp. 37–47) of this concise introduction to diplomatic practice, international organizations and law summarizes diplomatic privileges and immunities under the Vienna Convention of 1961 and briefly mentions those of representatives to international organizations and members of special missions.

Gore-Booth, Lord, ed., D. Pakenham, asst. ed. *Satow's Guide to Diplomatic Practice.* 5th ed. London and New York: Longman, 1979. The best single work on diplomatic practice, deservedly famous for its detail and authority. Its chapters on diplomatic privileges and immunities, 14 through 19, plus chapter 27 on consular immunities and chapter 40 on international immunities, are an excellent introduction to their subjects. Some of the strength of this work reflects the assistance the editors received from the Foreign and Commonwealth Relations Office and a number of eminent diplomats, international lawyers, and high officials.

Plischke, Elmer. *Conduct of American Diplomacy.* 3rd ed. Princeton, N.J.: D. Van Nostrand, 1967. A textbook on U.S. government procedures in conducting foreign relations. Chapter 11, pp. 334–69, "Privileges, Immunities and Asylum," is now of historical interest as a picture of the situation in 1974, i.e., only two years after the United States had put the provisions of the Vienna Conventions into force, and long before it had established the Office of Foreign Missions.

Sen, B. *A Diplomat's Handbook of International Law and Practice.* The Hague, London and Boston: Martinus Nijhoff, 1979. A good general work. One State Department expert commended it to this writer as having "lots of information and many interesting questions, but not so strong on answers."

Serres, J. *Manuel pratique de protocole.* New edition. France: Editions de la Bièvre, 1982.

Stuart, Graham H. *American Diplomatic and Consular Practice.* 2nd ed. New York: Appleton-Century-Crofts, 1952. Of continuing historical interest.

Wood, J.R. and J. Serres. *Diplomatic Ceremonial and Protocol.* New York: Columbia University Press, 1979. A guide to the practice of protocol offices, but mainly on ceremonial and etiquette questions.

Diplomatic and international immunities

Ahluwalia, Kuljit. *The Legal Status, Privileges and Immunities of the Specialized Agencies of the United Nations and Certain other International Organizations.* The Hague: Martinus Nijhoff, 1964.

Ashman, C. and P. Trescott. *Outrage: An Investigation into the Abuse of Diplomatic Immunity.* London: W.H. Allen, 1986. A journalistic collection of accounts, sometimes exaggerated, of abuses of diplomatic immunity by diplomats, consuls, and their dependents. These often useful and always readable case stories are interspersed with hasty condemnations of the general system of diplomatic privileges and immunities, but with no reference to its proven functional merits in practice. An American, updated edition under the title *Diplomatic Crime,* published by Acropolis Books of Washington, D.C., appeared in July 1987 and was critically reviewed by Richard Gookin in the *Foreign Service Journal* of January 1988. The review refuted some of the book's material, including its implications of State Department indifference to the problem and to the plight of victims.

Bean, Harold G. *Diplomats and Terrorists II – Overseas Security: Our People Are the Key.* Washington: Institute for the Study of Diplomacy,

Georgetown University, 1987. A practical guide to the programs and policies of the U.S. Government, particularly the State Department, in the difficult field of protecting diplomats and consuls and their premises and homes abroad. The Inman Report of June 1985 is excerpted and its conclusions summarized in an appendix. The author deals with how diplomats can best survive when their personal inviolability is not in practice being enforced by the receiving state.

Cahier, P. *Etude des Accords de siège conclus entre les organisations internationales et les Etats où elles résident.* Milan: A. Giuffrè 1959.

Draper, G.I.A.D. *Civilians and the NATO Status of Forces Agreement: A study of the exercise of criminal jurisdiction over dependents and members of the civilian component under the North Atlantic Treaty Organization Status of Forces Agreement, 1951.* Leyden: A.W. Sijthoff, 1966. A British legal expert makes helpful comparisons between British and American legal principles that should assist the British reader to understand such special American institutions as Supreme Court decisions. He remarks that Britain has had long experience of receiving visiting forces, including World War I and the interwar years with Commonwealth forces, and that Britain's "flexible constitution" has certain advantages in status of force matters.

Duffar, J. *Contribution à l'étude des privilèges et immunités des organisations internationales.* Paris: LGDJ, 1982.

Hardy, Michael. *Modern Diplomatic Law.* Manchester: Manchester University Press, 1968; Dobbs Ferry, N.Y.: Oceana, 1968. A lecture series revised for publication.

Hevener, Natalie Kaufman, editor. *Diplomacy in a Dangerous World: Protection for Diplomats under International Law.* Westview Special Studies in International Relations. Boulder, Colorado: Westview Press, 1986. Thoughtful essays by J.L. Hargrove and N.K. Hevener on the troubling, critical problem of attacks on diplomats, as considered at a March 1982 conference of distinguished experts at the University of South Carolina. The emphasis is on international community actions and policy (Hargrove) and on the situation with respect to pertinent international agreements and their application in practice (Hevener). The greater part of the book provides the texts of seven international conventions plus the full text of the ICJ judgment on the Tehran hostages and other documents.

Jenks, C. Wilfred. *International Immunities.* London: Stevens and Sons, 1961; Dobbs Ferry, N.Y.: Oceana, 1961. A good introduction to the fundamentals of this subject, as it was evolving in the 1960s.

Lazareff, Serge. *Status of Military Forces under Current International Law.* Leyden: A.W. Sijthoff, 1971. A thorough study of the NATO Status of Forces Agreement of 1951, with an emphasis on practice and on the historical and official reasons for its characteristics. Probably the best single introduction to the subject, detailed but readable.

Snee, Joseph M., S.J., and A. Kenneth Pye. *Status of Forces Agreements and Criminal Jurisdiction.* New York: Oceana, 1957. A short study which concludes with an interesting summary of reciprocity as it affects status of forces practices in the United States. The authors, then at Georgetown University Law Center, noted the presence in the United States of "several thousand military personnel of various NATO nations . . . in connection with their official duties."

Wilson, Clifton E. *Diplomatic Privileges and Immunities.* Tucson, Arizona: University of Arizona Press, 1967. A thorough, scholarly work. A portion of the discussion of practice is based on a survey of opinion by American career diplomats. He does not cover consular or international immunities or premises.

World Guide to Foreign Services: A Directory of Foreign Affairs, Embassies, Consulates, High Commissions, Missions, Legations, Delegations and Representations. First Edition 1986/87. Weissenberg, West Germany: World Guides International Publikationen, 1987. An 838-page worldwide directory listing names and addresses of diplomatic and consular posts of 170 states.

Some general works on international law

Bernhardt, Rudolf (editor). *Encyclopedia of Public International Law.* Amsterdam, New York, Oxford, Tokyo: North-Holland, 1986. Being published in instalments, of which number 9 in 1986 was "International Relations and Legal Cooperation in General. Diplomacy and Consular Relations." Articles on "Couriers," "Diplomatic Agents and Missions, Privileges and Immunities," with bibliographic recommendations. Instalment number 5, published in 1983 was "International Organizations in General/Universal International Organizations and Cooperation." The article on "International Organizations, Privileges and Immunities" (pp. 152–59) is a useful summary of this subject by Paul C. Szasz, with frequent cross-references to other relevant articles in the encyclopedia and a bibliographic list covering books and United Nations documents.

Brownlie, Ian. *Principles of Public International Law.* 3rd ed. Oxford: Clarendon Press, 1979.

O'Connell, D.P. *International Law.* 2nd ed. London: Stevens and Sons, 1970. Part 8, pp. 841–938, deals with "Immunity from Jurisdiction," and within it "Diplomatic and Consular Privileges and Immunities," pp. 887–938. O'Connell includes the immunities of international organizations and officials, pp. 926–33, and those of U.N. forces, pp. 937–38.

Oppenheim, L. *International Law: A Treatise.* 8th ed. H. Lauterpacht, ed. London, New York, Toronto: Longmans, Green, 1955. Vol. 1, Part III: chapter II is on diplomatic envoys, pp. 769–829; chapter III on consuls, pp. 829–46; and chapter IV on miscellaneous agencies, pp. 846–67. These last include armed forces in foreign territories, state ships in foreign waters, and agents without diplomatic or consular character.

Schwarzenberger, Georg, and E.D. Brown. *A Manual of International Law*. 6th ed. Milton, UK: Professional Books, 1976. Diplomatic and consular immunities are briefly discussed on pp. 78–81.

Historical background of modern immunity

Adair, E.R. *The Exterritoriality of Ambassadors in the Sixteenth and Seventeenth Centuries*. London, New York: Longmans, Green, 1929.

Khadduri, Majid. *War and Peace in the Law of Islam*. Rev. ed. Baltimore: Johns Hopkins Press, 1955. Reprint ed. New York: AMS Press, 1979. 1st ed. published as *The Law of War and Peace in Islam*. London, 1941.

Mattingly, Garrett. *Renaissance Diplomacy*. London: Cape, 1955; Boston: Houghton Mifflin, 1955; Sentry Edition, 1971. Thoughtful, readable history with many insights and good judgment throughout.

Mookerjee, G.K. *Diplomacy: Theory and History*. Vol. I. New Delhi: Trimurti Publications, 1973.

Numelin, Ragnar. *The Beginnings of Diplomacy: A Sociological Study of Intertribal and International Relations*. London: Oxford University Press, 1950; New York: Philosophical Library, 1950; Copenhagen: Ejnar Munksgaard, 1950. A wide-ranging history with special emphasis on the prehistoric and early periods. By Chapter 11, page 291, the author reaches the Babylonians, Phoenicians, Greeks, and Romans, or, as he calls it, "Diplomacy among the 'Historical' Peoples."

Queller, D. E. *The Office of Ambassador in the Middle Ages*. Princeton: Princeton University Press, 1967.

Russell, J. G. *Peacemaking in the Renaissance*. London: Duckworth, 1986.

Steiner, Zara, editor. *The Times Survey of Foreign Ministries of the World*. London: Times Books, 1982. Enlightening chapters by nonofficial experts on 24 different national foreign ministries. Unfortunately none are in Africa, Latin America, or the Arab World.

Reasonably relevant reading

Clark, Eric. *Corps Diplomatique*. London: Allen Lane, 1973. Also published as *Diplomat: The World of International Diplomacy* (New York: Taplinger, 1974). Popularly written and frequently amusing, with a chapter on diplomatic immunities, "The Privileged Diplomat" (pp. 100–18) and one titled "Embassies and Espionage" (pp. 184–207).

Eban, Abba. *The New Diplomacy: International Affairs in the Modern Age*. London: Weidenfeld and Nicolson, 1983; New York: Random

House, 1983. In an attractive style, a most seasoned diplomat writes about serious subjects. Mentions diplomatic immunity in passing.

Herz, Martin F. *215 Days in the Life of an American Ambassador*. Washington: Georgetown University School of Foreign Service, 1981. An extremely readable inside look at the realities of diplomacy, East-West relations, the U.S. Foreign Service, and everyday life in an embassy, in the form of diary notes from Sofia, told with wit and insight.

Mayer, Martin. *The Diplomats*. New York: Doubleday, 1983. The tone of Sunday press feature articles. A detached, journalistic viewpoint on the modern role of professional diplomacy.

Parsons, Anthony. *They Say the Lion: Britain's Legacy to the Arabs. A Personal Memoir*. London: Jonathan Cape, 1986. Wise, candid assessments, based on thorough experience, of several Arab countries and British policies. His British Agency in Bahrain was once threatened with mob attacks.

Official U.S. and British hearings, reports, and statements
(all published by the U.S. Government Printing Office or Her Majesty's Stationery Office unless otherwise noted)

U.S. Department of State. *Study and Report Concerning the Status of Individuals with Diplomatic Immunity in the United States*. Prepared in pursuance of the Foreign Relations Authorization Act, Fiscal Years 1988 and 1989, P.L. 100–204, Section 137. Presented to the Congress on 18 March 1988.

U.S. SENATE HEARINGS

U.S. Congress. Senate. Committee on Foreign Relations. *Hearings on Diplomatic Relations Act of 1967*. May 9, 1967. 90th Congress, 1st session.
——. *The Foreign Missions Act of 1982. Hearing*. July 24, 1981. 97th Congress, 1st session.
——. Subcommittee on the Vienna Convention. *Hearings on Vienna Convention on Diplomatic Relations*. July 6, 1965. 89th Congress, 1st session.
——. Committee on the Judiciary. Subcommittee on Citizens and Shareholders' Rights and Remedies. *Diplomatic Immunity. Hearing*. Feb. 6, 1978. 95th Congress, 2nd session.
——. Subcommittee on Security and Terrorism. *Firearm Felonies by Foreign Diplomats. Hearings*. July 24 and Sept. 21, 1984. 98th Congress, 2nd session.

U.S. SENATE REPORTS

U.S. Congress. Senate. Committee on Foreign Relations. *The Diplomatic Relations Act of 1967; Report to Accompany S. 1577*. 90th Congress, 1st session. Senate Report No. 346.

Bibliography of Suggested Reading 269

——. *The Foreign Missions Act of 1982; Report together with Minority Views, to Accompany S. 854.* 97th Congress, 1st session. Report No. 97-283. Nov. 30, 1981.

——. *Privileges and Immunities; Report to Accompany H.R. 5943 and S. 1526.* 93rd Congress, 1st session. Senate Report No. 93-471 (1973).

UK OFFICIAL REPORTS

Her Majesty's Government. *Diplomatic Immunities and Privileges.* Government Report on Review of the Vienna Convention on Diplomatic Relations and Reply to "The Abuse of Diplomatic Immunities and Privileges," the First Report from the Foreign Affairs Committee in the session 1984–85. Miscellaneous No. 5 (1985). Presented to Parliament by the Secretary of State for Foreign and Commonwealth Relations by Command of Her Majesty, April 1985. Cmnd. 9497.

House of Commons. Foreign Affairs Committee. *The Abuse of Diplomatic Immunities and Privileges.* Report with an Annex; together with the Proceedings of the Committee; Minutes of Evidence taken on 20 June, and 2 and 18 July 1984 in the Last session of Parliament; and Appendices. Ref. No. 127. Ordered to be printed 12 December 1984.

INDEX

271